ג

MY PINK GAS MASK

By Adrian Street

Contact Information:

U.S. Mailing Address:

Adrian Street
1496 Oak Drive
Gulf Breeze, FL 32563

Email: daffodil777@bellsouth.net

Website: http://www.bizarebazzar.com

ISBN-13: 978-1477413289
ISBN-10: 1477413286

Cover:
Dressing up made me unique as a wrestler. As a child when everyone else had Black gas masks, I had the only Pink gas mask. So even at the age of 3 - I was unique.

BOOK COVER REACTIONS:

Sister Pamela - *"I like - but SCARY!"*
Son Adrian - *"Now that's DISTURBING!!!"*
Linda Marx - *"Love the Book Cover - That's so EXCITING!!!"*
Judo Al Hollemby - *"That should make it sell!"*
Jeremy Deller - *"Looking good!"*
Rupert Smith, Author of 'Man's World.' -
"That's Fantastic and INSANE!!!!! - I love it."

DEDICATIONS:

To my Father & Arch Nemesis - Your constant opposition
guaranteed my success.

To my Mother - Without you I may never have been born.

To My Sister Pamela's LOVE.

To My Brother Terence's LEFT FIST.

To Raymond Plunkett. Who remembers more of my contests than
I do.

To 'Wresting Heritage' & 'Wresting Furness' whose Great
websites have immortalized 'THE GOLDEN AGE OF BRITISH
WRESTLING'.

To Victor Rook whose advice and book 'Musings of a
Dysfunctional Life' inspired me to complete my own stories.

I will be eternally grateful to those who told me I could do it. -
And even more grateful to those who told me I couldn't.

I want to pay a SPECIAL tribute to every wrestler I shared the
ring with. Friend or Enemy. You all taught me the lessons I
needed to reach the top. I couldn't have done it without you.

INTRODUCTION

My book has been self written and self edited - there maybe mistakes - the only time I spent in Oxford or Cambridge was when I wrestled there. Throughout my life I have always done things one way - My way. - So for better or worse, This is my story.

MY PINK GAS MASK

Everything was black – I couldn't see, I couldn't breathe, my whole head was pounding and ready to explode – I struggled, I squirmed, I fought for my life, but I was in the Mother of all strangle-holds and as helpless as a Baby! Which wasn't surprising considering that is exactly what I was at that time of my life and I was fighting for all I was worth to draw my very first breath. I was destined to be a wrestler, if I survived child birth, which I almost didn't, it wasn't an easy birth and the reason was that I was attached to my Mother with a much shorter, thicker umbilical cord than normal. When I did finally enter the World, instead of kicking and screaming, I was fighting for my life for my first breath, as the umbilical cord was wrapped around my neck and it tightened more and more the further I emerged into the world. Yes, I was caught in 'The Mother of all strangle holds' at an age never surpassed by any other living wrestler, after I had been cut loose by the nurse in attendance, she exclaimed,

"Well it's definitely a boy; I can see where the rest of the umbilical cord has ended up!"

THE WAR

"Hey Mam when is Hitler gonna drop the gas bombs?"

I had felt so important a few days earlier when a man in a black uniform and overcoat, complete with steel helmet had knocked on our door at 8 Queen Street, Brynmawr, South Wales. He had had a list of everyone in our household and a large pile of gas masks. He read out the names and ticked them off as he handed out a black gas mask each for my Grandmother and Grandfather, better known as Mamo and Dado. There was also a black gas mask each for my Mother Nora and nine year old brother Terence and a pink gas mask for me, three year old Adrian. It was a lovely pink gas mask with a little rubber beak, which had no other purpose than to appeal more to a young kid and make it look less frightening. I thought the black ones everyone else had looked really cool and sinister. But I was unique. I had the only pink one, so I was the most important and obviously the leader when the dreaded and for me much anticipated gas bombs were dropped. Oh boy I couldn't wait. My dilemma was that my Mother wouldn't let me play with MY mask.

"You'll only break it if you play with it, then you won't be able to breathe when Hitler drops the gas bombs." She told me.

"Well when is Hitler gonna drop the bloody gas bombs?!" I screamed, loud enough for my little screwed up face to turn the same color as my lovely pink gas mask.

I was born on the 5th of December 1940. Pearl Harbor was bombed two days after my 1st Birthday. My Uncle Alf was off somewhere in North Africa fighting the Germans and my Father, Uncle Alf's older brother was pulled out of the European theatre and on the way to Singapore to defend it from the Japanese, soon after that most infamous attack. We didn't have any air raid shelters near us, even though we were only about twenty miles from the docks of Newport and thirty miles from the docks of Cardiff. Both were prime targets of the German Luftwaffe's air raids. When the warning sirens began to wail each night, announcing the arrival of the Teutonic Knights of the sky with their devastating bombs, my Mother, older Brother and I would hide under a heavy table in the kitchen. A repeat of the sirens, would give us the all clear that another bombing raid had ended. That's where I decided to make my stand. Next night when the sirens began wailing, warning of another bomb bashing, Mam and Terence dove under the table, attempting to grab me on the way. Not this time Nora. With a pirouetting sidestep that many years later would become my trademark, I slipped out of her grasp and stood defiantly, fists on hips in the middle of the kitchen.

"Quick, get under the table before you get blown up, you silly little bugger!" Mam screamed.

"No!" I stated bravely, "Not unless I can wear my pink gas mask." So, from that night on, the only way I could be induced to sit under the table with Mam and Terence, while we endured another air raid was if I could wear my lovely pink gas mask. Then I would sit quietly, happy and content until the bombing stopped for another night.

"Another two enemy planes were shot down last night" wasn't an unusual thing to hear the townspeople shout to each other, the morning after a raid. 'Good!' I'd think, 'another little harvest for Adrian.' The townspeople would often take off in groups. Or even crowds to view them when they heard news of a new wreckage of a German plane that had been shot down while attempting to bomb the Welsh docks. And had crashed somewhere in the mountains surrounding Brynmawr. Everyone was always warned to stay away from them, at least until the appropriate authorities had inspected them.

"I think they crashed on this side of the Milfraen Mountin". They'd shout.

Ha-ha! Little Adrian was always there first, collecting any piece of wreckage I could move and hide to be picked up later after the crowds of gawking townspeople had lost interest and gone back home. Even at that age I knew my way around all the mountains, woods and valleys. My constant quest was to find a tribe of Red Indians so that I could join them. I would become a Brave and eventually the most famous War Chief in the whole World. The very reason I was collecting pieces of the German bombers was so that when I'd collected enough of them, I could rebuild and have a vehicle in which I could search for my Red Indian tribe from the air. God only knows I'd tried every other way of contacting them. I'd follow every imaginary spoor and track for hours every day, lay prone listening to the ground for the pounding of horses hooves. That would bring me my first contact with a bloodthirsty war party who would immediately invite me to join them. Then we would attack the palefaces wagon train, who'd had the effrontery to try to cross their ancestral lands in the Welsh Mountains. It was almost like they were hiding from me on purpose in order to test my determination and of course tracking skills.

"Have you been listening for Indians again?" Mam would shout, as I reared my imaginary horse to a halt outside our home. "Get in the house and wash behind your ears, you've got mud and Buffalo shit all over them!"

THE HILLS OF IRON AND FIRE

Dad and his family moved from Ystrad, a small town in the Rhondda Valley, to Brynmawr when he was about four years old. His Father had been working as a coal miner in Bulfar Colliery and upon moving to Brynmawr began working in Stone's Colliery in Blaina, which is about four miles from Brynmawr, the area was known as 'The Hills of Fire and Iron' - even before I came along.

A few months after their move, The 1st World War was declared. My Grandfather volunteered and joined The 3rd Monmouthshire Infantry Regiment and commenced his military training in Oswestry and Kimmel Park in North Wales. Army pay was very small and things were very hard for my Grandmother [Mamo] who was left to bring up my Father and his two younger sisters. Auntie May, Auntie Florie, Dad's younger brother Alf and youngest sister Pearl hadn't been born yet.

No wonder Dad was so tough, he learned from his Mother, the 2nd toughest Woman I've ever met. The title of the toughest without a doubt goes to Mam's Mother, Ethel Arnold. Her Mother Caroline was a Romany Gypsy, who danced around campfires as a young girl. She became an actress as a young lady and later married my Great-grandfather Jim Arnold. Big Jim Arnold was known as a Bare Knuckle, All-in-Mountain Fighter. In South Wales Bare Knuckle Boxing was against the law. To avoid prosecution the fighters, trainers, even the spectators would meet at a secret rendezvous, somewhere in the town's surrounding hills. Even when I was a kid we still attempted to emulate these dubious Heroes. Any dispute would be settled by agreeing to 'meet where the bull has his breakfast.' meaning, somewhere in the surrounding hills. The rules in Mountain Fighting were nothing that the Marquis of Queensbury would have approved of. Head butts, elbows, knees and Wrestling throws were not only allowed but compulsory, if the crowd were to really enjoy the spectacle. There was no time limit to the rounds, or how many rounds there would be. They would simply scratch a line in the dirt and that's where the fight would start. A round would be over when one of the contestants was knocked out. His seconds would then drag him to his corner and attempt to revive him in an allotted time and bring him back to the scratch line to continue the fight. The fight would only end when one of the Fighters could not be brought back to the scratch line leaving his opponent with the Victory. Hence the saying 'Up to scratch' indicating, that someone or something is fit enough for the task at hand. The most memorable fight ever, was a marathon Battle between "The Cowboy" and my Jim Arnold. Who won the fight? I guess I'll never know for sure. Some of the Old timers who claimed to have witnessed it, or got the result from someone who was there; say it was "The Cowboy" who won. Others claim Jim Arnold was the Victor. But one thing they all agree on, was the raw animal ferocity with which the fight was fought and the superhuman endurance they both displayed. They fought all day until it got too dark to be able to see each other. Then, they mutually agreed to call a halt for the night and then come back the following morning to finish the fight. They continued with the same vigor and violence they'd displayed when they had started their Battle the day before. When he was in his prime Jim Arnold stood an inch or two shy of six foot tall and weighed around 260lbs. His chest was so large he was able to decorate it with a tattooed design of a huge 18th Century Battleship in full sail. As well as his addiction to fisticuffs he raced Horses and raced pigeons. A story I always enjoyed hearing Mam tell when I was a child was about the times she spent visiting him. She and her Brothers shared a huge omelet made out of dozens of pigeon eggs freshly collected from his pigeon loft. I still remember my first encounter with Big Jim Arnold. To me he looked like a massive grey Giant. The conversation turned to his pigeons and the champion racers he was breeding at that time. It reminded me of Mam's omelet story, so I went out into his back garden to search for the famous pigeon loft. There it was, looking as splendid as I'd imagined. I let myself in and found that I had to slap most of the pigeons off their nests as they seemed reluctant to get off the eggs I had come to collect. I was simply gurgling with glee and anticipation as I staggered towards the backdoor with my arms full of prize pigeon eggs. How surprised and delighted Great-grand Dad would be, how I would glow with pride next time Mam told the pigeon omelet story, with me playing the starring role. I kicked furiously at the back door, dropping half a dozen eggs in the process. The door was opened by Great-grand Dad and although he did look surprised, I could tell right away by his expression, that there was a distinct deficit in the delighted department.

Thank goodness I'd already told him I was a Red Indian and I hated Cowboys.

****

I officially started school at the age of three, but had begun attending unofficially much earlier than that. St Mary's infant school and St Mary's junior school were just across the road from beside our house. From the time I learned to walk I'd follow all the other kids into their classes each morning. I'd listen to the stories being told, sometimes marching up to the front of the class and interrupting the teacher with,

"I'll tell you a wully tolly, - Puns a wot a time, there was a little Boy and his name was Adrian." and telling my own stories, usually about Red Indians. The only other story I told, that didn't include War parties and scalping. Was about a young boy who was swimming in a crocodile infested river and when attacked by a ferocious giant reptile. He managed to grab a stick that was floating in the water and thrust it upright into the crocodile's jaws just as they were snapping down on him. This enabled him to narrowly escape being eaten alive and to swim to safety. That was it, the whole story. I can't remember who told me that story in the first place, but I know I must have repeated it a thousand times. After listening to and telling stories, playing with school toys, especially my favorite, a very large and beautifully carved wooden rocking horse. I usually got bored and went home. The Governess of the school would often stop and talk with Mam on her way to the school and one day suggested that as I often wandered in and out of the school at will, why not let me attend officially. Mam replied that at three years old I might have been a bit too young, so the Governess asked me if I would like to be a proper pupil. I was always a sucker for attention, so like a sucker

I said

"Yes, I want to go to school" and regretted it for the rest of my childhood.

I don't remember learning to read, write, or count. Obviously I did, but I feel that I've always been able to do those things. The only thing I do remember about reading back then, was asking our teacher what this letter "g" was in the book I was reading.

I was familiar with a capital G and the small one, but had never encountered that little squiggle before until I was reading that particular book. When I first started attending school officially, the young pupils would have a nap period. Each would be given a mat to sleep on for about an hour, in an empty classroom adjoining the main hall. I could never sleep and was always full of restless energy, disturbing all the other kids by alternately hopping, leaping and screaming around them. I would perform my savage and primitive War Dance, then launch myself on top of them in turn and scalp them with my imaginary Tomahawk. I always thought it was more romantic than a scalping knife. Temporary relief for the other kids, during nap period only came after I'd made a wonderful discovery. The beautifully carved wooden Rocking Horse, which stood in the corner of the adjoining main hall, became the centre of my attention. Obviously I appreciated it more than anyone else in the World. So it was extremely unfair that during playtime I would occasionally be asked to get off it and let one of the other kids have a turn. You will never believe how much that can hurt. So, I began devising a plan to try to dismantle it and take a small piece of the Horse away at a time, so that nobody would notice. I could then rebuild it at home, for my own exclusive use. This would save this noble and magnificent creature the indignity of being mounted by anyone else. Except one who was destined to become the most famous War chief in the World. It's amazing how the teachers didn't become suspicious, that overnight the former mini-dynamo was suddenly the first to get sleepy. Stretching and yawning dramatically and staggering with feigned fatigue. As soon as everyone was asleep, buzzing with impatience and excitement I'd quietly creep out into the Hall to examine my wooden charger. I planned to take it a bit at a time and hide it under my fast growing pile of crashed German

Airplane pieces behind our outside toilet. Calamity! I found there was no way to dismantle the heroic beast. The most I could achieve was to make a small hole at the back of the leather saddle, - and that's when I made my wonderful discovery. The leather saddle was tightly stuffed with short lengths of shiny, embroidery silks in more colors than I could ever imagine. Red, a dozen shades of blue, greens, orange, mauve, lilac, purple, yellow, silver and gold. All of a sudden Pegasus became a little less important to me. I had other ideas. Day by day, over the next few weeks, I gradually managed to pull every strand of silk out of the saddle, from the scores of little holes I made all over it. With the saddle on the beautiful wooden horse so deflated and flaccid it became so uncomfortable to ride that only a tough, strong, brave Indian Chief would want to ride on it. But, that was not my reason for taking the silks. I'd heard the stories and envied Joseph and his coat of many colors. So when I was finally in possession of the last strand of silk, I took them all from their hiding place, dumped them on the table in front of Mam and demanded

"Make me a pair of Royal trousers,"

Even then I had an appreciation for the Exotic.

****

As a child there was one thing I wanted almost as much as becoming a Red Indian Chief and that was the man I was named after, my Father, Emrys Henry Street. I was named Emrys Adrian Street, that's the name that is on my Birth Certificate, but I have always been called Adrian. I used to like the story Mam told me, which happened during the time she and Dad were still courting. The Fair was in town and Dad took Mam there for an evening's entertainment. As they stood watching one of the rides in action Mam caught the eye of a man named Paddy Ryan who took a fancy to her. Being as dumb as a house-brick, instead of saying hello, he walked towards her at the head of his gang and flipped Mam on the nose with a ball fastened to a piece of elastic. Naturally Mam took offence and told him where to go. Instead of taking her advice he flipped her on the nose again. Dad stepped between them and pushed the man away.

"Give us some room!" The man shouted in order to attract as

much attention as possible, "I'm going to teach this idgit a lesson!" Everyone around them stood back and formed a circle.

"Don't fight him;" advised an onlooker, "don't you know who that is? That's Paddy Ryan, the Boxer!" Not only was Paddy Ryan a boxer, he had just won a championship and was now in training for his first title defense. He threw off his jacket, handed it to one of his entourage then began to bob and weave in front of Dad.

"Put up yer dukes and I'll put yer down!" he challenged probably imagining that thrashing Dad would impress Mam. As the weather had been very cold, Dad had been wearing his trilby hat and a wooly scarf tucked into a heavy overcoat. Instead of removing them to give himself more mobility as Paddy Ryan repeated his challenge to put up his dukes, Dad stepped forward and knocked him flat on his back with one punch. This not only rendered Boxing champion Paddy Ryan unconscious, but split his nose right in half, putting pay to his upcoming title defense for a long time to come.

At the time of my Birth Dad was working in Beynon's Colliery which had replaced Stone's Colliery after it had closed in Blaina. Because he was working on the coal face he was exempt from Military duty, even though World War 2 had already broken out on September 3rd 1939, just over a year before. Owing to a wage dispute, in which Dad was the self-appointed spokesperson, the pit management took him off the coalface and put him on nightshift, as an example to the other coal workers. There was no exemption from Military Service for a night shift worker, so Dad was called up as the Colliery Management had planned.

I was 7 months old when Dad was called up for The Armed Forces on the 19th of June 1941. He then began his 12 weeks of training in Rhyl, North Wales, before joining his regiment as a Driver/Gunner in the 6th Heavy Ac-Ac Regiment of the Royal Artillery. On the 12th of November 1941 he and his regiment boarded The Monarch of Bermuda from Prince's Pier at Liverpool Docks, destination Basra in the Middle East. The Monarch of Bermuda was about 28,000 tons and had been a luxury liner before the War, sailing between the USA and The British West Indies. Now painted Battleship grey and packed with munitions and Warriors, her former carnival aura had completely dissipated. Daily routines consisted of fire drill pickets, guard duty, plane and submarine spotting. The bitter cold, wintry weather and stormy seas that were left behind as they traveled south were replaced by waves that resembled the Himalayas, as they entered the Bay of Biscay. Other ships in their convoy, large troop carriers and Battleships like The Royal Sovereign looked like tiny corks bobbing in the sea. One minute a ship would be lifted to what seemed like the crest of the highest mountain then be alternately dropped into the deepest, darkest valley. A week or so after the voyage began the convoy began to enjoy calmer, warmer waters and on the 24th of November, twelve days after leaving Liverpool The Monarch of Bermuda dropped anchor when they reached Freetown, Sierra Leon, West Africa. The troops were not allowed on shore, or even to purchase fruit from the natives, who arrived at the sides of the ships in an armada of canoes. There was fear of the deadly tropical diseases that were so very prevalent, in that part of the World. A sight that really sickened Dad was the natives scooping refuse and waste food from around the anchored ships and eating it raw. Little did he know that before many more months had passed, he would have been very happy to share their meal. Once fully replenished the convoy sailed out of the bay and continued on their voyage. Out in open sea it was discovered that they were being followed by a German U Boat. The ships dropped depth charges that kept the U Boat submerged long enough for a Sunderland Flying-boat to fly out from Freetown in answer to a radio call and finish it off with bombs. A little later the convoy picked up some surviving Singhalese sailors whose ship had previously been sank by the U-Boat. They passed the Cape of Good Hope and arrived in Durban a couple of weeks after my 1st Birthday. Dad and three of his friends had a photograph taken all sitting in a rickshaw that was being pulled by a giant Zulu. Standing close to seven feet tall. He wore full Zulu regalia complete with a two foot high feather headdress and was a most magnificent Warrior. I still have a copy of that photograph that my Father sent home from Durban. On Christmas Eve they boarded another ship, The Orangi but instead of sailing north up the coast of East Africa towards Basra, they sailed due east towards The Maldives. News had just reached them that the Japanese had bombed Pearl Harbor. Instead of continuing on their journey to the Middle-East to engage the Germans, they were now redirected to defend the British possessions in Malaysia and Singapore from the Japanese. Singapore was now their destination.

Whilst at anchor and in the process of refueling in The Maldives another ship collided with The Orangi causing considerable damage. Fortunately with no Human casualties. On the 11th of January 1942 after passing through The Sunda Straits they entered the Java Sea. Then the South China Seas and approached Singapore. As they neared Keppel Harbor they were suddenly met with a large force of Jap bombers. They sailed back out to sea in order to make themselves a more difficult target. The Anti-aircraft guns on The Orangi and all the other ships in their Convoy kept up a ceaseless barrage of fire. This kept the enemy bombers at a considerable height. Although the Battle raged for more than an hour none of the ships sustained any damage or suffered a single casualty. The Japs on the other hand returned to their base with several planes and pilots short. Dad witnessed a couple of Jap planes dive straight into the sea. His baptism of fire was a short but very hectic encounter with a ruthless, cunning and cruel enemy. Their barbarism and brutality he would soon experience firsthand. As they were landing in Singapore the next day the Jap bombers returned with a vengeance and resumed bombing Singapore. Fortunately our guns had been assembled and were ready waiting for the attack. A heavy barrage of artillery fire was kept up and because the Jap pilots were taken by surprise they lost thirteen planes. In the process they caused considerable damage to both property and human life. The date was the 12th of January. So, while Dad was helping to blast the sons of Nippon out of the Tropical skies, his Wife Nora and his own sons, Terence and I celebrated Mam's 27th Birthday in the bitterly cold and bomb ravaged Welsh hills.

****

As a child there was only two things I was afraid of, one was heights, the other I will refer to later in my story. The only thing that frightened me more than my fears was the fact that I was afraid of anything at all. How could I be an Indian Brave, let alone a War Chief if I was afraid to chase an enemy Brave up a cliff or leap across a ravine in search of Eagle feathers for my War bonnet? I knew beyond all doubt that Red Indians were afraid of nothing and that's the way I wanted to be. I would have been thrilled to fight a Grizzly, or a Cougar, but I got chronic vertigo if I just so much as stepped onto a thick carpet. In order to resolve this problem I would climb anything that looked difficult. The higher and more precarious the better. Just to prove to myself that I wasn't frightened, of something I was really mortally terrified of. High walls, lamp posts, drain pipes and even tall trees were soon kids stuff. Cliffs, that's where I would prove myself and believe me there was certainly no shortage of them in my neck of the woods. Brynmawr is the highest Town in Great Britain, surrounded by a countryside with more cliffs than I could shake my War club at. Occasionally my terror would be replaced with wild exhilaration and pride and heart still thumping like a Cherokee war drum. I'd scramble to safety onto the summit of the highest and most hair raising cliff yet. I only wished that Sitting Bull himself had been a witness to my magnificent triumph. Unfortunately "The Great Spirit" who was into idiots and people who climbed rocks rarely smiled on my spirited efforts. More often than not I would find myself completely frozen with fear. I would cling to anything, roots, grass, stones or dirt trying to maintain my balance on the precarious, crumbling perch, hundreds of feet above the rocks or the river below. I was reputed to have a very good singing voice as a child. No wonder with all the practice I had singing hymns and praying so that God would save me.

"Oh, please, please, please God, get me out of this and I promise I'll never do it again, "AHHH! – WHOOPS! UM! The Lords myyyyy Sh-Shu-shepard I'll not want"

In spite of my promises, - to God even. Within a couple of weeks I'd be on the same ledge, consumed with the same terror. I'd sing the same hymns, croak the same prayers and make the same promises I'd made a hundred times before. I would also be destined to make hundreds more times to come. Maybe God has a sense of humor and he did get me out of my constantly self inflicted predicaments. I always made it eventually and was never ever rescued by anything tangible. This activity continued from the time I was a child until my mid teens. Then I left Wales to follow my dreams in London. There the lack of ravines and perilous peaks in the ancient city put an end to my courage seeking obsession, rather than the result of my own common sense.

Strangely enough many years later in the early 70's I was visited by some people from a civil rights group. They first asked my opinion on what I thought of the fact that many Russian Jews were being prevented from being able to leave Russia and live instead in Israel. I replied that as I thought that every human being was a citizen of the World. Therefore, provided they were not criminals and willing to respect other people's laws and customs should be able to go, or live wherever they pleased. They told me they were happy to hear me say that. At that time in Britain I had become extremely well known. I was household name in fact and if I were to join their protest adding my celebrity to their cause it might attract a lot more attention. Basically challenging me to put my money where my mouth was. Never being able to resist a challenge and genuinely sympathizing with their cause, I told them I would be delighted to help them in any way they thought fit.

"What do you want me to do?" I asked.

"We plan to plant some trees and display a large banner stating that the Russian Government should let the Jews who wanted to leave Russia and resume their lives in their ancestral home should not be prevented from doing so."

"Count me in" I replied feeling important like a modern day Moses.

"We plan to have the banner placed on the tallest peak of Mount Snowdon. This is the highest mountain in Britain south of The Scottish Highlands and plant the trees on the most visible ledges on the way up." They informed me.

"AHHH!-WHOOPS! UM! The Lords myyyyy SS-Shu-shepard I'll not want." I thought. "SHIT" I replied "Can't you think of anything else? Listen to this for a great alternative. If you can arrange it. I will be happy to fight both Cassius Clay and Sonny Liston. Both on the same night. in the same ring, at the same time. But please don't ask me to climb any fucking mountain, I can't stand heights."

"Oh, don't worry" they countered, "We've also got Don Willums, a Mount Everest veteran to take you all the way to the summit and keep you perfectly safe."

"Correct me if I'm wrong." I croaked, "But didn't Sir Edmund Hilary do most of his training climbing Snowdon before tackling Everest?" I soon began training with the great Don Willums. He taught me to be a very proficient but still reluctant climber. Our ascent of Mount Snowdon was a success. Gaining sufficient publicity to attract TV cameras, interviews and plaques presented to us baring a portrait of Her Royal Majesty Queen Elizabeth II. We then got a request that we repeat our performance. This time by scaling Mount Sinai and an offer from another group to fund the whole expedition. In return we would agree to explore the caves in the area in which the Dead Sea Scrolls had been discovered. As preparations were being made for this enterprise 'The Six Day War' broke out in Israel. The whole affair was then postponed indefinitely. A damn shame as by then I was, to my own amazement actually looking forward to climbing Mount Sinai and especially exploring the caves.

If you think that my obsession as a kid with cliffs and ravines was a little loony, let me tell you about one of my other Wartime hobbies - collecting bombs. Sometimes fragments, like the small metal fins with a hole in each of the four blades. They were designed to make a loud whistling sound in order to terrify and demoralize. Also whole unexploded bombs. There were many muddy bogs amongst the surrounding hills. With the volume of bombs dropped in those areas it was not unusual for them to just stick into the soft earth and not detonate. My friends and I would just pull them out and take them home. I lost count of how many I had confiscated by adults. They would constantly warn us to leave bombs alone as they were obviously very dangerous. They didn't look much, just a cylinder about a foot long with a warhead on the bottom and a grey metal fin on the top, resembling the flight on an arrow. I had managed to hide five whole ones for years amongst my other treasures behind the backyard toilet. My plan was when I did finally join my Red Brothers, instead of taking them gifts of crappy beads, they'd probably be much happier with the bombs. I'd devised they could be fastened to their arrows and fired straight at the encircled covered wagons and explode. That would make a gap that we could charge right through. Like UM charging Buffalo, instead of getting the shit shot out of us by riding round and round their wagons like sitting ducks.

****

My Mother, Nora Fowler was born on 12th of January 1915 in Nantyglo. She was the first child and only Daughter of Ethel Arnold Fowler and Father James Fowler, better known as "Gentleman" Jim due to the fact that he had an obsession for always being a very stylish dresser. He also loved to see Mam dressed like a little Princess, as she was the apple of his eye. He would often put her on his knee hold her hand gently and say,

"While I'm alive these little hands will never do a hard day's work."

Unfortunately "Gentleman" Jim died when Mam was only fourteen and she worked very hard for the rest of her life. Grand-dad "Gentleman Jim Fowler was a Construction Engineer. He was in charge of construction work in the Gold mines on the Gold Coast and the Ivory Coast. He built the port in Freeport, Sierra Leon where he contracted a deadly tropical disease which killed him. By that time Mam had three Brothers, Fred the oldest, then Arthur and young Jimmy who was named after his Dad. Young Jimmy was always the Black sheep of the family, at least until I came along. Always in trouble as a child, Jimmy came home from school one day in tears. Between sobs told his Mother the reason for his distress. Because of some transgression in school Mr. Jones the Headmaster had brutally canned him in the assembly Hall. He had pulled Jimmy's pants down in front of the whole school's pupils. This caused young Jimmy as much embarrassment as pain. Black sheep or not little Uncle Jimmy was Gran's baby. Next morning she escorted Jimmy to school herself. She arrived when the assembly hall was already full of students. They were in the process of receiving a lecture from Mr. Jones himself. As luck, or misfortune would have it, according to whose point of view you'd sympathies with he was swinging a cane to emphasize his message. The same cane he had used the day before on Jimmy's bare arse. Gran descended on him like an avalanche. She punched his glasses right off his face. Then snatching the cane from his hand she whipped the living shit out of him. Around the assembly hall, down the corridor into the playground and from the playground into the street.

In her prime Gran stood an impressive 4 feet, 10 inches tall. But she was the Daughter of Caroline the Gypsy and Big Jim Arnold, Mountain Fighter extraordinaire. As many more were to discover, to their dismay she had inherited all of the toughness, fighting ability and fiery temper of her Herculean Father.

Mr. Jones never, ever laid a hand or a cane on any of Gran's children again, so in spite of all of his academic accomplishments this little episode goes to prove that you never stop learning, - even if you're a Headmaster.

Uncle Jimmy eventually moved to Bristol with his Mother when she remarried, to our Step-Granddad Jack Davis who we always called Uncle Jack. In Bristol, although becoming a very skilled welder Jimmy also realized his boyhood dream. He became a Gangster. Many times in later years when I was visiting, if Uncle Jimmy came in and found me alone he'd make a big show of getting his revolver out. He would empty the chambers, clean it and reload it just for attention. That might not seem like a big deal, but in Britain even the Police don't carry firearms. A story Uncle Jimmy loved to tell was of a Bristol Police Detective whose sole reason for living seemed to be to nab Uncle Jimmy and put him away for good. If there was a murder, a burglary, a bank robbery or a phantom flasher in the park, Uncle Jimmy would be at the top of this overzealous Cop's list of suspects. So much so as he would even stalk Uncle Jimmy when he was off duty. One night Uncle Jimmy became aware that he was being followed discretely by the detective and a uniformed Constable. He decided he was going to do a job anyway. He began to move furtively, picking up the pace as he turned corners. He snuck down alleys all through the backstreets of Bristol. Jimmy kept this up for over two hours. Finally he sprinted down an alley and vaulted over a high fence. About twenty minutes later he struggled back over the fence dragging a heavy sack. Straight into the waiting arms of the detective and

Constable.

"Gottcha!" the detective thundered with glee, "I've been waiting for over six years for this.- Empty out that sack and let's have a look at what you've got."

"I'd rather not" replied Uncle Jimmy quietly,

"No, I'll bet you'd rather not." chortled the detective, "But empty it out anyway."

"Oh, well if you insist." Sighed Uncle Jimmy and poured the sack of earth all over the Detectives shoes,

"What's the meaning of this Davis?" shrieked the bewildered Dick.

"Well," drawled Uncle Jimmy innocently, "I promised Mam that I'd get rid of this earth 'cos as you can probably tell by the smell that the dog and the cat's been shitting in it. I couldn't go to the front door and wake Mam up at this time of the night. That's why I climbed over her fence instead." The color and the expression of the Detectives face making further baiting totally superfluous. Uncle Jimmy would simply quiver with mirth and giggle like the overgrown kid he really was as he told his story and not resembling in any way the dangerous desperado he thought he portrayed.

****

Mam worked each Evening cleaning a Bank after it had closed for the day during the war. Sometimes I would accompany her and when I did I'd always make for the offices at the top of a few flights of stairs as soon as Mam closed and locked the Bank doors behind us. I would occasionally bring a ball of plastercine with me and sculpt a group of little figures which I would equip with trombones made from paper clips that I'd find in the office. Other times I would pull out a certain volume from a set of encyclopedias and turn to the same well scrutinized section time after time. Yes, you've guessed correctly, the anthropology section, it illustrated not only a variety of different Red Indian tribes but portraits of people from all over the World. Zulus, Dyaks from Borneo, Incas from Peru, Jivaros from the Amazon, Cannibal tribes from New Guinea, Arabs, Turks, Mongolians, Egyptians, Chinese, Tibetans, Eskimos in their furs, Sikhs in their turbans and many, many more. I loved all the colorful costumes which I never got tired of gazing at as Mam worked downstairs. One night as I sat lost in my dreams of far distant lands and exotic races, all the lights suddenly went off. Plunging me into complete darkness. After a few seconds of hesitation to recover from my surprise I slide off my chair felt my way out of the office. Then carefully groped my way as I descended the stairs to the ground floor and into the main part of the Bank. A faint light though the window from the Moon cast a dim yellow glow over the tiled floor as I slowly wandered around the main hall. I started to go around a marble pillar, when all at once about two feet above me hovered a strange, pale, yellow face. After blinking a couple of times to assure myself it was really there, I enquired politely,

"Are you a Ghost?" At which time the Ghost exploded into fits of laughter. Then it suddenly turned into Mam who said,

"Aren't you afraid of anything?" She admitted later that she had conducted a rather foolish experiment. I could have fallen down the stairs in the dark, especially if I had panicked. She was curious to know why in the dark house where we lived. I would plunge straight into a room or hallway with no hesitation. She wondered if my apparent lack of fear was the result of my familiarity to the house we lived in. She wanted to see my response in a place that was less familiar in the dark. I was never afraid of the dark or of anything else that would have terrified most kids my age. The last thing anyone would need to say to me was,

"Don't go into the woods, or caves or 'The Bogeyman' will get you!" The first thing I would do was to rush into the woods or caves. The reason being that I was curious to know exactly what 'Bogeymen' looked like and I was very anxious to check the sucker out. I don't mind telling you that going to the Bank required a lot less courage than staying home while Mam was out working. Especially if my Brother, Terence was left to look after me. Ter was six years older than me and was a very cruel, spiteful Boy. He very much resented having to mind me. In fact he seemed to dislike it almost as much as I did. His only consolation was tormenting me. That would range from him telling me for hours how small and ugly I was, to beating the crap out of me. A scenario that was performed more times than I could possibly count was when Ter seemed to be occupied with some recreation of his own. I would breathe an optimistic sigh of relief and move as quietly as I could so as not to disturb him. I'd then begin to build my armies out of my ball of plastercine. Horses and covered wagons for the Cavalry. Horses and feathered head dresses for my Redskins. An hour would fly by in a flash. I was Completely absorbed. Arranging all my Soldiers and Warriors into their Battle lines. A prelude to the glorious action I was about to play. THUMP! That's when it would happen. The book he might have appeared to be reading would sail past me smashing my warriors. Scattering them half way across the room. Sometimes he'd kick them. I even remember being slammed face first into them. But then he would always gather them all up. Then with a look of unconcealed relish on his face he would roll my Warriors back into a ball. That destroyed the hour or more of work I'd done. Before I had the pleasure of playing with my self created toys. Sometimes after he stole them he would play with them himself. That was to draw the torment out. Strangely enough there were occasions when I actually enjoyed watching him play. That's when he discovered one of his worst tricks. All of a sudden, in Ter's hands, my valiant and constantly victorious Indian Braves became pathetic losers and cringing cowards. Their punishment would be mutilation. As I'd watch him tear off my warriors heads and legs I found myself not just crying but screaming hysterically, in a way that I had never heard from anyone, let alone myself. I remember thinking that my head, chest and face was going to burst. I had told myself long ago that brave Indians would never cry for any reason. Normally even as a child I never would, but Boy oh Boy! Terence could do it for me. Then the fun would start, he would wait patiently for me to recover and settle down. Then he'd ask me if I would like to have my plastercine back. After receiving my affirmative reply he'd say,

"O.k. you can have it but you've got to fight me first." So I would fight him. The fight would continue until I was bawling again. Then he'd give me back my plastercine again in an effort to shut me up. Once I'd recovered and was in the process of rebuilding my armies, he would grab the plastercine and we would play the whole episode over again and again. Complaining to Mam was not only a waste of time, it could be downright dangerous. She was convinced that my complaints were due to the fact that I didn't like being left at home. She didn't want to hear about it after returning home tired from work. And agitated at the thought of the probability of having our meal interrupted by the next wave of Nazi Bombers. Upset Mam and you'd get a hiding far worse than anything my Brother could dish out. She was her Mother's Daughter.

One night In order to counter the panic I always felt as the front door slammed and I found myself once again at my sweet Brother's mercy. I decided to forgo the preliminaries and I attacked him savagely. Needless to say I found myself sailing backwards halfway across the room into the kitchen door. As I bounced off and landed on my arse, I noticed hanging on the handle of the door, a string bag containing a Swede. I made a grab for it as he rushed me. I took a step forward and swung the string bag around my head in a way that I thought would have resembled Richard the Lionhearted, as he smote the snot out of the Saracens. WHACK! He charged straight into it and he must have sailed right back to the place he'd started from. I stood triumphant and weighed the Swede in my hand. I watched the Evil Infidel Saladin laying flat on his back. In a flash he was on his feet but I was ready for him. WHOOSH! I hurled the Swede at his head with all my might and what seemed like eons of pent up frustration. SMASH! OH – SHIT! Ter ducked and the Swede hurtled through the window and into the back garden. We both stood staring at the window. Ter was shaken and I was horrified! When Mam came home!!! -- It didn't bare thinking about as Ter was thrilled to remind me, as soon as he found his voice.

"You're dead" he gloated, "When Mam comes home she's gonna kill you."

So there I sat in terror, waiting for the inevitable. The hours soon passed till I heard Mam return.

"Look what Adrian did to the window Mam. He threw a Swede through it!" yelled, Ter, not wanting to risk being blamed himself. Mam looked at both of us with disgust but to my surprise glanced at the window and said,

"Why can't you daft buggers behave yourselves when I'm

out? Now I've got to pay for a new window." To my relief and Ter's disappointment, that was the end of it. I think Mam was too tired that night to get angry. Back at the Bank. A few nights later I was sitting in the Office upstairs with my favorite book opened to my favorite page and my big ball of plastercine at hand. I was attempting to sculpt some of the many races of people illustrated in the Encyclopedia. I was especially intrigued by the different physical varieties, the seven foot tall Wituzi contrasting with the vertically challenged Pygmies and Bushmen. The powerfully built Zulus and the Hottentots with their huge buttocks. Mam entered the office and told me to get ready to leave. She had seen and admired my models before, but this time I had a new one to show her, one that wasn't depicted in the book. I was sure of that because I had searched for it many times. I couldn't understand why they were not included with all the other races because I saw them on the Newsreels, every time I visited the Cinema. I had rolled and stretched my little sculpture's neck, torso, arms and legs as thin as I could manage without them breaking off.

"Look Mam," I invited dangling my masterpiece in front of her, as Mam entered the office "An Atrocity." Mam didn't know whether to laugh or cry. It was a long time before I realized that a German Atrocity was not a Race of pitifully skinny people.

****

Night after night the early Monsoon rain came down in torrents. It threatened to wash away the tents and equipment belonging to Dad and his regiment. Huddling, dozing, plagued constantly by marauding, bloodsucking mosquitoes they'd try to sleep and hope that their new billets would be completed as promised. They were now entering the rainy season. The huts contained a rough wooden bed for each soldier covered by a mosquito net to protect the soldiers as they slept. They proved to afford scant protection from those vicious and persistent little insects. The nights were nightmares of buzzing, swearing and loud slapping. The heat of the day was terrible and perspiration ran like the Monsoon rain as the new troops from wintry Britain began their training in Jungle warfare. On January 22nd Dad and a number of other soldiers were detailed to go to the docks to pick up some supplies. But when he went to collect his truck to join the rest of the convoy, the Officer in charge countermanded the order and told him to get some petrol instead. Three other soldiers, Gunner Anstey, Bombardier Thornton and Gunner Lance were ordered to take Dad's original detail. As they were making their way to the docks the Jap bombers arrived and made a devastating raid on the dockland area. Dad later learned that amongst the many casualties were the three soldiers who had taken his place. Gunner Anstey and Bombardier Thornton were killed. Gunner Lance had a leg blown off. Whether he survived his terrible wound Dad was never able to find out. Dad said he was extremely thankful to Almighty God for such a miraculous escape from death. I have often wondered what Gunner Anstey, Bombardier Thornton and Gunner Lance's thoughts would have been on that subject. From that very day the Japs increased the intensity of their air raids. On the 22nd 9 enemy Bombers were shot down, 5 more on the 23rd, another 3 on the 24th. Over the next few days Batteries of the 3rd, 12th and 15th Heavy Ac-Ac Artillery accounted for 33 Jap Bombers. Meanwhile the well equipped, Jap Forces were advancing down the Malaysian Peninsula. They drove the British and allied Australian troops before them, as they retreated Southward to where a causeway joined the southern tip of Malaya to the island of Singapore. By December the 8th 27,000 Jap troops under the command of General Yamashita Tomoyuki had invaded and gained a foothold on the Malaysian peninsula. They captured the British air base at Kota Baharu the same time that the Jap air force began bombing Singapore. The main Jap force moved quickly down the Western side of the peninsula and swarmed down the single North-South road. The Jap divisions were equipped with approximately 18,000 bicycles. Whenever they encountered any kind of allied resistance on the road they simply detoured through the jungle on their bicycles, or took to the sea in collapsible boats. This enabled them to outflank the British and allied troops, encircle them and cut off their supply lines. Penang fell on December the 18th, Kuala Lumpur on January 11th 1942, Malacca on January 15th and Johor Baharu by January 31st. The Japs enjoyed the advantage of more tanks, guns and troops, plus superior planes. The British lacked vital air support since the British air bases in

Northern Malaya were now in the hands of the Japs. The Royal Navy had already lost the Battleships 'The Prince of Wales' the pride of the British Royal Navy and 'The Repulse'. Casualties were huge, every day they would come pouring over the causeway and down the Bukit Road to the hospitals in the city. When Dad's regiment had first arrived in Singapore they had brought 50 Hurricane Fighters that had to be made ready for combat. They were ill equipped for tropical flying. They were intended to supplement the few Brewster Buffalo Bi-planes which could only fly at between 90 and 100 mph. The Buffalos were soon blasted out of the air by the superior Jap Fighter planes. The 50 or so Hurricanes were all destroyed on the ground, as the Japs didn't even give them the opportunity to take to the air. Fifth column activity was rampant amongst the Jap sympathizers on the Island. Japs disguised as Chinese traders had been gaining vital information who then flew in knowing exactly where the planes were and destroyed them. The great guns at the naval dockyard that had inspired Winston Churchill with the confidence to tell the World that "Singapore was an impregnable fortress" had already been well studied by Jap tourists on the Island. So the Japs were well aware that the big 15" guns defending Singapore were only pointing out to sea. They were only maneuverable to a 90 degree angle. Therefore the obvious choice was to make multi pronged landings from directions which rendered the big guns useless against their attack. With their vastly superior air, land and sea forces the Japs finally drove the remnants of the Allied Forces out off Malaya and onto the Island of Singapore. Fighting had been furious at the large reservoir in Johor Bahru, which supplied water to the Island and despite the stubborn resistance. The casualties soon proved to be so great that any of the survivors still capable of fighting, crossed the causeway and set up their defenses on the south side of the Straits of Johor, as a last post. In an effort to slow the advance of the fast approaching enemy the 27th Australian Brigade laid ambush on the forked road beyond Gemas and scored considerable success. Meanwhile on the south side of a wooden bridge spanning a stream the 2nd/30th Australian Battalion were entrenched and concealed from enemy view. The bridge itself had been mined and a battery of field Artillery had been sited on some higher ground commanding the Jap's approach to the bridge. The ambush was laid under General Percival's own instructions. He was convinced that ambush was the only way for them to fight the Japs. It was about 4 o'clock in the afternoon on the 14th of January when the enemy's Advance Guard approached mounted on bicycles. They flowed across the bridge and well into the ambush area. Then came the main Jap column several hundred strong also cycling. They were followed by tanks and engineer trucks. At that point the bridge went up, exploding with a tremendous blast sending timber, cycles and bodies hurtling through the air. Our troops in the ambush lane and the anti-tank traps then poured a devastating combination of machinegun and rifle fire mowing down the enemy who advanced along the roadside like grass. The Jap loses would have been very much greater if not for our own sappers inadequate attempt to camouflage the field telephone cable that ran through the scant undergrowth at the jungles edge. It was unfortunately spotted and promptly cut by a very observant and quick thinking Jap. As a result our Artillery did not receive the signals and the big guns never came into the action at all. The Japs advanced in ever increasing numbers with tanks and guns blazing and now well aware of the allied positions. Even under the heavy return fire their engineers set to the work of repairing the damaged bridge. Orders were given for the small British and Australian force to withdraw to a position near Gemas where they repelled a few more Jap assaults. More and more Jap reinforcements kept advancing with tremendous air support, whilst the allied air strike was practically nil. Allied losses were very heavy. HQ of the 6th Heavies were issued fresh orders to withdraw south down the Bukit Jimah Road. There was a definite feeling that the Allied Forces were not going to be able to hold back the immense hordes that were coming against them. Further orders commanded them to collect as many men and as much arms as possible and get off the island of Singapore and cross the Malacca Straits to Sumatra. This decision was made on the 27th January 1942. Upon their arrival at Keppel Harbor they found thousands of civilians men, women and children as well as soldiers trying to board the only few ships that were available. Most of the civilians were directed onto two ships destined for

Australia. The troops were to board a larger ship with whatever guns, ammunition and supplies it could carry. The tension mounted to fever pitch and everyone who had a God, prayed that they would escape the island of Singapore, before the swiftly advancing hordes of Japs would overwhelm them.

****

"Mam, when is Dad coming home?" To everyone I saw in a uniform, I'd make the same request, go find my Dad. "Hey Mister, will you go and bring my Dad home, his name is Emrys, he's with the Japs and when you get him, tell him we live up there." I'd say, pointing towards Queen Street. Of course there were lots of uniforms around in those days, but the new kids on the block were the Yanks. It became an almost weekly event to hear the loud rumbling of the huge, heavy American Tanks and Military trucks as they made their way through the streets of Brynmawr. The whole town's populace would line the sidewalks cheering and waving British and American flags. Ter and other kids his age would always chant,

"Give us some gum-chum!" Prompting the American soldiers to throw packets of chewing gum at them from their assortment of military vehicles. We'd all scramble for the precious gum, with me due to my size usually the last to reach it. Even if I did grab some I rarely managed to keep it if Ter was there. But I'll always remember one time when gum was flying and I was having no luck at all. Leaning against a lamppost and chatting to a couple of Brynmawr's beautiful belles was an American soldier. He had obviously noticed my vain attempts to acquire the elusive gum and probably felt sorry for the scruffy little mountain urchin, who in spite of all his best efforts continued to come up empty handed.

"Here kid." He said as I stood looking for my next chance. I looked up at him as he placed a perfect, white cube of sugar into my hand. My mouth fell open in amazement as I gazed at it in awe. "Its sugar, kid," he said, "You can eat it." I had never, ever, seen or heard of a cube of sugar before. I was well aware of regular sugar even though it was on ration during the War – but a cube of sugar! I was thunderstruck. There was no way I was going to eat my precious treasure. I did touch it gently with my tongue to make certain it was indeed sugar, but one did not devour a beautiful and rare work of art. No indeed, I must have kept that cube of sugar for a eon and a half. I carried it with me always and constantly handling it with my grubby little paws, it soon became jet black instead of snow white but I loved it all the same.

The argument started when Mamo, for whatever reason threw a massive cast iron saucepan containing about twenty pounds of still boiling potatoes after Dado as he dived nimbly down our passageway, in an attempt to escape her wrath. She had started to apologize to Mam, for the terrible mess the spuds had made all up the hall that was in our part of the house. My Mother interrupted Mamo and said,

"Listen; don't waste your time and energy saying you're sorry for the mess you made. You made it – you clean it up." Mamo who still hadn't really recovered her temper flew into another rage. This time it was directed at Mam. She was a very large woman with a very large voice with very large bulging eyes on a face that had turned a gorgeous shade of purple. I leapt up from the floor completely abandoning my plastercine General George Armstrong Custer, who was in the process of being scalped by Crazy Horse. I placed myself solidly between Mam and Mamo, who looked as if she was about to breath flames from her mouth and nose.

"Don't you talk to my Nora like that," I growled at Mamo, "get out, you old cow!" I was staring up at the closest thing I had ever seen to the top totem pole. Well Mamo laughed so hard I thought she would burst. I didn't ever remember her laughing before and I thought she was doing it to confuse me. I turned inquiringly to Mam and to my surprise found that she too was laughing and holding herself in such a way as not to wet herself. They also seemed to reach a compromise. A little later I saw Dado in a flowery apron cleaning the mashed potatoes off the walls and ceiling. Bouts of violence were not unusual between Mamo and Dado. Even though Dado had been a very good amateur lightweight Wrestler in his younger days he was hardly a match for Mamo. As well as throwing anything that came to hand I've seen them have fist fights, wrestling with Mamo usually coming out on top.

About that time my Auntie Florie died in childbirth. Unlike her parents she seemed to be a lovely gentle lady. She had been married to my Uncle, Arthur Humphries. Auntie Florie had lived in Llandrindod Wells with her son Raymond and had died giving birth to his little sister, Mary. Cousins Raymond and Mary came to live in our house and were adopted by their Grandparents Mamo and Dado. Raymond was a little younger than me and I often kidnapped him and took him to school with me. After much scheming on my part I got him enrolled as a pupil. 'Why should I suffer alone?' I thought.

"I wonder what happened to that lovely suite of armor?" Mam would ask Terence. WHOOSH! In a split second my wigwam would dissolve and I'd find myself back in our kitchen sitting crossed legged under the table.

"What suit of armor?" I'd yell, leaping from under the table in a flash.

"Oh, you mean the silver one with the red ostrich feather plumes and the red velvet cloak?" He'd answer, as if I wasn't there.

"Yes, I think that's the one, it had a silver shield with a big red Dragon on it."

"What suit of Armor?!" I'd yell again, only louder. Back and forth they'd conduct this conversation, completely ignoring me.

"It wasn't really a full sized suit of armor so we couldn't sell it to a knight."

"Oh, that's right," Ter would agree, "it was just about Adrian's size."

"What suit of armor are you talking about?" I'd yell once again frustrated.

"I wonder what happened to it?" Mam would muse, still treating me like the invisible man.

"I think it got thrown in the trash can." Said my Brother. "I think I threw it away because it was rusty and only fit someone as big as Adrian."

"What bloody suit of armor are you talking about and where's the velvet cloak and shield?" I'd demand, losing my temper.

"Oh, I expect it'll be buried in the rubbish dump now, a pity that, it was a lovely suit of armor." Mam would say.

"Yes, it was the best suit of armor I've ever seen." Ter would agree.

Why they tormented me that way I'll never know. No TV in those days I suppose. They both knew I was crazy about armor. I would have gladly swapped my pink gas mask and my Brother for the rustiest suit in existence. But when they were bored and had nothing better to do either one of them would start and they wouldn't let up until I was crying or screeching with temper. Then, like as not, I'd get a smacking for misbehaving. What they didn't know, or at least I hoped they didn't know, is that I knew where the town rubbish dump was. I'd often seen the tip up trucks drive out of Brynmawr and dump their load over a precipice above the river. Even though I was deathly afraid of heights, I would climb over the edge without a moment's hesitation. I wanted that imaginary armor in the worst possible way. It was probably about a hundred foot drop into the river but it wasn't all shear. There were places where there was such an accumulation of rubbish that it sloped almost down to the river. I explored and excavated all of it. Dozens of times I almost fell down a shear drop. Other times I would be up to my arse in refuse and feel the whole section of garbage I was burrowing into start to slide a little further down the slope. I would go home disappointed time after time, filthy and stinking like a polecat who'd been shagging a skunk. I always was a scruffy little sod, so in spite of the fact I had been burrowing in filth for hours, no one really became suspicious. I never would have stopped my searching as anyone who has ever known me can testify to. If I want something bad enough I will never, ever leave it alone until it's mine. But I became very ill at that time and although I must have spent a few weeks in bed no one guessed what my illness was, as a Doctor was never called. Eventually my health began to improve and I was almost back to normal. Then Raymond became ill displaying the same symptoms that I had suffered. His illness became worse and worse so that our family Doctor was finally called. Poor Raymond almost died and was diagnosed with diphtheria which he must have caught off me So, say no to trash kids! It can kill ya, even if it's second hand.

Grancher Gould was Mamo's Father. Even though he was my Great-Grandfather we all called him Grancher Gould. He lived in a part of town that was called The New Houses. Why they were referred to as The New Houses I don't know as they looked to me as though they'd been built six weeks before Stonehenge. Thinking about it Grancher Gould looked as though he belonged to that period also. He was a large robust man with an even larger Walrus moustache. Always very neatly dressed and sporting an impressive Gold watch and chain that spanned his ample middle which he even wore when he was busily working in his beloved garden. He always seemed happy to see his Great-Grand Children, unless of course they were found scrumping the delicious fruit that was so abundant in his garden. Then he'd let out his big walrus roar that would have been heard in Siberia. I don't remember Grancher's wife Ellen, as she had died on the 25th of July 1926, many years before I was born. 8 Queen Street was a big house and as well as being occupied by three families Mamo would also let a few rooms to lodgers. Often Showbiz people, Circus performers, occasionally long distant Truck drivers. A mixture of strange and sometimes very interesting people. There was once a Brother and Sister who were a Carnival's Fat Man and Woman. I don't know how much they weighed but they were huge, absolutely elephantesque. I remember them leaving in an enormous automobile, both Brother and Sister had to stand either side of the car with both the back doors open. Then they would have to shout, "One, two, and three!" so that they would both slide into the car at the same time. If they got in separately the weight would almost turn the car onto its side. When they were leaving, they were all subjected to the same request.

"When you come back, bring my Dad with you. He's with the Japanese."

****

Joined by two escorting Battleships, relief was short lived as the fleeing ships finally cast off and sailed out of Keppel Harbor, in the desperate attempt to escape from Singapore and the swiftly advancing barbaric hordes from Japan. Almost without warning Jap bombs began to fall from a great height into the sea all around them. They were leaving Singapore as they had arrived, under a hail of Nipponese bombs. One of the two Australia bound ships was hit causing it to list badly. Dad wondered but never learned whether either of the ships ever reached their final destination. Although they were pursued for many miles, they continued their voyage without further incident. Breaking away from the rest of the convoy they reached the mouth of The Moesi River and sailed upstream to Pelembang, the capital City of Sumatra, arriving late in the evening on the 28th of January1942. They were met at the quayside by an extremely excited populace. This included an official Dutch Military Commander, whose overall command they were placed under but still retained their own Officers. That night they were all billeted in a Chinese school. Next morning after Breakfast they marched back to the dockside and began the job of unloading the supplies, larger weapons from the ship, which took them until late into the evening. By February 2nd anti-aircraft guns had been deployed in both of the two airfields P1 and P2. P2 was about 40 miles south of Pelembang and was defended by 12 Heavy Ac-Ac Battery and the Light Ac-Ac guns of 35 LAA Regiment. There were several thousand RAF ground personal in the area mostly unarmed that had also been recently evacuated from Singapore. P1 airfield was 7 miles north of Pelembang and was defended by one troop of 15 Heavy Ac-Ac Battery whilst its other troop was deployed in the large oil refineries just outside Pelembang. Both the airfields had been covertly developed by the Dutch before the Japanese attack; to guard against such a contingency. Upon its discovery P1 began being bombed regularly by early February. P1 airfield was attacked and quickly taken by a force of Jap paratroopers. It wasn't until about that time that the Japs even learned of the existence of P2. Dad was on his way back to Pelembang with his company. They had been delivering supplies to the 2nd airport. when they learned that the Jap forces were coming up the Moesi River towards Pelembang, the day prior to the Japs attacking and taking P1. On his arrival in Pelembang Dad found the British and Allied Forces assembled on both sides of the river just as the Japs came into sight. Then all hell broke loose as the enemy received a heavy bombardment from trench mortars and machinegun fire. They quickly withdrew leaving behind them many casualties. The next day they heard that P1 airport was now in enemy hands and there was a much larger Jap force coming back up the river to take the City and the all important oil refineries. After another fierce battle, the enemy was once more repelled. The allies heard of the advance towards Pelembang and the refineries by the Jap paratroopers. The Japs presence made P2 airport untenable, so the decision was taken to abandon Southern Sumatra altogether. No air support, no chance to hold on to Pelembang. Orders were given to blow up the refineries and their containers and evacuate the City. After waiting for hundreds of native men, women and children to cross the river to the railway station Dad was amongst the company who were detailed to blow it up. Their only chance seemed to make a mad dash down a tenuous 350 mile road and rail journey to Oosthaven in the south and escape across The Sunda Straits into Java. As Dad prepared to evacuate Pelembang they heard on the radio that Singapore had fallen. During the evening on February the 8th the Japs using their collapsible boats had landed under the cover of darkness on the northwest coast of Singapore. By dawn despite the determined resistance offered by Australian troops the enemy was able to advance two divisions with their artillery onto the island. By the next day the Japanese had overran and captured Tengah Airport and gained control of what was left of the Causeway itself. They repaired and rendered it usable to their invading army within 4 days. The British and Commonwealth forces at first offered a very strong and determined resistance but were plagued by poor communication and coordination. They failed to prevent the enemy from taking Bukit-Timah, which is the highest point in Singapore. By February 11^{th,} the Allied Forces had fallen back and prepared to make a final stand around the city perimeter, stretching from Kallang to Pasir Panjang. General Yamashita issued an invitation to the Allies to surrender, but orders from Winston Churchill demanded that the city be defended to the death, whilst executing a scorched earth policy. No surrender was to be contemplated. Every inch of ground defended and defenses blown to smithereens in order to prevent its capture by the Japs. In accordance as the Naval base which was less than useless in the absence of a single ship, the Allies set about the task of destroying it to deny the advantage it would afford the enemy in the advent of capture. On February 13th as the Allies were building defense works to help protect the northern coast, the Japs broke through the final perimeter at Pasir Panjang. This put the whole city in range of their artillery. The Japs continued to bomb the city by day and shell it by night and in the region of 2,000 of Singapore's civilians were reported killed each day. General Yamashita accepted Lieutenant General Arthur E. Percival's unconditional surrender on the 15th of February. But, as the bombing and shelling ceased, hostilities of another kind broke out all over the vanquished Island of Singapore. Between 5,000 and 25,000 civilians, mostly Chinese betrayed by informants and accused of being anti-Jap were executed. Many more were imprisoned. A party of Jap soldiers entered Alexandria Military Hospital and bayoneted many of the sick and wounded patients, including Private A Lewis who was bayoneted to death as he lay on the operating table. All Australian and European prisoners were interned at Changi POW camp on the eastern side of the island. The 600 Malayan troops and about 45,000 Indian troops were lined up. They urged to transfer their allegiance from Britain to the Emperor of Japan and fight for the independence of India from The British Empire. Under pressure almost half of the Indian troops joined the Japs. Those who refused were executed, tortured, imprisoned or sent as slave labor to Thailand, New Guinea or Sumatra. Singapore regarded as Great Britain's "Gibraltar of the East" until its fall in 1942 was now designated as the capital of Japan's southern region and was renamed Shonan, which in Japanese means 'Light of the South.' Being amongst the last of the troops to evacuate Pelembang, Dad marched to the station and boarded the train. The trucks and guns had already started on their long trek to Oosthaven by road. Later they rejoined the convoy and relieved the drivers as they continued their nightmare journey, over roads that had turned to slimy quagmires by the relentless, tropical rainstorms. The deep, muddy and waterlogged ruts in the road caused the heavy guns and trucks to sink to the axles making progress very slow and exhausting. Their only consolation was that any pursuit by road from the Japs would be suffering the same diabolical conditions. For 4 long days and torturous nights, they toiled their way to Oosthaven and with great relief they finally drove into Felongbetong Port. As they prepared to embark on the Dutch ship, Darvel they were told, that their efforts in towing the heavy guns and heavy trucks were all in vain, as the Dutch authorities refused to allow them on board the ship.

****

I've never been fond of candy and unlike any of the other kids I knew at the time, I found it completely resistible. The fact that it was on ration during the war seemed to make them even more voracious for it, but for me, I only had two interests in it. One was the fact that it was on ration, which meant that I had my own personal ration book and that made me feel important. Once a week I would take my ration book and a few copper coins and walk to 'The Sweet Shop' at the bottom of the street. I'd enter and make my choice, which was easy as 'Raspberry Ruffles' were wrapped in the best metal foil. If it was removed very carefully, I could shape it to form wonderfully shiny armor. It would transform my little plastercine mannequins into the most heroic of Knights in silver armor, which explained my second interest in it. Almost all foodstuffs available were on ration. Many food items were rare, like meat, or absolutely impossible to obtain, such as bananas and grapes, which I had never even seen. American Soldiers seemed to be able to acquire an abundance of hard to get items. This included nylon stockings, which made them even more popular with the local ladies. Black-market was obviously rampant and my most memorable recollection of that, was when the entire family clubbed together to buy a carcass of a whole sheep from one of our local Black-marketers. Money paid and rendezvous arranged, the family haggled, squabbled and argued as to which cuts they would receive for their share of the illegal booty. As they waited in mouth watering anticipation for its delivery. The hall clock striking midnight coincided with a knock on the back door. In crept not two or three large men struggling under the weight of the huge carcass but one shifty, skinny, little rat faced runt. He quickly laid a small newspaper wrapped parcel on the table and rushed back out of the back door. Everyone stood as still as a room full of statues, looking at each other, waiting for someone to make a move. They pounced on the parcel tearing it open to reveal a pitiful, scrawny, blue hued little carcass. It looked as though, whatever it was, had died of malnutrition and old age at the same time. After saying a few words over it to show our respect, it was quietly buried in the back garden. In those days and for many years to come, meat of any kind was considered a very expensive luxury. If a family could afford it at all, it would be enjoyed only as part of a Sunday dinner, which was regarded by everyone as the special meal of the week. Sunday dinner was such a special event that the question of what meat one had eaten the day before was always the major topic. Monday morning upon arrival at school A typical greeting would be,

"Hya Dai, what did you have for dinner yesterday?"

"A lovely bit of lamb, Ade. What did you have?" would be the reply. I remember announcing to Mam, that when I grew up and was very rich, I was going to buy a whole leg of lamb and eat it all by myself.

"Where are you going to eat it, under the table?" she asked.

'Hmm!' I thought, and that appealing vision lingered with me for a long time.

I loved flowers, or any kind of plant. I could look at a tree for an hour, just examining the shape, the size, its leaves and colors. Any flowers I saw which appealed to me, and they all did, whether growing in the hedge growths, on the hills, meadows, riverbanks, in the woods or even in any neighbors garden. I would pick it and take it home for Mam. Roses, Buttercups, Kingcups, Primroses, Bluebells and Foxgloves, Daisies, Dandelions. Even a lowly Dock leaf would sport some gorgeous colors as autumn advanced. My first conscious recollection of any type of flower was the Nasturtiums that grew in abundance amongst her rockeries in my Auntie May's back garden. That's where I found my furry little stray Kitten and I loved animals too.

I had never owned a pet before and I was having trouble trying to think of a name for it. I thought the names suggested to me, like Fluffy or Tibbs were really stupid but I couldn't make my mind up. I preferred to name it after one of my Redskin Heroes, or one of my favorite movie heroes like Tarzan, or Paul Robeson. I really admired him after seeing him play the part of Bosambo in the 1935 movie, 'Sanders of the River' or my idol Joe Louise, 'The Brown Bomber,' maybe an inappropriate name for a white kitten.

My little Kitten went missing before I ever got chance to name it and we searched everywhere for it in vain. The mystery was finally solved when Brian Gore, a kid that was a few years older than me and lived opposite us admitted that he had catnapped my Kitten. He had put it in a trash can that was half filled with water and then put the lid on it. He said that he heard it crying and trying to get out when he was laying in bed that night and by the time he went to check on it the next morning it was dead. What his motive was I could never guess. I was inconsolable and couldn't banish the picture out of my mind of the horror of that poor little Kitten swimming around and around until it got exhausted and drowned. But, I do bare a grudge. I stood in the middle of Queen Street with Mam, when Brian Gore standing between his Dad and his Granddad Gore made his confession. Brian's relatives seemed half embarrassed and half proud of the snotty nosed ogre, because he was man enough to admit what he had done. Brian seemed to be relishing the attention he was receiving as he related his story. I flew at him with a speed and fury that shocked everyone. Especially that bastard Brian. He was smashed into the ground with me on top of him Punching, kicking, gouging, he was a mess. It took the combined efforts of Mam, Brian's Dad and Granddad Gore to drag me off him. He had been reduced to the sniveling, blood spattered coward that he really was.

"Behave yourself, settle down" Mam scolded, "Go on home." As soon as she released me I was at him again. I strove to tear him away from his Granddad Gore who had picked him up and was attempting to console him. His Granddad wasn't doing him any favors holding him to prevent him falling down, as he now made a very convenient target for my flailing fists.

"You little blackguard!" Granddad Gore roared, as I was once more pried off him.

"Who are you calling a blackguard?!" shouted Mam as she advanced on Granddad Gore her hands balling into fists. "Go on Ade!" she called to me, "Give him another one!" and damn if I wasn't on him again. That was the beginning of my terrorization of Brian Gore, anywhere and anytime I saw him I would attack. I might have been playing happily with other kids and in the best of possible moods but just the sight of him would instantly turn my guts into a cauldron. I became a charging beast, thirsting for vengeance. Fortunately for him and unfortunately for me he was older, bigger and faster than I was and I could very rarely catch him. The few times I did manage to corner him, I most certainly made it worth my while. Invariably his parents or Granddad would complain I'd get a scolding and carry on my hunt of him regardless. He was difficult to catch. He would mostly make it through the gates and refuge of his iron railing surrounded garden, before I'd even get close to bashing him. I remember making a plan of ambush. If he ever stepped out of his house or garden, he would always scrutinize the whole street and any possible hiding places I could use. So my plan was to squeeze through the iron railings, into his garden. I'd creep behind some flowerbeds and shrubs which lined the garden and that would afford me cover until I could reach the trees at the back of their yard. Then I'd wait behind them in hiding, until that bastard Brian would unsuspectingly come out into his garden to play. That way, as long as I could cut him off from his back door there was nowhere for him to run except into the iron railings where I wanted him. Sounds great doesn't it? But it didn't quite work out the way I planned. I managed to force my head through the railings, but they were too narrow for my chest and shoulders to follow. Push as I may I could not force my way in. When I finally realized that my little plan wouldn't work, I attempted to retrieve my head but couldn't get it back out. Well I must have been there for an hour or more. I shouted, yelled, pushed and pulled, but I was stuck fast, there was nothing I could do. Terence was the first to discover me and tried in vain to get my head free. Soon my family, the Gores and most of the denizens of Queen Street were out making suggestions and watching. One after another tried to turn my head and body in every conceivable position. They even covered my head and ears in grease and they tried to pull the railings apart but to no avail. Some of the neighbors who knew me well, including the Gores, suggested, it might be a good idea to leave me there. They finally decided to call the Fire Brigade. Upon arriving and after much sweating and straining managed to pries the railings apart and get my head lose. Once free I immediately began scrutinizing the crowd for the arsehole Brian.

One of the Firemen who helped to release me asked me how I had got stuck in the first place. I told him exactly what happened but he shook his head and insisted, that I must have been inside the garden, had managed to squeeze my body through the railings but not my head. And that, to my disgust, was the official verdict, as no one would believe my version. It must have been a year or more later. I was sitting on the kitchen table, wearing nothing but my underpants, while my Mother was washing my dirty knees. I heard Brian Gore's voice calling to someone up the road. I was off the table, out through the front door, across the street and laying into the horrified Brian before he knew what hit him. As I triumphantly marched back into the house I knew I was going to have to think quickly when Mam asked me,

"What was all that about?" I had been warned over and over again that I must forgive and forget. I had to think of another reason for bashing slimy Brian.

"He threw a snowball at me last Christmas." I replied, trying to look as indignant and as justified as I could. It was now the end of summer but it was the best I could think of. Mam turned her back on me and pretended to busy herself with some other chore, but I could see her shoulders shaking with silent laughter at my feeble excuse. I couldn't help laughing myself but our merriment was cut short by a thunderous hammering on the front door. We walked to the door and Mam opened it to a furious Granddad Gore who was holding a very, blooded Brian by the hand.

"This isn't good enough, Nora!" he complained gruffly, his eyes blazing.

"Well, Brian is bigger and older than Adrian," she replied, "He should learn to look after himself." Granddad Gore shifted his gaze to me and made an effort to soften his expression. "Adrian," he said, pleadingly, "When are you going to stop all this nonsense and be friends with Brian, instead of beating him up all the time?"

I looked him straight in the eye and replied,

"When my Kitten comes back to life."

****

On the 22nd of February 1942 "The Darvel" sailed into the Port of Merak on the Island of Java. From there Dad and the other troops traveled by train to the capital city Batavia. They were met by a contingent of Dutch officers and taken by bus to 'Mister Cornelius' army barracks. As they arrived the whole place was suddenly plunged into darkness as a prelude to a Jap air raid. Bombs were dropped but fortunately no loss of life occurred and very little damage to the base. A few days later they made another trip by train to Tjimhai and on arriving marched to No.12 Infantry Barracks rejoining what was left of 3rd, 12th and 15th Batteries who had also managed to escape from Singapore. The first day of March, Dad and three other drivers were detailed to carry reinforcements to Kalidjah Aerodrome. They were given the choice of returning the same night or the next day. After conveying the troops they ate a meal while they decided what they would do. Two of them voted to return that night after they had finished their meal. Two of them said they would prefer to stay the night and start back in the morning. The deciding vote fell to Dad and he chose to return as soon as they'd eaten. After arriving at the Barracks the next morning they were informed that earlier that day a large number of Jap troops had advanced on the airfield supported by Jap paratroopers. The Japs had captured the airfield and annihilated the troops they had just transported there. Only a few managed to escape. Major Coulston the commanding officer was killed when a Jap tank ran over him. Again Dad thanked God for what appeared to him as another very narrow escape. A couple of days later bombs dropped by the Japs and intended for their military camp instead landed on a nearby native village. The whole village and its inhabitants were literally blown to pieces. Next day the regiment and all its attachments pulled out of Tjimhai in attempt to get to Tjilatjap on the west coast of Java with the hope of boarding a ship on which they could make their escape to Australia. As they fled from the advancing Jap forces through the dense, Javanese jungle they were suddenly attacked by a Jap plane as they emerged from the concealment of the thick wooded canopy which covered most of the road. As the Jap dive-bombed the convoy on his first pass he made the mistake of bombing the back of the convoy instead of the front, which would have blocked the road and left the whole of the convoy at his mercy. The last two trucks were taken out, but by the time the Jap pilot was ready to make his second pass the rest of the convoy had time to gain the shelter of the jungle. Soon after the Jap plane abandoned its search for them as it was obviously getting short on fuel. On the 8th of March as their mad flight through the jungle continued they were met by a Dutch dispatch rider. He handed their commander, Lieutenant Colonel Hazel, a note announcing that the Dutch had capitulated. All Javanese cities, towns and villages were 'open.' As far as the Dutch were concerned. The War was over for them and they naively believed that they would now share administration with the Japs. The note also requested that all Allied troops on the island behave in a likewise manner and would receive in return a more favorable and benevolent treatment. The Dutch obviously didn't know the Japs very well, as they would soon find out. The Japs had done a very thorough job of cutting off all lines of communication and every avenue of escape. Their planes had bombed every ship in the ports of Tjilatjap and Surabaya. This news was broken to them by an allied convoy heading towards them as they were retreating from the ports. Dad's convoy in turn were able to inform them that the Japs were just behind them and if the convoy advanced they would most surely meet them head on. It was March the 9th 1942 and Dad's 32nd Birthday when they reached a tea plantation in Garut. There they were told that the Allied Command had decided to lay down their arms in surrender and to wait where they were for further Japanese instructions. Wow! What a Birthday present as Dad wondered, 'What now?' That night they slept under their vehicles and waited.

****

I examined my reflection carefully in the bathroom mirror as I held a straight razor in my right hand. I intended slashing my face with it and was trying to decide which way the cuts should go. Maybe, three or four gashes diagonally across my nose and down my cheek, or perhaps, vertically from my forehead, past my eye and down my cheeks to my chin. Whichever way I decided, they would need to be parallel and a couple of inches apart. I had folded a face towel and placed it on the bathroom sink in front of me. I guessed there would be a lot of blood, but reasoned that a blood soaked towel, would add not only drama but also considerable evidence to the credibility of my story. Who would refute my tale of bloodcurdling bravery, when confronted with my freshly scared face and a cloth dripping with blood? If they wanted to know where the pelt was. Or the carcass of the giant, Kodiak bear, that I had vanquished, as part of my initiation rites, as a Cherokee warrior. I could tell them it fell over a cliff in the life and death struggle. It landed in a fast flowing river and I couldn't find it, after it got swept over the waterfall.

Even as a kid I realized that first impressions were very important when establishing an identity. I was starting my first term in Saint Mary's Junior School and I thought it important, for staff and pupils alike, to appreciate the fact that they now had a celebrity in their midst. A famous War chief no less and the scars on my face, from the Bear's slashing claws would attest to the fact. I was confident that my story would be believed at my new school, but Mam was a problem. She had an uncanny way of guessing that I wasn't actually a real Red Indian War Chief. If she saw me with half my face hanging off, from the razor slashing, she'd probably beat the crap out of me. I could never understand how she wouldn't believe I was a real Redskin. Oh well, I'll fight a Kodiak bear, but I won't risk getting a hiding off Mam. I decided instead, to do the war paint smeared face and stick chicken feathers in my hair. The first time Mam had seen me dressed up like that, I could tell by the look on her face, that even she was impressed. Thank goodness the Junior School was just on the opposite corner of our street, as it was a bitterly cold January. All I was wearing, apart from every garish color in my paint box smeared all over my face, every chicken feather I owned in my hair, was my short trousers, shoes and socks. I also sported my Diana 22 air rifle. As soon as I hit the playground, the startled students made a path for me and I went straight into my most energetic and violent wardance. Partly for effect and partly because I was freezing my arse off. I danced and danced, I whooped, hollered and screamed my blood curdling war cries. when with sudden relief, for me as well as the other students, my performance was interrupted by the morning school bell. It beckoned all the children into the assembly hall, to commence the days schooling. Striding majestically to the front of the assembly hall, I made my grand entrance. I could tell immediately by the wide eyes and open mouths that my efforts had paid off. Even the Headmistress and all the teachers couldn't believe what they were witnessing. Head held high I leaned my air rifle against my crotch, leaving both my arms free to fold high and proudly across my chest. I knew I had captured the very image of 'The Noble Savage' even though the cold, wintry wind had caused my running nose to smudge my war paint all over my chops. After long silent minutes passed, the Headmistress was the first to find her tongue.

"Who do you think you are, Sitting Bull?!" The old paleface squaw boomed, fixing me, with excited eyes. I was flattered by her mistake and was about to explain that Sitting Bull was a Sioux, not a young, Cherokee War chief like me, when she added.

"Go home and wash your silly little face and don't come back, until you're wearing some warm, paleface clothes!" Shocked and crestfallen, I walked towards the exit, dragging my air rifle behind me. The whole assembly hall exploded with laughter. As I reached the doorway, I turned and eyed them all sullenly. 'Cowboy lovers', I thought, 'just you all wait, till I come riding out of the hills, through the streets of Brynmawr. Wearing my huge war bonnet, at the head of my bloodthirsty war party. You'll all find your scalps hanging outside my teepee.'- 'Maybe I should have stuck with the bear scars and blood?' I wondered.

****

March 10th-11th 1942, just after Dads 32nd Birthday, the bewildered soldiers were instructed to take all their arms, ammo and some of their transport to Tjikadjang railway siding. Dad threw his bayonet, rifle bolt and ammo into a rice field and then poured water down the barrel of his rifle. He didn't intend the Japs to get any use out of it. They were ordered to walk twenty miles back to Garut through the hot, steaming, jungle. Exhausted they arrived late in the evening and ate whatever was made available from their meager supply, before attempting to make themselves comfortable for the night. They thought the prolific growth of the towering bamboo would solve that problem. They were cut and split to fashion bench shaped beds and they all settled down, to enjoy some much needed sleep. Their rest was short-lived, as they were soon awakened by swarms of vicious, stinging, red ants, which unbeknown to them infested the bamboo. Pandemonium broke out as they frantically tried to beat the horrible, biting insects from their faces, hair and every other body part imaginable. Needless to say, there was no more sleep for anyone that night. Instead as their bodies itched, burned and throbbed, they sat miserably, listening to the nerve wracking night time chorus of Frogs, Crickets and the ever-present, biting, buzzing, mosquitoes. The nightmare conditions continued and as the days past many of the soldiers became sick, with malaria and dysentery. Still they waited. On the 18th of March, they made their first face to face contact with their Jap captors and were immediately made to feel humiliated. The Japs forced their prisoners to sweep up leaves along the jungle roads, whilst waving their bayonet-fixed rifles in their faces. They issued commands that the prisoners did not understand. Everything was confusing. Many a vicious and seemingly unwarranted beating was handed out. The bewildered prisoners were pummeled with fists, boots, riflebuts and spiteful jabs from the Japs sharp bayonets. The Japs became especially vicious towards their prisoners when in sight of any civilians. They never missing an opportunity to demonstrate who, were the conquerors and who were the conquered to the native populace. Just when Dad thought that things couldn't get any worse, he began getting terrible pains. His stomach felt as though his inside had turned into red hot water. He had to keep rushing into the jungle, which was their only toilet. The Regimental Doctor informed him that he had malaria. He was put in a field ambulance which took him to No 1 General Hospital in Bandoeng. He learned he had amoebic dysentery. At first Dad was very sick but after about three weeks began to recover quickly. This was just as well, because the Japs took over the Hospital. Dad, along with all the Allied patients were immediately ordered out and forced to walk about fifteen miles in the hot sun carrying all their kit. Most of the prisoners were in a very sick and weak condition. Halfway to their destination one of the Jap guards shouted "Yasme" which means 'is rest'. An immensely arrogant and extremely short Japanese officer strode into sight. He was approximately 4 feet 8 inches tall. From his belt hung a magnificent Samurai sword. The sword was so huge in proportion to its owner, that it had been fitted with a little wheel, at the bottom of the scabbard. It revolved along the ground, as the diminutive Jap strutted along. The Jap officer beckoned to a very tall Australian prisoner who stood about 6 feet 4 inches tall. As the prisoner approached him the officer stepped up onto a large, mound by the side of the road. He ordered the big Aussie, who was now standing to attention in front of him to 'Kerry'. This means, to bow very low to the Jap officer. As the prisoner did so, the Jap brought up his knee with tremendous force into the Aussie's face and knocked him flat on his back. This brought a huge grin of satisfaction onto the Jap officer's evil little face, as the Jap guards howled with glee. Their amusement was short lived, as the big Australian leaped from the ground and with a great round house punch smashed the little Nipponese gremlin into space. The rest of the prisoners wanted to laugh and cheer at the top of their voices, but they had to bite their lips and turn away. Punishment for making either mistake would have been unimaginable. The poor Aussie had been pounded into the dirt by the guard's riflebuts before the angry and disheveled officer had found his feet. The Jap officer barked out an order and the helpless giant was dragged to the other side of the road and nailed to a tree facing the hot sun. That's where he was left. The remaining prisoners were herded on by the Jap guards, to continue their journey. Hours later, those who were able, marched through the gates of their first concentration camp. Many, especially the sicker patients, had fallen by the wayside and had been loaded onto some of the Jap trucks, like so much garbage. The Japs had a mania for' Tenko; that was getting the prisoners on parade and counting them, to make sure there had been no escapes. After Tenko had been completed for the third time, they were all marched to their allotted cells. My Father was to share a cell, which measured fifteen feet square, with eighteen other prisoners. They lived in that vermin infested hole like sardines in a can. This was their first taste of prison life under their cruel and ruthless Jap conquerors. The daily ration of food given to each of the POW's by the Japs which they declared was sufficient for the long hours of hard work they would be made to do, was as follows: 600 grams of boiled rice, with a little watery vegetable soup would be split into three meals a day. Water, about three cups of tea or coffee, sometimes with sugar, but never with milk. Any animal that wandered into their camp, dog, rat, lizard or snake would soon find itself flavoring the otherwise tasteless soup. Even the maggots that infested the latrines became a valuable source of protein when added to their meager diet.

Many beatings, tortures, hunger, privation and terrible diseases while being forced to endure many hours of forced labor in the hot, humid, tropical sun caused many thousands of deaths. Even those fortunate enough to survive would be broken in health, in both body and mind. After they had settled into their cells, they were called out into the prison compound. They were informed by the Australian Officer in charge, Lieutenant Colonel E. E. Dunlop that the orders given to them by the Japs must be obeyed without hesitation. The penalty for breaking the rules and regulations laid down by the Japs was the same for the whole camp. Failure to comply meant that not only the offender but also the Officer in charge would also be executed. One of the first orders was that every POW had to have his hair shaved off. The regulation length was not more than one eighth of an inch. If an inspection guard could pinch a prisoner's hair between his finger and thumb, then that POW would be put in solitary confinement and issued half rations after receiving a thorough beating. On such occasions the other prisoner's food rations would also be cut in half. Needless to say all the POWs studied very hard to learn as much of the Jap language as possible. They would then know what they were being ordered to do, and comply quickly enough to satisfy their sadistic captors. At a nearby POW camp, filled mostly with Dutch Colonial troops, seventeen Abonese who had disobeyed an order were taken outside the camp, tied to trees with barbed wire and used for bayonet practice. A Dutch officer and soldier who managed to get outside the camp, in an effort to contact members of their families who had not yet been interned were shot. Those of the prisoners who were reasonably fit, Dad included were made to work long hours, under heavy guard. Mostly digging trenches for the Japs air-raid shelters and making anti-aircraft gun placements. Occasionally they would be taken into the town of Ban dung and ordered into houses that had belonged to Dutch and Indonesian families and remove the furniture and valuables for the Japanese officers. On one such occasion Dad and some other prisoners were enjoying a 'Yasme', or rest period, when a Jap guard decided he wanted to show off his wrestling skills to his fellow guards. He walked up and down, scrutinizing the seated POWs, singled Dad out and ordered him to stand up. He adopted a wrestling stance and beckoned my Father towards him. Dad was wearing a thick leather belt, to hold up his shorts and as they began to grapple. The Jap placed his thumb into the back of the belt, stepped behind Dad's legs with his left foot and with a powerful shove of his free hand threw Dad flat on his back. To the cheers of approval, the guard strutted about and declared himself the winner of the first fall. Dad slid off his belt and threw it to the other prisoners as the Jap motioned him to wrestle some more. As they approached each other my Father flew right at his opponent and dropped him in a similar fashion, to the way he had been thrown before. Much to the amazement of the Jap guard. As the guard regained his feet, he held up his finger to indicate that they would wrestle one more time to decide the winning fall. After a terrific struggle and much to everyone's surprise Dad once again succeeded in throwing the Jap wrestler. If everyone was surprised by the result of the match, they must have been shocked when the vanquished Jap got to his feet and said to Dad in the Malayan language,

"Orang bagus." This means, 'Good man, well done.' So instead of a spiteful reprisal which everyone, including my Father thought he would receive, he was congratulated by an honorable man who believed in fair play.

Another example of benevolence from the Japs was the time, when one of their guards took Dad aside and asked him in Malay, to teach him to sing some English folk songs. Dad taught him to sing, 'Rule Britannia' and 'God save the King.' Much to the amusement of the other prisoners. The Jap guard could soon be heard, singing at the top of his voice. 'God-ah save-ah the gracious King-ah; long-ah live-ah the noble-ah King-ah.' Their amusement soon turned to concern, when they wondered what would happen, if he was overheard by another Jap, who understood English.

On the 1st of June 1942 the Japs decided it was time to move the prisoners to a different camp. They did this on a fairly regular basis, so the inmates would not get too familiar with their surroundings, in case of a planned escape. They were marched back to Tjimhai, whilst the prisoners from Tjimhai were being marched to the camp vacated by them. As both camps marched past each other halfway through their respective journeys, they were prevented by the guards from exchanging any greetings or information. Especially regarding the war in Europe. News of the war with Germany filtered in from friendly natives and from illegal radios kept hidden by the POWs. Frequent checks by the Japs failed to impede the ingenuity of some of the prisoners. Some had built receiving sets into water bottles and the soles or heels of wooden shoes which were worn right in front of the Jap guards. The Jap Commandant at camp 18 was much more kindly disposed towards the POWs and for a little while they enjoyed privileges hitherto unknown in a POW camp. For a few weeks life became a little more bearable, until he was replaced by Lieutenant Soni. He was a very strict disciplinarian who brought with him a number of cruel and sadistic guards. These guards took a vicious delight in beating up POWs for no other reason than the pure enjoyment of it. Food rations were cut and the workload increased. The hunt for anything vaguely edible that could supplement their starvation diet, whether dog, cat, rat, lizard, snake or maggot, was resumed with the renewed vigor that only the really hungry could appreciate. A POW who failed to salute one of the guards was beaten without mercy and crammed into a small pen in the middle of the compound in the hot sun with no water for hours. He was then ordered to hold a heavy bar above his head for most of the day. Each time his arms dropped from exhaustion he was beaten until he managed to lift the bar again. This went on until he fell completely and utterly exhausted into insensibility. They left him in that condition for hours before he was taken to receive medical treatment. He was in a very bad way. With this in mind, it was with horror that Dad and three Australian prisoners were suddenly confronted with a furious Jap guard, who had quietly approached them while all four of them were laying down, taking a break from work. He became more and more enraged as he demanded in both Malay and Japanese the reason why they had not jumped to their feet and saluted him. They were marched at the double to the guard room where there were several more guards on duty and brought before them for questioning. All four prisoners were told to stand to attention while some of the guards arranged themselves each side and behind them. Dad stood rigidly to attention but the three Aussies fearing the fact that they were now surrounded stood defiantly with their arms folded and looked at the Japs with contempt. Defiance under those circumstances proved to be a terrible mistake. The three Australians were pulverized, they were beaten from all sides with the butt-end of the Japs rifles till they were a tangled, bloody heap on the ground. One of the guards turned to Dad who was still standing as stiff as a board and to his amazement said in the Malay language,

"Angkau Orang bagus soldator, bayk pergi." which meant,

"You are a good soldier, you can go."

Wally Sherratt was one of Dad's best friends; he was a huge, strong man with a very kindly nature, who Dad called the gentle giant. But his massive bulk seemed to melt like a Popsicle in the hot, tropical sun. Forced labor and starvation diet was followed by dysentery and malaria, in a very short time he died. Dad was taken very ill with dengi fever, which is caused by the bite of a striped mosquito. He was examined by several doctors who were greatly puzzled by his blood count. Although he was barely conscious and his eyesight had been badly affected by the disease, he remembers the doctors and orderlies shaking their heads in disbelief. There was no way he should still be alive according to his blood count. They considered his recovery as nothing short of miraculous. Dad's first Christmas in captivity come and went, when they were transferred to 'Boei Glodak' prison in Djakarta, where their existence droned on and on. By November 1943 my Father found himself once again in St Vincentius Hospital after suffering severe stomach pains. After a four and a half hour operation he had two rough surfaced gall stones removed. Another Christmas came and went.

Lieutenant Soni was a lunatic. Every time there was a full moon he would go on a rampage and usually vented his madness on the medical section of the camp. He would charge screaming into the supplies of precious medicines and medical equipment, smashing and destroying everything he could lay his hands on. Anyone unlucky enough to be caught in his path would be punched and kicked as he continued on his way leaving a trail of devastation in his wake. On one occasion during an insane fit, as he was crashing out of the medical department an old Dutchman was in his pathway, which he attacked with all the fury he could muster. The old man was beaten to death before the madman left the building. This was only one of many similar incidents committed by this Japanese brute. He with many others including the notorious 'Tiger of Malaya' were executed for their crimes when the war ended. It was a very unfortunate time for Dad to suffer more stomach pains. An Australian physician Dr. Peodivin after confirming he had appendicitis was prepared for an immediate operation. Thanks to Lieutenant Soni there was now no General anesthetic only local, which they soon found didn't work. Dad was strapped to the operating table, while two orderlies held him down by his arms. He was told to hold on, while the surgeon went to work with sharpened knives and razor blades, which was all the surgical equipment they possessed. Dad thought that he would grind his teeth down to the gums with the intense agony he had to bear. After the offending appendix was removed he was congratulated by everyone present on his toughness and fortitude. Dad believed his recovery was a miracle; especially considering the meager ration of food he was given. Many deaths from malnutrition and disease were being suffered by the POWs every day; men became so weak when they got sick they had no resistance to fight any illness. This coupled with the vicious beatings was like murder by degrees. Sometimes the Japs would come into the compound and demand a large contingent of prisoners to go out and work in their various garages and workshops, helping to repair their trucks etc. On one particular day along with 123 other prisoners Dad was chosen to work in a big motor repair department a few miles outside the prison camp of Boei Glodak. As usual they were all assembled outside the guardroom and counted, 124 prisoners in all. They were then all marched out and onto trucks that were waiting to take them to where they had been detailed to work. As they were marching out 5 Dutch prisoners who had managed to escape outside the prison the evening before crept stealthily out of the jungle and tagged along with them while the guards were supervising the loading of the prisoners into the trucks. Apparently the 5 Dutchmen had friends and family that they had visited in the nearby town. Since early that morning they had been hiding outside the prison trying to devise some way of getting back in without being detected by the Japs. When they got off the trucks at the depot the guards lined them all up again for Tenko. When they counted the prisoners and found that they now had 129 prisoners instead of 124 they went completely berserk. They demanded to know who the 5 extra men were and where they had come from. The other prisoners refused to give them away. Instead of assigning the prisoners to their various tasks they packed them all back into the trucks and sped straight back to camp. They were lined up and made to stand on the boiling hot cobblestones outside the guardhouse in the hot tropical Sun under heavy guard. One of their number went to report the matter to the camp commandant. Before he had chance to respond the rain suddenly came down in torrents and they were left standing on the parade ground until it stopped. Finally out came a very angry commandant who stood in front of every prisoner in turn demanding to know who the 5 culprits were. Still the Dutchmen wouldn't confess and the other prisoners refused to give them away. The commandant was furious as he kept asking questions for hour after hour but received no answers. They had not been given any food or drink since early that morning, which had consisted of rice and water. Now made to stand to attention in the hot sun for hour on end their hunger and even more so their thirst became unbearable. Eventually the interrogation wore the commandant out. He ordered the prisoners to be marched to some cells where they would be locked up to await further interrogation. There would be no food or drink until a confession was forthcoming. By now it was late at night, but in spite of their exhaustion sleep alluded most of them due to the terrible thirst they were all suffering. At 1 o'clock in the morning they were awakened, marched out and once again forced to assemble in front of the guardroom. Then out of the guardroom burst a furious cursing commandant shaking his fists angrily,

"Who are the 5 culprits?!" He demanded, still no one

answered. They were all ordered to kneel down on their bare knees on the hard cobblestones with their arms held rigidly by their sides. They would remain in that position until a confession was made. He continued with his questioning but still no answers came. After a couple more hours of interrogation with the same unsatisfying results the commandant flew into such a frenzy that he rushed back into the guardroom and returned with a heavy wooden club. With it went up and down the lines of prisoners bringing the club down on their unprotected heads. He alternated the blows of his club with vicious kicks into the ribs, stomachs and spines of his helpless victims with his heavy jackboots. Men fell bleeding and unconscious as he continued on his way closer to where Dad was kneeling and praying. The commandant stopped and prepared to deliver the blow, Dad prayed that it would not inflict too much damage. Down came the club crashing against Dad's skull and sending him sprawling backwards onto the cobblestones. Whether it was God's intervention as interpreted by Dad, or pure shock, Dad swore that he hardly felt the blow. He soon found he had plenty of time to contemplate. The extreme exertion caused by his furious and savage assault on the prisoners had completely exhausted the commandant. Before going off to rest and recover he ordered the prisoners back on their knees in a rigid upright position until he received the confession he was determined to achieve. Four hours later after enduring the agonies of torture and thirst the Dutchmen could stand no more of it. Much to the relief of the other 124 prisoners they confessed to the Japs. The 5 Dutchmen were badly beaten, interrogated, beaten some more and finally placed in solitary confinement on half rations. The rest of the prisoners were sent back to their quarters but were still not given food or drink. Much later they received some rice and water that were quickly consumed prior to being counted. Thank goodness there was still only 124 of them this time.

Early in the morning on 14th of September 1944 1,750 POWs, including Dad were marched to the dockside of Tandjong Piok, where a ship of about 5,000 tons was moored. They were amazed as they watched about 5,500 Indonesian coolie labor, comprising of men, women and children being driven aboard the vessel. These were followed by 600 Ambones' POWs. They were positive that there would be no room to transport so many. To Dad's utter astonishment they were the next to get marched onto the ship, they were packed in like sardines. Including the Jap crew and guards, there was well over 9,000 souls on board a vessel of only 5,000 tons. They were packed into makeshift platforms about 5 feet high and beaten into place by the impatient Jap guards. They were made to sit in long lines between each other's legs so as to utilize every square inch of space. This is the position they were kept in the whole time they were on the ship, except for work duty, or to answer the call of nature. Sanitation was indescribable, vomit and excreta was everywhere, as most of them had malaria or dysentery, or both. Their daily food ration was one cup of water and one cup of rice per man. This they endured for three days when one of the prisoners went mad and jumped overboard. The Jap guards thought this was hilarious and couldn't stop laughing until they realized he was swimming to shore, which was just about visible in the distance. They were forced to put out a boat in order to bring the poor wretch back to receive a severe beating. They had been hugging the shore in order to avoid being exposed to Allied submarines known to be lurking in those waters. Now they needed to put out well to sea to prevent any more attempts to escape. The POWs and native coolies were being transported to Northern Sumatra to work in the coal mines. Coal was a very valuable commodity for war time Japan. On the 18th of September, Dad was listening to the monotonous, pulsating beat of the engines and sitting in between one prisoners legs while the prisoner in front of him sat between his. Suddenly there was a terrific explosion in the hold where the coolie labor had been crammed. There was pandemonium as all the POWs in front rushed for the wooden stairways that led to the decks above. Dad was very much enclosed on the bottom tier and had very little chance of making it to either of the stairways. Bewildered Dad looked for a way to escape. Then with a rendering crash the stairways on both sides suddenly collapsed with the sheer weight of the struggling bodies trying to climb them. That's when Dad noticed a huge mountain of bedding and kit belonging to the POWs. He began scrambling to the top of it as fast as he could. From the peak he was able to leap into space and make a grab for an iron girder that straddled across the width of the ship. He just managed to reach the girder and haul himself astride it when the second torpedo struck the ship killing hundreds more men. By the time he had climbed across the girder and reached the deck he saw that many people had already jumped into the sea. The vessel was already listing as many more men were running up and down the deck. Wringing their hands in despair and crying out in their different tongues "What can we do?" A field generator broke its mooring chains and crushed a man against the rails killing him instantly just as he had prepared himself to jump. Men were still yelling and screaming as the deck swung into a more impossible angle. Dozens were jumping each second to join the hundreds of bobbing heads and flailing arms already in the sea. Dad prayed to God to help him as he knew he couldn't swim. As the ship lurched violently he launched himself into the air and as he dropped the vast waters of the Indian Ocean closed over him.

****

Mam answered the front door and I looked up from her side to see standing on the doorstep, dressed in his usual black suit the Pastor of the 'Tabernacle' Old Mr. Noble.

"Oh Nora," he cried, as though preaching to his flock from the pulpit of his grey corrugated iron chapel, "I have got some terrible news for you, your husband and my brother in the Lord, Emrys is dead and won't be coming home."

"How do you know this and why haven't I been informed?" Mam asked him.

"God revealed it to me in a dream last night Nora." He replied, adopting his most sympathetic and his best holier than thou expression.

"Oh yeah, what exactly did God say? Asked my Mam, eyeing Mr. Noble, with a flat, stony expression. I felt as though the air had been squeezed out of me. I obviously didn't remember Dad when he was home. But, with everyone else in the family I dreamed for Dad to come home. It had never occurred to me that he could die. Even though, in spite of being so young, I knew he was at war and had been fighting the Japs.

"Is Dad dead?" I asked my Mother panic stricken.

"No! Of course he isn't love." Mam replied. I wasn't convinced, I looked at the grey, gaunt looking Mr. Noble as he compressed his lips inclined his vulture like head and folded his hands in front of him as if in silent prayer. I had been going to Sunday school at "The Tabernacle" for as long as I could remember. I was taught it was sinful to tell a lie. Not only did I appreciate that Mr. Noble was the head honcho of the chapel so he could only tell the truth. But I had caught Mam out in a little white lie quite recently. I had read in an encyclopedia some facts about a Red Indian tribe and in conclusion it had stated, 'Alas the Indians are a dying race.' Obviously with my obsession with Indians I was devastated and wanted reassurance that it wasn't true. I knew that if I asked Mam outright if it was true that Indians were indeed a dying race, she being aware of my love of Indians, would reassure me that it wasn't true. So I went about it in a roundabout way and asked my Mother,

"Mam, is everything in an encyclopedia true?"

"Yes, of course it is love." She answered absently. I was inconsolable, I screamed, I cried, I wanted to die, I was so upset.

"What's the matter love, what's wrong with you?" She asked. I couldn't even answer for hours; every time I tried the impact of what I had read hit me with renewed force and started me off again. When I finally managed to blurt out the reason for my distress through sobs that almost choked me, Mam did a complete one eighty and said,

"Oh no love, I didn't understand what you asked me, I wasn't listening properly, not everything in encyclopedias is true, there's still plenty of Red Indians about."

"Well how come I can't bloody find any then?" I sobbed, still unconvinced.

The next time I was in Sunday school knowing that only the truth was spoken there, I asked the same question 'is everything you read in an encyclopedia true?' and got an answer that partly consoled me. Mr. Noble shook a Bible in my face and declared,

"This is the only truth!"

"Well are there any grapes in Heaven?" I asked, while I had his attention.

"No my son," he boomed, "we'll have no need of earthly food in the Kingdom of Heaven; we will be nourished by the word and the spirit of God!"

"Well if they haven't got grapes I'm not going!" I replied, hoping that as Mr. Noble had the ear of God he might confer on my behalf. Although I had never seen grapes, let alone tasted them, due to the war, they were another of my obsessions, as pictures I'd seen of them really appealed to me.

"If you don't go to Heaven you'll go to the Devil and burn in an everlasting lake of fire!" Ranted Mr. Noble.

"Do they have grapes?" I inquired.

****

Dad broke the surface of the ocean coughing and spluttering. Literally the drowning man clutching for a straw, or anything else he could grab to help keep him afloat. Everywhere he looked there was heads bobbing, bodies floating, swimming splashing. And thank goodness plenty of debris to help him stay buoyant long enough to look for some form of salvation. There it was, floating about fifty yards away a wooden latrine box, how he reached it he'd never know. Being a very religious man it's obvious to where he attributed the credit. As he grabbed the latrine so did a few others with the same idea in mind which caused the latrine to roll over in the water. Dad was sent back into the depths below the surface of the ocean. Up he popped again then back below the surface as soon as he reached for the rolling latrine. He realized that this was not going to work, as a raft floated into sight, again about fifty yards away. So, praying as he went, he floundered and groped his way through the ocean, until he managed to reach his goal. There was already about twenty others hanging on the raft when Dad grasped it and they realized that they needed to get as far away from the sinking ship as they could. The resulting suction could drag the raft as well as the survivors down with it. This is what they endeavored to do as the ship sank below the waves. She had been torpedoed by an American submarine at 5.30 p.m. and sank within 20 minutes. The Jap commander, his crew and his guards, got away in the lifeboats. Some of the POWs tried to save themselves by clinging to the sides. The Jap guards who were armed with axes, chopped their hands off or split their heads open. The carnage was awful.

There were 20 other POWs clinging to the raft besides Dad, a few were British, the rest were Dutch or Eurasian. Although they had only been in the water about half an hour, they realized that darkness would come very quickly. The question arose as to what they were going to do. In the distance they could see the escort that had accompanied them from Java. A destroyer and a corvette. The corvette seemed to be the closest to them, but in their weak condition, could they reach it? One of the POWs named Boyd knew Dad was a Christian and asked him to pray for them, as he realized they were all in a very desperate situation. So Dad said to the others around the raft,

"Boys, now is the time for you all to pray to God on your own behalf and commit the keeping and saving of your bodies and souls to him who is mightily able to save." So they had a prayer meeting around a 6 foot square raft in the shark infested waters of the Indian Ocean. They struggled in the water for over an hour in their effort to reach the corvette, but the strong current seemed to carry them away. When darkness descended upon them they could still see the corvette's silhouette in the moonlight. Four times more they struggled towards the ship. Each time as they thought they were about to make it, the current pulled them out of reach. By then they were exhausted and could not carry on. Of the 21 who had prayed around the raft only one Dutchman had seemed to have lost all interest in his soul and body. A few times he tried to break away from the raft, but Dad had hold of him with one hand while he clung to the raft with the other until he thought his arms would break off. Some of the others also tried to hold on to him, but he seemed determined to drift away. Finally they became so weak that they could hold on to him no longer. There was a feeling of real grief as he slipped away and they saw him no more. Everyone prayed to God, for the strength and courage to make one last attempt. They had by now been floundering in the water for over eight and a half hours. With the prayer still on his lips Dad thought that their prayers had been heard and answered as the raft finally touched the side of the corvette.

"Help!" Dad shouted in Malay, "Please throw us some ropes." Down came the ropes and some of the prisoners who had managed to stand up on the raft, caught them. Soon all the POWs were on board with the exception of Dad and a Scotsman named Dick, who was completely naked. Dad had fixed himself to the rope that ran around the edge of the raft with a hook on a belt that had been given to him by a very good friend. His arms had finally grown too weak to hold on to the raft by themselves. The rope had swollen in the water and it was now impossible to get it out of the hook. Dad had to unbuckle the belt which he regarded as his prize possession. He left it attached to the rope around the raft in order to stand and get himself hauled aboard the corvette. Luckily for Dick, Dad was wearing two pairs of shorts, one of which he gave to Dick, so the Jap onlookers didn't have to feel inferior for too long. Dad and Dick were interrogated on the spot by two Jap guards. What were their names, their homeland, etc. After the interrogation Dad and Dick were beaten viciously and were left lying on the deck, while the guards went off to deal with the other survivors. In spite of the vicious beating they received, after being rescued from a terrible ordeal in the Indian Ocean, Dad and Dick managed to crawl under the tarpaulin which covered the ships derricks. That's where they stayed until dawn came. They were awakened by cries for help and as they groped for consciousness they realized that they were at anchor. The only movement of the ship was caused by the rise and fall of the swell. Both Dick and Dad scrambled out onto the deck. As their eyes adjusted to the faint light on the horizon they became aware of a dark skinned young man floundering near the stern of the ship. He was still crying for help. They raced towards the stern they noticed a long pole with a length of rope attached and found it fairly easy to place the rope within the young man's reach. As they commenced to pull him towards the ships side, the Japs, who are always ready for a little sport at someone else's cost, decided to move the corvette. Desperately they tried to hang on, but the ever increasing speed caused the weight of the man being dragged through the water to become so heavy, that the pole just slipped out of their grasp. So close to rescue, the young man merely became another one of the many causalities. Out of the 5,500 coolies only 300 were rescued from the sea. Only 278 of the 1,750 European POWs. 312 out of the 600 Abonese POWs. The Jap commander, his crew and his guards were also picked up. There was no way of knowing how many casualties the Japs may had suffered. That morning Dad learned that during the interrogation the night before, the Jap guards had thrown 17 of the survivors back into the sea. All around the cabin area were strewn the badly mutilated corpses of Abonese POWs. Whether their deaths and mutilation was caused by the Jap guards or from shark attacks while they were still in the water, or from wounds sustained when the torpedoes exploded in the transporters they would never know. Dad and some of the other prisoners were ordered to throw the bodies over board and forced to clean the decks of the remaining blood and gore. In all that time the hard working POWs had been offered no food or drink as the hot equatorial sun rose to its zenith. They thought they would go crazy with thirst. The eight and a half hours of floundering in sea water had only added to their agony. An Abonese POW named, Manuputi became so desperate that in spite of warnings that his thirst would become worse as a result, he urinated into his cupped hands and drank it. Later that day, the 19th of September 1944 the corvette anchored off the coast of Sumatra. All the prisoners were dumped unceremoniously overboard and made to swim for the beach. With no debris to cling to and no swimming skills whatsoever Dad after all he had already been through, would have lost his life drowning within sight of land. If not for a Dutchman who saw him struggling in the water and immediately swam to his aid. When they reached the beach Dad hardly had time to thank God and his Dutch rescuer, before they were rounded up and counted by the Jap guards. Once more they were counted and then marched inland to a Jap outpost and counted yet again. What a sorry looking crowd they presented, those who were not completely naked wore only shorts or jockstraps. What they stood in was the total sum of their worldly possessions. They didn't have a cup or a can, or any other kind of utensil to use even if the Japs did offer them any food or drink. They were told later that they would be given a little boiled rice with dried fish and some water to drink but they didn't know what they could eat and drink out of. The problem was finally solved by the abundance of coconut palms that grew everywhere. With so many cocoanuts on the ground they were able to crack the nuts open and after scooping out the rotten pith use the empty shells as dishes and cups. There were also plenty of mussel shells in the sandy soil that they used for spoons. The Jap outpost was not designed to accommodate prisoners and they were told that they would be moving to another destination the next day. They discovered that their sleeping accommodations that night would be under the huts of the Jap guards. They had nothing to cover their naked bodies from the swarms of voracious mosquitoes. The Jap's huts were built on platforms about two feet high and as the prisoners crawled underneath they found their hands and knees sinking into the chicken shit that was inches deep over the sand. As if all this had not been enough to endure. The guards in the room above them amused themselves by pouring sand onto them all night, through the cracks in the floor of the hut. This deprived them of any little chance they may have had of getting some much needed sleep. They were all glad when dawn arrived and they were allowed out of their wretched quarters. Lined up and again counted to make sure no one had escaped during the night. When the Japs were satisfied that all were accounted for, they were marched to a local river where a Jap landing craft was awaiting them. It carried them several miles upriver. After they disembarked they were forced to endure a nightmare journey through the jungle to another river. With no shoes or socks on their feet the thorns and spikes in the undergrowth caused the POWs unimaginable injury and pain. Many of the prisoners fainted by the wayside and the Jap guards tried to beat them back to sensibility. When they failed to respond, they were left in the jungle to die. Eventually they reached the Indrapura River and were ferried across to the opposite bank by native canoes that had been waiting for them for that purpose. On the other side of the river lay a native village where they were allowed to rest and were even given a little rice and water. They were also given a pair of multi colored native shorts to replace the tattered ones that some of them had been lucky enough to own. Then they were bundled onto the backs of trucks where they had to force themselves amongst large drums of oil and petrol. With 35 POWs forced into each vehicle it was even more of a tight squeeze than on board the transport ship. When all the trucks were ready they set off on what was to prove the beginning of the most terrible journey by road that they had ever undertaken. They traveled through steaming hot jungle roads and over high mountain passes for over 200 miles before arriving late that night at Padang. Dysentery was rife in the camp, so bad in fact that many died in the two days spent there. When they continued their journey there were only dying men left in that camp. They had only been given two small bowls of rice the whole time they had spent at the camp. Then a little rice and dried fish, which stank to high heaven to last them on this next stage of their journey. After traveling about 150 miles inland they arrived the next day at Payakombo. There they were paraded barefooted through the streets, much to the amusement of the native population. Then reloaded 50 to a vehicle onto some Lorries, waiting the other side of town to transport them towards Paken Baru. There followed another nightmare journey as none of them could move an inch to relieve their acing limbs. Cursing and groaning was all the POWs could do to pass the 200 mile trek. This took them to the other end of the island and their destination No. 4 camp at Paken Baru. After arriving Dad met up with some friends he had first met in a camp in Java and one of them gave him an aluminum panikin and spoon. The panikin contained rice flavored with an evil smelling concoction called ikan tressi which he later found out was fish manure used for growing vegetables. Nevertheless he ate it with gusto and soon got used to eating it as there was little else but rice and an ongo-longo-pap, that looked and tasted like wallpaper paste. A couple of weeks later all of the remaining shipwreck survivors were taken further up the River Siak to camp No. 43. Forty-four of the survivors had already died within 10 days of their rescue due to the appalling treatment. The horrible journey and starvation diet, they could no longer endure. On arriving at camp No. 43, they were formed into working parties, to work the railroad project between Paken Baru and Muaru. In that very difficult part of the country, the Dutch had failed to build a railroad, so the Jap commandant got all the working parties together and said,

"This stretch of railroad has been given to me to lay and will be completed, even if it means a POW for every sleeper laid." With a few thousand sick and diseased POW and coolie labor he succeeded, but only at the cost of many hundreds of lives. There were several camps spread out along the line and at one camp alone Dad counted over 600 graves. If a Jap wanted 500 men on a certain rail section at any time he got them, even if that number was made up of very sick men. Some had to be carried on stretchers by the rest of the POWs. If they weren't capable of doing anything else they were made to straighten out bent nails. Many of these poor wretches died and were buried alongside of the railway track. As the tracks grew longer and further away from base camp, it became necessary to put rails and sleepers onto trucks. Then pulled by engines that burned wood for fuel. Dad was amongst the prisoners detailed to cut and collect the wood. On one such occasion, Dad had just laid down a machete he had been using to chop off the small braches from the bigger lengths of wood. He then threw the smaller branches into a large fire that they had built for that purpose, when a Malaysian coolie reached over and took it. Dad asked him to return it to him, as each POW was held responsible to the Japs for the tools they were using. After being completely ignored by the coolie, Dad bided his time until he got an opportunity to snatch it back. As he reached for it the coolie suddenly let out a blood curdling screech and began throwing Kung-fu like kicks at Dad from all directions. Dad managed to avoid or block most of the kicks that were being rained on him in rapid succession by the irate native. He realized that the vicious little Malaysian was purposely attempting to drive him back into the fire. As Dad began to feel the heat scorching his back the coolie took a couple of quick steps back and then came hurtling forward in a flying dropkick. If it had connected it would have smashed Dad right into the middle of the blazing fire. Dad anticipated such a move and managed a side step with perfect timing. He threw a right handed fist which exploded straight into the Malaysian's face. The force of the punch combined with the impetus of coolie's flying dropkick turned the would be Kung-fu assassin upside down. He landed on his head and was knocked out, as cold as a Penguin's buttocks.

There was very little to eat and the only water available was from some very oily streams flowing out of the jungle on the opposite side of the track. When the Jap guards were otherwise occupied they would take a chance and steal some boiling water from the engine via a valve underneath. At least they knew that the water from that source was sterilized but the guards were generally too vigilant. Then prisoners were forced to drink the impure jungle water. Dysentery was very prevalent; Dad had it badly together with attacks of Malaria. He was amongst the many sick transported back to base camp hospital. They were placed in a large hut with patients who the Doctor had diagnosed with Typhus. Dad became very ill as men around him were dying like flies. Those who had that terrible disease slipped into a coma, which would last for about 21 days and at the end would not recover. Although Dad was oblivious to the world and everything in it for a full 3 weeks he miraculously recovered. Although very weak and feeble he gradually got better to learn that with the exception of a Welsh Major named Armstrong from Cardiff, everyone else in their hut had died. As the days passed and Dad became a little stronger he was given light duties in connection with other hospital huts, dispensing camp-made medicines to Malaria and Dysentery patients. In that way he made many friends and was permitted to give spiritual help and comfort to many who needed it. Some just before they died. Although it could be a heartbreaking experience, Dad was happy to think that God was using him in such a desperate situation. Time went by and they hardly knew what day or even what month it was. Rumors and bits of information began to filter into the camp that the War in Europe had ended and that things were turning against the Japs in both India and Burma. The Japs reacted in various ways, some became even more homicidal while others became more kindly. Some asked the POWs what they thought would happen to them if the Americans won the War. They told them that the Americans would not treat them as badly as the Japs had treated their prisoners. A few of the Japs even asked if the POWs thought they should commit 'Hari-Kari'. At that suggestion many of the prisoners became quite enthusiastic and suggested that it was definitely worth considering. That was sometime in June 1945. Rumors and the weird change in many of the Guards attitudes gave them hope, but work resumed on the railroad with a vengeance. At one point the Jap Commandant arrived to give the POWs a lecture, telling them through an interpreter that the railroad had to be completed by August 14[th.] Then the prisoners were made to work from dawn to dark every day carrying rails and sleepers. They were hustled on by vicious blows from the guards armed with lengths of hard rubber, heavy sticks or, the butt end of a rifle as they shouted,

"Lekas, lekas, Speedo, Speedo." Or their form of swearing, like, "Kanara bagero, orang, oranga tida cagoes." Meaning, "No good lazy, men, work faster." They were kept at it for about another 5 to 6 weeks. On the 15th of August, one day after schedule, the two stretches of railway line met. There was great jubilation amongst the Japs, who were so elated that they gave out cigars to the POWs. The last nail that the survivors drove into the last sleeper on that railroad of death through the hot, steamy, Sumatran jungle was made of copper. This, 'The other railway of death," built by British, Australian and Dutch POWs and by press-ganged Javanese slave labor. Through the swamps, mountains and jungles of central Sumatra under the orders of their cruel Jap captors had taken a terrible toll, probably more than 10,000 people altogether. This does not include the victims who perished on the way to Sumatra. Torpedoed by our own Allies whilst on board the Junyo Maru and the Van Waerwijck. After returning to camp where they were allowed a few days well earned rest. They began to notice a marked difference in the attitudes of the Jap guards, who suddenly became much friendlier towards them. Obviously they began to wonder why? It was August the 28th, less than two weeks after the completion of the infamous railway when an Allied Officer from base camp arrived. He went immediately to see the Jap Commandant. Soon the Commandant emerged from his office with the most unbelievably good news any of them had received since before the War had began. He simply informed them that hostilities between the axis forces and the Allied forces in Europe and South-East Asia were at an end. He no longer had the power to make them work. However he still did expect them to maintain camp discipline and look after the general welfare of the camp. It was then it dawned on them why all of the most cruel of the Jap guards had already disappeared. They left only a few elderly and more kindly guards, but it was another two weeks before they learned the whole truth. The War with Germany had ended in May of that year. Hitler had committed suicide the month before. Japan had agreed to an unconditional surrender on the 14th of August after America had dropped the first of the big bombs on Hiroshima on the 6th and then Nagasaki on the 14th. That was the day before the completion of the Sumatran railway of death. It was with surreal joy that they began to realize they were now free men. They were about to live the dream that most of them thought they would never realize after three and a half long, terrible years of captivity. A locomotive hauling a long line of trucks pulled into a siding near their camp. The POWs got into them after gathering their meager possessions and were soon traveling back to base camp, along the very track that they and so many of their now dead comrades had built. They made the journey for the first time as free men, but with mixed emotions as sadly some died on their last ride to base camp and freedom. Waiting for them was a good meal of steamed rice and stew, plus a good bath and some decent clothes to replace the dirty, tattered, lice infested rags they had been wearing. When they reached base camp they learned that the Japs had kept the news that the war had been over for a couple of weeks for fear of reprisal. The ex-POWs spent a few days at that camp enjoying delicacies they hadn't eaten for four years, especially Australian meat, sausages and coffee. Then news came up the line that they were to expect a very important visitor, Lady Mountbatten. After inspecting the camp she told them that they would all be repatriated as soon as possible. She had instructed liaison Officers to take everyone's name, rank, regiment and home address in order to get cablegrams sent home to their relatives. There would be good news for some and terrible news for others. She was appalled at the conditions that had existed in the camps and amazed to see so many men who had not completely lost their reason after suffering such horrific experiences. They were informed that an army landing craft would soon be coming to take them back to Singapore. Dad arrived back in Singapore on the 19th of September. It was one year to the day since they had landed on the beach in Sumatra after their ship had been torpedoed. Upon disembarking they were picked up by ambulances that were waiting for them quayside to take them straight into an emergency hospital. It was so full that they all had to sleep on the balcony. The next day they were examined and given medicine to combat the effects of Malaria, Dysentery, Beriberi and tropical ulcers. For the past few months Dad had noticed that his arms, legs and tummy had swollen. They were causing him a lot of pain, the Doctors told him it was beriberi, which had led to kidney malfunction that resulted in the swelling of his stomach and limbs. He was still also suffering with both malaria and dysentery. During the time they spent in the Hospital they were given some army pay and allowed out to look around the City. Dad and his friends became ravenously hungry. As only Dad had spent any time in Singapore it was left to him to suggest the best place to eat. Dad took them to a place that was a car park in the daytime, but was almost magically transformed into the most exotic food market at dusk. Food stalls sold every kind of Oriental delicacy imaginable. The smell of roasting meats and vegetables, fresh herbs and spices assailed their nostrils like a gastronomic orgasm. They decided there and then that they were going to have a meal to remember. There was all kinds of meat, fish, vegetables and exotic tropical fruits too numerous to itemize. It was as though all the longing and dreaming for food, glorious food over the past three and a half years had been granted. They found themselves sitting in an Aladdin's cave of grub. Dad declared it was a meal that was never surpassed in his lifetime. He told them all that although he never dreamed of being wealthy he would love one day to be able to afford to bring his wife Nora to repeat the wonderful experience. Also to see with him some of the strange and wondrous places he seen, but in time of peace. They were told they were soon to go home and were given the choice of flying which would take but a couple of days or a much longer journey on a large ship. Dad opted for the longer route. It would give him an opportunity to put a bit more weight on his dreadfully skinny malnourished frame before being reunited with his loved ones. Before Dad was taken prisoner he had weighed a solid muscular 156 pounds. As he sailed out of Singapore in the transport ship Antinor he was a scrawny, 90 pound, pot bellied skeleton. Their first port of call was Ceylon, Dad thought it ironic that after they had first left Britain they were not allowed to go ashore in West Africa for fear that they may have contracted some deadly disease. Upon arrival in Ceylon they were not allowed on shore in fear of them spreading some deadly disease. After taking on fresh water, oil and food supplies they were on their next leg of their voyage which took to Egypt. From there into the Mediterranean and on to Gibraltar.

Sailing through the straights into the Atlantic they thought that they would be landing in Southampton and were disappointed to learn that they would be sailing to Liverpool instead. On the 23rd of October 1945 as they sailed up the Irish Sea and came in sight of Liverpool a terrific storm blew up so instead of landing once again in Britain after four years absence they had to wait until the storm abated. So close and yet so far.

PEACE?!

"The War's over!" They were shouting in the streets of Brynmawr. I'd heard the same thing a few months before when the Germans surrendered. Not much had changed except we now had no blackout and no more air-raids. "The Japs have surrendered the war is over, now its peace." Now what? I thought, almost apprehensively. When I was born we were at war, I hadn't experienced anything but war. What was this peace thing going to be like? I'd been hearing all my life, that things will be like this, or like that, when the war is over. It had gone on year after year and nothing changed. So what was supposed to happen now? Your Dad will be coming home now the war is over, I was told. After all this time I found the news just a little bit too good to be true. There was rejoicing in the streets. Excitement and celebrations going on all over the place. Flags were flying everywhere. Long lines of trestle tables decorated with anything patriotic were placed in the middle of the streets. They were covered with as much food as was available in ration riddled Britain. We sat and gorged ourselves as we sang 'We'll meet again' along with the recorded voice of Vera Lynn. There were more and more soldiers coming home but where was Dad?

"I've received a telegram, Emrys is on his way home!" Mam told the family excitedly. My own excitement was great but still a little reserved. Too many people for too many years had told me that they would bring Dad home. It hadn't happened yet. After all this time, would my wish finally come true? - What's that saying? 'Be careful what you wish for.' For everyone else the War had ended, little did I know mine hadn't quite begun.

After almost arriving at Princess Pier, Liverpool on the 23rd of October 1945, The Antinor rode out the storm within sight of land for two whole days. Dad disembarked too late to be able to catch the last train home that night of the 25th. We learned that we would be able to meet him the next day when his train arrived at Abergavenny Railway Station. As we didn't own a car, Tommy Griffiths our next door neighbor kindly offered to take us in his. Dado sat in the passenger seat next to Tommy, while Mam, Ter and I sat in the back. We reached Abergavenny in plenty of time to meet the train but when it arrived there was no sign of Dad. I began to think to myself 'I knew it, I knew he wouldn't come.' We found out that the train's final stop would be Newport, so we took off for Newport as fast as we could go. We arrived at the station before the train came in. I remember standing at the bottom of the steps that lead down to the street from the platforms above. Amongst the avalanche of passengers that poured down the steps I was the first to recognize Dad. I watched him until he came right up to us. Then there was hugging, laughing, kissing, crying. My Dad was home I couldn't believe it, I thought I was dreaming. When we all got in the car Dad sat in the back on a pull down seat with his back to the driver, but facing the rest of us. He looked down at me and asked me if I would like a scone or a cream cracker to eat. I had never heard of either at that time so I chose a cream cracker as that sounded deliciously exotic. You can imagine my disappointment when he handed me a little square, dry, salty biscuit. Oh well, never mind Dad had come home at last and was actually sitting right in front of me, isn't that marvelous? All the way home everyone was swapping news so fast that I couldn't get a word in. I couldn't wait to tell him I was a Red Indian. Every time I'd open my mouth to speak to Mam she used to say,

"If it's about Red Indians I don't want to hear about it!" Ha-ha, things will be different now I've got a Dad. He'll want to know all about my brave, Redskin exploits. Maybe with Dad's help we can finally find the elusive Welsh Cherokee tribes together. Maybe --- Oh no I almost exploded with panic, what could I do to shut everybody up? Dad had been asking after the well being of every member of the family and had just asked the question I'd been dreading,

"How's Florie?" We had all loved Auntie Florie very much.

"I'm afraid your Sister Florie died in childbirth earlier this year Emrys, we are sorry." I can still see Dads face. Why did they have to tell him? I thought.

When we arrived home the whole street was gaily decorated. Family, friends and neighbors were there to welcome him and children carried lighted candles in glass jars. I still hadn't spoken to him. I was completely overwhelmed with shyness, hero worship and a feeling of complete unreality. Dad had really come home. I just watched him fascinated. Looking at the expressions on his sun burnt face, listening to him speak. He smiled, he talked, but as the days past and I sometimes found myself alone with him, he just sat quietly and never said a word. It was almost like I wasn't there. I was never shy with anyone else; I'd either speak to someone or hit them according to how I felt about them at the time. But with Dad I was tongue tied, the first thing I remember saying to him when we were alone was,

"Hey Dad, how many Japanese did you kill?" It was just like talking to myself, I got no response at all. That only made me feel even more wary still about talking to him. The first time I ever got any response from him was one day as he sat in the kitchen I went to get myself a drink of water. I had to get a chair and put it up to the sink in order to be able to reach the tap. It was quite large and made of brass. I was aware that he was watching me and as I tried to turn the tap on I found that it was really stiff and would not budge. Dad must have known the tap was very hard to turn on but there was no way I was going to ask for help or fail to get my water while Dad was watching. 'I've got to show him how strong I am,' I thought. I struggled and strained there was no way I was going to give up. All of a sudden the tap gave in and opened right up. The force of the water hit the sink so hard that a great fountain engulfed me and almost blasted me off the chair. I floundered against the tide trying to shut the water off. When I finally succeeded I heard a strange hissing sound coming from Dad. I spun around in shock. I was even more shocked to see Dad holding his stomach and wobbling and shaking all over his chair. I leapt off my chair and ran from the kitchen screaming for Mam.

"Quick Mam," I yelled, "Dad's got Malaria again." It was the first time I had ever seen him laugh.

Dad was in and out of various Hospitals for tropical diseases for almost a year. He was still suffering from the effects of malaria, dysentery, beriberi, typhus, dengi fever and hook worms eating away at his intestines. I remember Mam changing the sweat soaked sheets on his bed umpteen times a day. Dad writhed deliriously, oozed more sweat by the gallon while his teeth clattered like castanet's as fits of chills seemed to wrack his whole body. He had began to work in Beynon's Colliery again. Still suffering regular attacks of malaria, he asked William Powell, the Colliery manager if he could start with a light job until such times as he might recover his health. The manager was totally unsympathetic. He told Dad that the only job he had available for him was the same gut busting job he had been doing before he had left the pit more than five years earlier. Dad had read in his Bible, James 5: 13-15, of Gods instructions to the sick. He decided to throw himself on God's mercy and prove his words in his own life. He went to the elders of his chapel, was anointed with oil and was prayed for in the subscribed fashion. Dad claims, as a result he never lost another days work from any of the tropical diseases he had contracted while being held prisoner by the Japs. The usually stern and dour Mr. Noble was fizzing with jubilation after performing the ceremony. In his desire to bask in the limelight and to take full credit for intervening with God on Dad's behalf. Bringing him safely home from the clutches of the cruel Japs and as he put it 'out of the house of bondage', he said to Mam,

"Nora, I told you our prayers would bring Emrys back home to us didn't I?"

"No!" My Mother replied, "I seem to remember you saying something completely different. I don't think God spoke to you in a dream when you told me Emrys was dead, that wasn't a vision, I think you probably ate too much cheese before you went to bed!"

I had been attending Sunday school for as long as I could remember but it suddenly became a chore. Dad seemed to believe we all needed to pay penance for his decision to 'Render himself unto the Lord.' Dad believed it was a sin to go to a movie theatre and even worse to visit a pub. This was in spite of the fact that it was a yearly ritual for him to visit every member of our family and friends on Christmas morning. He drank to celebrate the festive season with each of them. A sherry here, a brandy there, a port, a glass of rum, or his favorite, some sweet sticky liqueur. Dad would stagger back home in time for Christmas dinner with his eyes hanging down to his chin and his arse dragging on the ground. All the Port, Sherry, and sweet sticky Liquor Brandy that was left over from Christmas would disappear regularly whenever he was at home alone. But, at least he hadn't been to a wicked pub. I should have been more appreciative of the fact that I was a member of 'The Tabernacle'. I was soon to learn that the 50 or so members were the only Christian worshipers in the whole world that really understood and appreciated the word of God. Other Christians were probably well meaning enough. But obviously deluded in their belief and quite ignorant of the true meaning of God's word. The religious rivalry didn't end there either. Even in the Tabernacle itself each member seemed to strive to be thought of as the most righteous of the righteous. Speaking in tongues really pissed me off. The first time I ever remember hearing it I was unfortunate enough to be standing right next to the 'Blessed one.' It came so suddenly, loud and nerve rending. The lady possessed quivering so violently with the force of the spirit that had descended upon her that I nearly shit myself with fright.

"What was that lady shouting about?" I asked Dad when we got home; chapel was the only thing I could ever get him to talk to me about.

"She was speaking in tongues." He replied, as if that would mean anything to me.

"Was it a foreign language?" I asked.

"No, it was the spirit of God, talking through dear sister Blodwyn." He answered.

"Can't God speak English?" I inquired.

"God can speak every language." Dad assured me.

"Well why can't it be one I can understand?" I said.

"Because that is the way God speaks to us." He replied.

"Do you know what it meant?" I asked.

"No, but one glorious day God will reveal it to me." He answered.

"Did Blodwyn understand what she was saying?" I asked.

"No, but one day God will reveal its blessed meaning to everybody." He stated.

"One glorious day." I corrected.

"Yes, that's right," he confirmed, "one glorious day when we are all called to face our maker and answer for our sins."

"Well why doesn't God just tell us what he means on one glorious day, instead of Blodwyn having to shout stuff that no one can understand?" I demanded.

Speaking in tongues was an almost weekly occurrence. Especially if you attended the evening service when a spirit or two with dinner would pave the way for the spirit from above. It usually began with silent prayer. Everyone would be standing with head bowed Someone would start to pray aloud and then maybe someone else when they finished. I began to believe that speaking in tongues was probably invented by someone who couldn't actually think of anything really impressive to pray aloud about. Or to do so in a way that could sound more righteous or intelligent than the preceding prayers. One of the members might start it off. Then it wouldn't be unusual for a few more to join in with their own versions of their mystic mumbo jumbo. They seemed to almost compete with each other until they'd work themselves into a total frenzy in stereo. Before the frenzy reached its ear shattering zenith most everyone would still be standing with heads bowed. I always maneuvered into a position where I could observe the faces of the 'Holy stricken'. I found it wasn't at all unusual to see the eyes of the possessed ones flashing sidelong glances this way and that. I supposed to ensure themselves that their holy spirit inspired outbursts were having the desired effects on the rest of the congregation. Each 'tongue speaker' seemed to have their own patented version. It wasn't long before I could tell who was possessed without even looking at them. In fact I could eventually have imitated any one of them, word for unintelligible word. Except for the fact I didn't want to be struck blind, spend eternity doing a dogpaddle in the lake of fire or get zapped on the head by a thunder bolt. I was left in no doubt at all as to what would happen to anyone who stole, lied, took God's name in vain, made fun of the righteous, forgot to pray, or swore. THEY ALL WENT TO THE DEVIL! Also God knew everything you did as soon as you did it. Even what you were thinking. If a deed or a thought was evil, - ZAPP! Justice was not just swift it was immediate. Whatever you do, if you attend the Tabernacle don't get ill or suffer any kind of accident. That would be a clear sign to all the other members that

God was punishing you for some evil transgression. I've even heard them talk about their own members,

"Where's Mrs. Jones? I 'aven't seen 'er in chapel for weeks." Asks Blodwyn.

"Oh 'aven't you heard? Megan answers, gratified that she is about to impart bad tidings. "She's in 'ospital with cancer, in terrible pain she is."

"Oh! She must 'ave sinned somethin' awful for God to make 'er suffer like that." Blodwyn would gloat with relish.

"Beware!" Wailed Megan, really starting to get into the groove, "Lest your sins will find thee out, you may hide it from the rest of us but you can never hide it from the Almighty!" Whatever happened to, 'let him who is without sin cast the first stone?'

God, they made me sick. Oops! I wrote that in vain, I guess I'd better slip into something tropical.

Although rationing still seemed to go on for years after the war had ended, little by little items began to appear in the shops that had been impossible to acquire since before the war began. Things like pineapples, bananas, peaches and grapes, delicacies I'd only ever seen in books, magazines. Or on the top of Carmen Miranda's head. For a young boy brought up on bread and drippin' they were all items I craved for, especially grapes. Imagine my excitement when Mam came home one day triumphantly brandishing a bunch of four bananas. One each for her, Dad, Ter and myself.

"Are you sure you want to give Adrian a whole one Nora?" Dad asked, "He's only five, why don't you give him a half?" I hated people saying I was only anything, especially five. I wished people would talk to me not at me and give me my own personal banana like everyone else, not a half.

"Oh yes Em,' let him have a whole one he's got an appetite like a horse. He's done nothing but yap about bananas since he learned to talk." Mam replied.

"And grapes!" I injected. In spite of the glowering look I received from Dad I grabbed the offered banana with trembling hands and bit into it skin and all. 'YUCK! My grimace of disgust almost brought Dad's stony face back to a semblance of normality.

"You're supposed to peal the skin off first, you silly sod!" Mam informed me, "Like this look." She added, demonstrating with her own banana and taking a bite. I pealed the greenish, yellow skin off my precious banana and took my first taste of the lush, exotic, tropical delicacy, "Yuck!" The unripe banana didn't taste much better than the skin. It took a Herculean effort to roll the unpleasant morsel around my mouth and swallow it.

"Do you want the rest of it, Mam? I asked, Mam's eyebrows rose inquiringly,

"Why, don't you like it?" She asked,

"Yes it's lovely," I lied, "but you can have the rest of it if you like." I didn't want to disappoint Mam after all the years I'd spent talking about them but it was horrible.

"You wanted it, you eat it!" Dad interrupted. I hated the gratified smirk on his face as I gulped down the dreadful banana I swallowed it in lumps, with tears in my eyes. I said, "I'll bet you didn't have to eat a whole one when you were only five!"

The grapes were another story. Mam, Dad and I were standing in the street outside the greengrocers shop looking into the window and there in their fruity magnificence lay bunches of gorgeous, gleaming, grapes. The first I had ever seen in my life. I gazed as in a hypnotic trance at their purple perfection, only to be induced out of my reverie as I heard Mam say to Dad,

"Shall we buy him a bunch Em'?" I buzzed with excitement as Dad let out a huge exaggerated breath, as though he was Atlas with the weight of the world on his shoulders.

"I don't know," he replied, "they're awful' expensive."

"Well let's get him a little bunch." Mam said and we entered the greengrocers shop serenaded by Dad's huge sigh. Grapes purchased, I couldn't wait to get home. Only to discover with disappointment that grapes were not what I thought they'd be. I'd only ever seen pictures of grapes. I thought that the classical tapering shape was one fruit, not a group of separate round berries. 'Shall we buy HIM a bunch?' That didn't exactly pan out either as I got a total of five. The rest of MY bunch were shared between everyone else. Did I enjoy them? Yes, they were okay, but not worth boycotting heaven for.

When Dad was still convalescing during the summer of 1946 we all went to stay with Gran in Bristol. What a mess, not Gran, -

Bristol. The great port city was devastated. Block after city block had been reduced to heaps of rubble. I have never forgotten the sweet sickly smell of hops wafting over the water from a brewery, as I walked along the docks. Every time I get a whiff of that, my most nostalgic scent; it takes me back to that day. That was the day I met the first love of my life, Rosie. We had walked on past the port of Bristol. Up the hill, past the museum and on towards Clifton Downs. We caught a bus to our destination which was Bristol Zoo. Along with Mam, Dad, Terence and Gran was cousin Margaret. Margaret wasn't a real cousin. She was actually a young gypsy girl who had been abandoned by her family and was being brought up by Gran. I was sitting opposite Margaret on the bus. She had a very disturbing habit. Whenever she was sitting down, she looked at your eyes and allowed her knees to wander further and further apart. I was in a dreamland of excitement and believe it or not, it had nothing to do with my gypsy Cousin. I loved animals of all kinds, but had never seen anything more exotic than a Welsh mountain pony. I never ceased to be enthralled by Tarzan and all his jungle friends and enemies alike. Frank Buck in 'Bring 'em back alive' was beyond belief. Of course the giant bears, the stealthy cougar and the powerful bison who shared the forests and prairies with the noble Redman went without saying. I had never been to a Zoo before and to say I was impressed would be the biggest understatement of my young life. The sheer size and beauty of the animals I saw that day almost struck me dumb and that took some doing. As awestruck as I was, everything I saw that day faded into oblivion. I finally came face to face with the first great love of my life, Rosie. Unfortunately it proved to be a tragic epic of unrequited love. maybe she thought she was too old for me. Or too tall. Whatever it was, it was a love that was never to be. I think she must have liked me as she didn't try to kill me as I clung to her leg. She was a dainty creature, a little over eight feet tall and weighed about five thousand pounds.

"Come out of there you silly little bugger!" Mam screamed, "Quick Emrys get one of the keepers to get him out!" The huge steel bars that divided 'Rosie the Elephant' from the public were designed to keep Rosie in, not small enamored boys out. I had taken off like a rocket the second my eyes had adjusted to the dim interior of 'The Elephant House'. She stood there in all her elephantine glory. Huge, grey and magnificent. Every bit as lovely as I knew she would be. Two zoo keepers appeared and attempted to coax me back out between the bars. I easily ran through them at the first sight of my much anticipated meeting with Rosie. I had spent the last couple of days 'working' with Gran's husband Uncle Jack, in the large garage he worked in. The garage was under the apartment in which Gran, Uncle Jack and Cousin Margaret lived in. The work we were carrying out, was on a large store room that was being built inside the garage. Uncle Jack had assured me we were preparing living quarters for Britain's most famous elephant since Jumbo. Unsuccessful in their quest to entice me back through the bars. The zoo keepers had to gingerly enter Rosie's enclosure. Then pry me off Rosie's leg, before I could be restored to my worried family.

"Are we taking Rosie with us now or will they send her to us?" I inquired.

"No, we can't take her home with us now." Replied Mam, being well aware of Uncle Jack's phantom promise, "You and Uncle Jack haven't finished her home yet."

I found everything an anticlimax after leaving Rosie, until we happened upon 'Alfred.' Alfred the Gorilla was Bristol Zoo's other most famous resident. 400 pounds of hair and muscle and shit flinger extraordinaire. I gazed in awe at the sheer massive size and power of the magnificent, silver backed primate. Attracted to the intelligence that exuded from his shinning brown eyes set in his huge black, grey head. King Kong sprung into my mind. Especially as standing right next to me regarding the giant simian with wonder that mirrored my own, was a tall and very beautiful blond haired lady. She put me in mind of Fay Rae who played the beauty to King Kong's beast. Dressed in a flimsy, filmy, yellow frock. She wore a matching straw bonnet decorated with yellow and white daisies and accompanied by a man wearing a soldier's uniform. She finally turned from Alfred and smiled into the eyes of her beau. They walked away, gently swinging their finger linked hands. That was when Alfred performed his famous party piece, reaching behind him he produced a huge handful of crap which he threw with vicious intent. I watched its flight with fascination as it whipped the yellow, be-flowered bonnet right off of the blonde's head and splattered the startled soldier's nose.

"SHIT!" Screamed the lady, "What was that?"

****

The winter of 1947 was the coldest in Britain since before the Battle of Waterloo. It snowed every day from January 22nd till March 17th, with temperatures rarely reaching a degree or two above freezing. Brynmawr being the highest town in Britain probably suffered the most. There were blizzards that left snow drifts roof high. We along with most the other town's people had to dig tunnels from our front doors to be able to escape the confines of their own homes. I thought it was a great adventure. Even being rescued by Ter and Cousin Desmond from a snowy ravine. I'd fallen into it when my weight had caused a minor avalanche. It had carried me gently but firmly down a slope burying me up to my shoulders. After an hour of high drama they managed to get me back to safety. I then had to be restrained by Ter and Desmond as I wanted to do it again. The freezing wind would create an icy crust on the surface of the snow, which prevented my feet sinking in it. On my walks I would pass what looked like large bushes, which I knew, were the tops of tall trees. Familiar places looked and felt entirely alien. A frozen pipe had burst beside our outside toilet in the backyard. I remember gazing, mouth hanging open, flabbergasted with wonder at the magic ice palace that had appeared there as a result. Great bubbling ramparts cascaded, dramatically decorated with huge robust icicles that hung like the pillars of the Parthenon. It sparkled like jewels in the weak, Welsh sunlight. It was breathtaking and beautiful beyond belief. I immediately envisioned an army of my best plastercine Vikings defending this frozen Valhalla against a horde of Barbarian Snow Giants. I was enraptured. Then here comes horrible Ter with an ice pick and like a scruffy Vandal sacking Rome began to demolish natures beautiful work of art. I was horrified. I tried to stop him but that only increased the intensity of his attack. Pillars began to fall and icy splinters flew everywhere. Again I tried to pull him away but he would not be restrained. I begged him to let me have a turn with the ice pick as I would have ran as soon as I'd got hold of it. I would throw it where it couldn't be reached. He brushed me aside but I was determined to rescue what was left of my ice castle. I grabbed him and tried to tear him away. He spun around and lashed out at me with the ice pick. As he is left handed the ice pick stuck into my right eye. Hot blood spurted everywhere. I reeled back in shock and pain, I had never felt anything that had hurt that much. Like Ter I thought I had lost my eye. I began to scream as he dropped the ice pick grabbed hold of me and carried me indoors to the kitchen. He aimed my head under the tap and turned it on full blast. I screamed again as icy cold, pink water sprayed the kitchen. Dad burst in to find out what all the commotion was about. He was shocked to see so much blood pouring from the socket of my eye. Ter dropped me and shot past Dad. Dad hurled a large bread knife after him. It shuddered as it stuck in the kitchen door. Ter had managed to slam it behind him in time to prevent another similar tragedy. Damn! Is this supposed to be the peace we were promised? As that famous African-American philosopher Rodney King so sagely put it,

"Can't we all just get along?" Fortunately I never lost my eye, so I never got to wear one of those cool, black pirate eye patches. I still have a small scar on the outside of my right eye. I would soon just casually brushed it off. The result of a war arrow fired from an enemy Red Indian's bow, in a bloodthirsty intertribal battle, next time I went to school.

A little ice princess was born on Saint Valentine's Day, February 14th 1947, at last I had a baby Sister. She was named Pamela Christine by my Mam and Dad. I was more than a bit miffed at the time. As it was MY Sister, I thought it only right that I should name her. I wanted to name her Sylvia. The reason being, I was in love again. This time with a human being. - Well there's a first time for everything. As I was saying, the reason I was in love again was Sylvia. She was in a class above me in school and she loved to dance. I had noticed her before as she was a very pretty girl. BUT, the first time Sylvia danced for me she spun around and around so that her dress flew up around her waist. It revealed a complete absence of underwear and as I had never seen anything like that before I obviously fell hopelessly in love.

"Sylvia is a lovely name," I whined, "it's like silver and that's precious." I added not wanting to reveal the real reason why I liked the name so much.

"Well, Christine is like Christian," countered Dad, "and that's more precious than silver or even gold."

"Ok, we'll call her Sylvia Christine." I said, more than willing to compromise. I told my Sister the story years later and she said,

"Thank goodness you didn't get your wish, I hate the name Sylvia." Well I was sad at the time, but never mind, now she'll always be my little Pamela.

****

Hundreds of sheep and mountain ponies must have died amongst the Welsh hills as a result of that savage winter. It wasn't unusual to see the poor beasts wandering around the town trying to scrounge some form of nourishment. Or find shelter from the continuous blistering blizzards. As I stepped out of the house one day I was attracted by the excited yells of two boys leaping about on top of a mountainous snow drift against the school wall opposite.

"Come and have a look at this!" one of them yelled to me as I approached them. I climbed up and joined them on top of the drift and looking down the other side I saw the reason for their excitement. A huge raggedy, grey ram was trapped between the bottom of the snowdrift and the side of the school. The boys were rolling snowballs till they were as big as they could heft up above their heads. Then they hurled them down on the helpless Ram. Both boys were chortling with glee. They smiled at me as though to invite me to join them in their merry sport. As the nearest boy bent down to pick up some more snow I kicked him in the face. I hoped that the ram was watching my every move. Quickly I grabbed the other boy by the woolen balaclava helmet he was wearing and swung him backwards and began to choke him with it. I pummeled his big red snotty nose, which became redder and snottier as I pummeled. Finally I dragged him up and gave his arse a hefty kick. It helped him on his way tumbling down the mountain of snow to the road below. I turned back to face the ram, gratified that I had its full attention. I squared my shoulders and puffed up my chest into what I thought would present my most heroic pose. I'd seen the movies and read the books. This was where the hero comes to the rescue of some wild beast who's unfortunate enough to find itself in some life threatening predicament. He would bravely save it, thereby enjoining their souls forevermore. Now destined to fly to each other's aid at a seconds notice. If either one is ever threatened, or in any kind of danger whatsoever. I had seen it happen with Tarzan, Sabu the elephant boy and countless Red Indians. Now it was my turn. I climbed down into the snow pit to greet my new found friend. I reached out to touch its head gently between its enormous curling horns. In a gesture I thought reminiscent of Tarzan. Stroking his elephant's head or trunk after it had just squished a whole tribe of cannibal pygmies on his behalf. WHAM! The giant ram lurched forward as though it had been fired out of an ancient Roman siege engine. It smashed its massive horned skull into my left leg. Then it tossed up its head with such force that I was sent spinning. Cart wheeling through the air to land face first in the snow. The lower half of my body seemed to jackknife in the opposite way in which it was designed to bend. I felt my stomach stretch and my back almost snap as my head buried itself deep into the snow. SHIT THAT HURT! But what hurt even more was my pride, dignity and my faith in the noble beast. It worked for Tarzan, but this stupid, bloody animal obviously hadn't seen the movie. I barely had the strength to hurl a parting snowball at the ungrateful bastard. Crestfallen and injured I staggered back home. I took comfort in the fact that I have a long memory and I do bear a grudge. The words to Vera Lynn's wartime song came back to me 'We'll meet again."

It seemed as though the slowly diminishing mountains of snow would last forever. We had already snapped the last of the snotty icicles from our frozen noses before the last of the blackish, grey drifts finally disappeared. A warm spring brought torrents of melting rain causing streams and rivers to overflow. The cascading waterfalls so abundant throughout The Clydach Gorge were the most spectacular that I had ever seen at that time. The force of the hurtling water crashing down and rushing through the ravines and chasms would dislodge huge rocks that had probably sat in place for centuries. The warm, wet spring gave way to the longest hottest Summer I had ever experienced in my short life. Wildflowers in the woods, on the hills and crowding the hedgerows. They sustained the busy, buzzing bees and made a spectacular background for Peacock Butterflies and Red Admirals which I had never seen before. They vied for attention with the more common but dazzling, bright yellow Brimstones and the gaudy Small Tortoiseshells. That summer coincided with our move from my siblings and my Birthplace in Queen Street to 'Aneurin Place'. I still had to share a room with gentle Ter but at least now I had my own bed. I found 'The Prefabs' a much nicer place to live as they were almost completely surrounded by mountains, small woods, fields and country lanes. Equally attractive to me was the two large gardens that I'd always wished for, one in the front and one in the back of the house. But, once again I was soon to become aware of the old saying, 'Careful what you wish for!' Both the front and back, rock strewn gardens which surrounded 39 Aneurin Place were wild and choked with scrubby grass and weeds. The back garden was divided from a large field by a wire fence. It was to be left in the same wild and wooly state in which we'd found it and a place for us kids to play. The front garden, facing the road was to become Dad's horticultural pride and joy. It needed a lot of planning and an incredible amount of sweat, tears, blisters and backbreaking work. As it turned out my Father did the planning. I did the rest. I was flattered and felt quite grown up at first when Dad who rarely took much notice of me had declared that I was to give him a hand in the garden.

"You may as well learn to use a shovel," he said, "I'll have you working down the pit with me as soon as you leave school."

"No, I'm not going to work down the pit," I argued, "I'm going to be an Indian Chief or a film star and earn lots of money!" Hearing Dad say so many times, that if he ever had enough money, he would take Mam to the Far East. I had made my mind up that I would find a way to make lots of money and take them both myself. I had no idea at the time how I was going to get lots of money but I had not the slightest doubt that I would.

"Don't argue with me, you'll do what you're told." He growled. I knew I couldn't expect him to be grateful of my holiday plan as it was going to be a secret surprise.

"I'm not going down the pit!" I glowered, SMACK! "Ouch!" His hand bounced off my head.

"Shut up and fill those buckets with rocks and dump them at the bottom of the back garden!" he ordered.

"Stop hitting him on the head," Mam shouted through the kitchen window, "he's daft enough already!"

"That's right, pick his sleeves up when I'm correcting him; he's going to grow up to be another blackguard like your Brother Jimmy in Bristol!" He yelled back to her.

"I'd rather be a Gangster like Uncle Jimmy than work down the pit!" I chimed in.

SMACK! "Ouch!" I said. I hardly took much notice any more of the consistent smacks on the head I received off Dad. I seemed to get one every other time I walked past him. Sometimes I knew what it was for sometimes I didn't. I began to believe he had become addicted to the noise my head made when he slapped it.

From the age of seven when I returned home from school and finished my dinner I was made to work in the garden. Even after the shapeless, rock bound, weed ridden mess was transformed into a neat lawn. Surrounded by colorful flower beds and rockeries there was still the constant dreaded, back wrecking, mind numbingly boring weeding. My Thirteen year old Brother Ter was never made to work in the garden. As soon as he came home from school and had eaten he went off to one of the towns Billiard Halls. He played billiards or snooker till it was time to have supper and go to bed. Dad did ask him once when he was about fourteen if he would help in the garden. He promptly inquired how much would he get paid for his work. He agreed to do a couple of afternoons for 5 shillings and was paid on the spot. He got paid but never, ever got around to earning it. I had been forced to work in the garden without receiving a single penny for my efforts. I said that I would expect pocket money from now on for all the work I was doing. At first he refused point blank to give me anything. He told me I should be happy to work for my keep. I pointed out that Ter had already been receiving pocket money for years. He had never been forced to work for it. He had just been given an extra 5 shillings for just two days work in the garden which he didn't do. Dad reluctantly agreed to pay me 2 shillings a week pocket money for six days work. The Sabbath was for Sunday school. He warned me that I would be expected to be in the garden promptly after I had eaten every day if I expected to be paid; I agreed and held my hand out, Dad said,

"Work first, pay after." he had already been stung by Ter and wouldn't fall for that trick again. On the very day I expected to get paid, I was invited to dinner after school by a classmate. Knowing that his very pretty older sister would be present I readily accepted the invitation. As a result, I must admit I was late getting home that day. Dad was waiting with his arms folded and that angry buzzard look on his face. He stood inside our garden gate and couldn't wait to tell me as a result of my lateness I would not be receiving my promised wages. As a further punishment I would be made to do the work but there would be no question of me ever being paid for it. I obviously couldn't be trusted. I truly believe, that Dad only promised to pay me just for the pleasure he would derive from denying me my just deserts at the last minute. He would use any pretext he could invent, knowing that I had anticipated what I might do with my 2 shillings, when I received it. Shit! I hated being a kid; I couldn't wait to grow up. For some strange reason I felt that I hadn't been fairly dealt with. Punctuated only by frequent slaps on the head, which I stubbornly refused to let deter me, I continued to complain bitterly. Mam who's nerves were fast becoming shredded by the constant conflict my complaints were causing came up with a solution to the problem. She hated polishing the linoleum floors in the house and offered me sixpence a day to do it for her, if I also agreed to shut up.

"Oh WOW!" I exploded, "That's 3 shillings and 6 a week!" I had always been good at mathematics, especially where money was concerned.

"You mean 3 shillings, not 3 shillings and 6 pence!" My Father injected, obviously pissed off with Mam's solution. Determined to at least drizzle if not rain on my exuberance, "No one in this 'ouse shall do work on the Sabbath! Don't think you're getting out of working in the garden either!" he added for good measure.

'Oh boy, I'm going to be rich," I thought, 'it would serve Dad's right if I took Mam to the Far East and left him home by himself.' Oh boy, shit! - Mother's work very hard I found out. On my hands and knees I polished all the linoleum floors in the kitchen/dining room, the sitting room and the hallway every day. Except of course the Sabbath. Then I'd wallow in the luxury of going to The Tabernacle and listening to Blodwyn and company spout their scintillating 'Holy Ruckus.' Dad also decided on another little aggravating twist. He declared that I would have to get up in front of the congregation and recite a whole verse learned from the scriptures. Cousin Ray had done so a couple of weeks previously when he recited the whole of the 23rd psalm. So I learned one off by heart and every Sunday much to Dad's chagrin I recited the whole verse flawlessly, "Jesus wept."

Unlike Dad, Mam could be trusted. On the following Saturday as soon as I'd finished the polishing, Mam gave me my 3 shillings pocket money AND told me I'd done a very good job. Dad who consistently hovered in the wings, always ready to put a sprag in my wheels suggested that I save some of it. - To put in the Sunday school collection box the next day! Every Sunday Mam would give me 6pence to put in the Tabernacle's collection box and now Dad was suggesting I use my money instead.

"Why do we have to take any money to Sunday school?" I asked him, "God can do miracles so why can't he make his own money, and if he knows everything, why can't he find all the gold and all the hidden treasure in the whole world?" Even though Dad made barely enough money for Mam to make ends meet. He still insisted on putting 10 percent of his hard earned wages in the Chapel collection box each week. I think that may have been a sore point with Mam, so that when Dad answered me it was more for her benefit than mine.

"The money is used to run the Tabernacle and for upkeep, maintenance and repairs!" Dad informed me impatiently.

"Well why doesn't God do a miracle and do the repairs himself?" I argued, 'repairs' being the only thing he said that I understood.

"God doesn't do it that way," He persisted, "it's up to us to show faith with him."

"Well why don't we all pray for God to fix the Tabernacle then? And then we can keep all the money ourselves." I suggested and then asked, "Who gives God all our money anyway, Mr. Noble?" The only converse I ever had with Dad was this kind of childish banter and as I was a child the only one with an excuse.

You may remember me mentioning earlier that I loved armor, - well that has never changed and I also love any kind of historical uniforms and weapons. Especially helmets, swords and daggers. During our stays with Gran in Bristol, we would spend hours looking around antique shops. There were dozens of them in Bristol in those days. The nearby City of Bath was also oozing with them. Japanese Samurai swords, German Field and Dress swords and daggers were so abundant and so cheap. So soon after the war many of the returning soldiers had brought them back as trophies or souvenirs by the thousands. The novelty soon wore off for them. They were so common, the soldiers must have almost given them away. Samurai swords would rarely cost more than a pound or two and German swords and daggers were sold for somewhere between 7 shillings and 6pence, and 25 shillings. The same weapons are now extremely collectable and would easily fetch in excess of a hundred times what they were worth in those days.

So common, so cheap, but for me so unobtainable. I'd had no money and Mam, nor Dad would give me any to buy swords or daggers. Mam loved Victorian Lustre Vases and as a result we were always exploring curio and antique shops. That way I was able to learn a lot about weapons. I hadn't been able afford to buy them, but now I had a job so things would change. I saved my money like a miser but couldn't wait for the family to take its yearly trek to Bristol. I began making trips on my own to towns closer to home. I searched for a good source where I could start my collection. After many disappointing journeys to many antique free towns I hit pay dirt. The Cathedral City of Hereford was only 32 miles from Brynmawr but it took exactly 2 hours to get there by bus. The only Antique shop in Hereford that catered to my taste was called 'Aladdin's Cave'. It was almost hidden away in a shabby, narrow, little back street, but it was great. Unfortunately for me I had spent my hard earned money on bus fares and train tickets to all those other towns. Now I had very little of my savings left. The variety of edged weapons was impressive for such a small store. Enough to raise my pulse at the thought of owning one. The undisputed star, without a doubt, was a 3 foot long Samurai Sword. It had a white sharkskin handle, the matching brass pommel and tsuba was decorated with chrysanthemum flowers and leaves. But at the astronomical price of 3 pounds this 'Shinto Excalibur' was way out of my league. At least for now. I'd heard Mam and Dad haggle the price when they were interested in a Lustre Vase, but my remaining 5 shillings wouldn't tempt the proprietor to part with it. I couldn't bear the thought of returning home empty handed after at last finding this treasure trove. In desperation I asked the owner what he had for 5 shillings. After examining a big wooden box full of 19th and 20th Century Bayonets I explained I was looking for a Sword. The proprietor took pity on me and I soon left 'Aladdin's Cave' closely clutching my newly acquired, brown paper wrapped treasure. No, it wasn't the Samurai Sword, it was in fact a 17th Century Turkish Scimitar, black with rust and age. The last foot of the ugly, curved monstrosity was bent sideways above a huge split in the blade. It wasn't pretty, but it was a Sword, my first Sword and I was happy, - for now.

Our school offered its students an educational day trip to visit Windsor Castle and I was going. I was very excited, the only castles I had ever seen was Abergavenny Castle which was built by the Normans and was now in ruins and Cardiff Castle which was also a Norman Castle but was built upon an original Roman foundation, it was in excellent condition, - but no arms and armor. Windsor Castle I had been told was different, - and it was. I had never seen a real suit of armor before and Windsor Castle was crammed with them. I was in Heaven, Wonderland, the Happy Hunting Ground and Valhalla all rolled into one. I could have happily wandered from hall to hall for the rest of Eternity. Unfortunately, I had, after much pleading, persuaded Mam to accompany me on the trip. Parents were not only invited they were encouraged to join our outing. They could take care of their own children and so leave less kids to the care of the Teachers. Mam, in turn had persuaded Mrs. Woodyat to come with us, so that she would have some company. Obviously I wasn't considered worthy of that roll. In complete contrast to myself, Mam had no interest in History at all, I asked her why,

"Who cares what happened hundreds or thousands of years

ago? If it had only happened last week there's nothing anyone could do about it, so why worry?" I'd respond with that bit about those who ignore History's mistakes are destined to repeat them and Mam would respond with something like,

"Well remind me when the Battle of Hastings comes back around and I'll be sure to wear protective glasses to save my eyes from arrows." Anyway I wasn't destined to wander the Magical, Mystical halls of Windsor Castle for eternity. On the contrary. We hurtled around the halls and out of the Castle in search for a Lyons Tea house, as fast as Mam's bulky 4 foot 10 inch frame would allow. I was promised we would return to the Castle as soon as we'd eaten. I have always had a large appetite but not when there are Castles to explore and suits of armor to study. When at last we quit the tea house, Mam and Mrs. Woodyat said it wouldn't be right to come all the way to Windsor and spend all the time in the Castle. On the way to 'Marks and Spencer's' we passed a shop that sold 'Military Miniatures.' Now that's not your regular toy soldiers, these were scaled military works of art, 54 millimeters high, they were fantastically detailed right down to the insignia on the infantryman's brass buttons. But, Mam, who needed no encouragement from Mrs. Woodyat, who was already dragging the sleeve off Mam's coat, in her haste to go get her big 'let's go look at women's clothes fix.' I was promised that we would pop in and buy some soldiers on the way back to the Castle from the beckoning clothes stores. I had been saving my earnings religiously and now it was burning a hole in my pocket. Every few minutes whether I could get a word in between Mam and Mrs. Woodyat yapp-yapp-yapp-yapp-yapping or not, I was moaning about getting back to Windsor Castle via The Military Miniature shop. I was told, to my horror, to shut up, as I was spoiling 'THEIR day out!" I appreciated they were just about as interested in a armor as I was in Ladies shoes and petticoats but they could go and look at clothes any time they wanted to in Brynmawr or in an identical 'Marks and Spencer's' in Ebbw Vale. But, where was I going to find a castle crammed with armor in Brynmawr?! It came as a great disappointment, but no great surprise to find that Military Miniature Shop closed, by the time we got back there. We would also have to forego our return to the Castle, as it was now time to make our way back to the railway station. DAMN! I hated being a kid; I couldn't wait to grow up.

Dad decided to build a wooden shed in the back garden. First we built the section that included the door and left it on the ground until we completed a frame that was loosely attached to an existing brick wall. We lifted and positioned the first section parallel with the frame that was propped against the wall. Dad told me to steady the first section while he tried to lift a very thick and heavy plank up on to the frame and door section in order to join them together. He could manage one side, but was not tall enough to place the other end on the other side and we didn't own a ladder. He began to get more and more frustrated as he tried to toss the other end up onto the finished section. Every time it bounced right back narrowly missing both of us. Eventually, much to my amazement, his ludicrous scheme actually worked. Then he lined it up by moving it carefully with the head of a broom. Once it was in place he told me to hold the frame steady as it was only leaning against the wall. He wanted to make sure that the door section was perfectly vertical before nailing the plank to it. So we swapped sides and I put all my weight against the frame. After testing the door side section with his spirit level he found that the section was way out. It needed to be pushed away from the frame I was holding. Without even telling me what he intended doing Dad gave the door section a mighty push. The heavy plank came crashing down on my head. I obviously didn't even see it coming and it's surprising it didn't crack my skull or break my neck. What was even more surprising was the fact that I was still on my feet after it struck me. I thought I was going to vomit and as I fought to control it, my eyes went out of focus. I felt myself lurch backwards into the corner. Dad began to scream like a banshee, his face a mask of fury. I thought for a moment that it was out of concern for my welfare. I was soon brought back to reality when I felt the sting of his thick leather belt as he laid it across my back and shoulders. I had never seen him so angry and according to him it was my fault that the plank had fell on my head after all the time and hard work it had taken him to get it on the frames in the first place.

A couple of days later, after a disagreement with a boy in school we arranged to settle our argument in our usual battle ground on the site of a war bombed house. As always the news of a fight would draw a crowd of just about every other student in the school. Everyone arranged themselves in the best vantage point on the highest piles of rubble to view our scrap. The other boy and I began to circle each other, but as soon as we rushed together with fists a flailing my nose began to bleed in torrents from both barrels. I hadn't even suffered a single blow. My opponent backed off and claimed victory. That was a normal procedure, in those kind of schoolboy fights, after someone had scored first blood. But, I wasn't hurt, - I hadn't even been hit and was furious. Everyone I appealed to agreed with my antagonist that he had won and I had lost. My nose was still pouring as I chased him in and out of what was left of the bombed out building. I was only to be appeased by his promise to meet me on the same battlefield the next day. Same battlefield, same result. It seemed that every time I got excited or exerted myself for months to come my nose would just pour blood like a tap. I can only put the reason for it down to the blow I received to my head.

I didn't like school in spite of the fact that I was doing quite well at that time. I had just been moved up a grade into a class whose pupils were a year or so older than me. I had become so far advanced of all the other students in my former class. Probably due to the fact that I had been attending school since the age of three. I got on fine with most the other teachers. Especially our music teacher, who one day during choir practice, silenced every other pupil in turn, until I was the only one singing. She even brought most of the other teachers in to listen to me sing alone. They all congratulated me on having a beautiful singing voice. It's a shame I thought that none of them betrayed the same enthusiasm for my talking voice. But, I admit it was hard to shut me up at times.

It was about that time that I would often not go home after school. I was sick of Dad and his remorseless slave driving. Dad was home from work a little after 3 in the afternoon. He was usually waiting for me by the time I came home just over an hour later. I would get into trouble if I was late and he had chores for me. But, I had long since learned that I was in trouble just being around him. I figured if I'm going to get a slap or two, I may as well get them for getting home when it was too dark to work in the garden. What I'd usually do, was to go home lunch time from school, polish the floors, make myself lunch and a bag of sandwiches to take on my travels to eat after school ended.

I didn't realize it at the time but I think Dad may have got back at me in other ways. The combined evidence didn't dawn on me till years after, and I may be wrong. I guess I'll never know. As much as I loved animals I had the worst luck in caring for them that a boy ever had. I found a beautiful Jay that had hurt its wing and I brought it home. I fed it all the worms and bread to eat and water to drink that it required. Its wellbeing improved with each day, until I came home from school and found it dead. The same thing happened with a homicidal Raven I'd named Genghis, which I changed to Attila and then changed again to Khan. Maybe I caused it to suffer from an identity crisis. Then to a Magpie named Merlin, a Rabbit named Thumper. A Squirrel that was named Cyril until it burned its nose by pushing the lid off a saucepan of boiling water. Then I named it Chip after the red nosed Chipmunk cartoon character of Chip 'n' Dale fame. Even my pet Tortoise named Timothy. I complained that a Tortoise was supposed to live a hundred years. Dad suggested that it must have eaten Lupine leaves in the garden which he said were poisonous. My Snakes, Newts, Lizards and Hedgehogs must have escaped from the homes I'd made for them, in a way that would have bewildered Houdini. Many people who think they knew Dad would argue that he would never harm an animal. That is not true and I'll tell you why I know different.

I had built myself a hut in the back garden by weaving elderberry branches together to form the side sections and the roof. It was a neat little jungle, looking affair, which would have done credit to my favorite Ape-Man. One day I started to enter it and found a large frog living there. A little while later I found a cat had taken over and seemed happy to stay there. I began bringing it milk and any leftover scraps for it to eat. I've made myself a critter magnet I thought. I wasn't far wrong because a few days later when I brought the cat her milk, I found her laying there suckling three gorgeous, newborn Kittens. Each one was a different color, one was a grey Tabby, one was Black and the third one was a ginger Marmalade color. The Mother was a grey Tabby. She hardly finished weaning her motley pride when my nights turned into a ghoulish nightmare. Screaming, growling, mewing Toms fought and snarled from dusk till dawn to win her favors. She soon left with them and I found myself a foster Mother. My Sister Pamela who still loves cats to this day, fell in love with the little Marmalade. It was the runt of the litter. Ter took a liking to the grey Tabby and I favored the black Kitten, who I named Shaka after my favorite Zulu. I gave my Brother and Sister the Kittens they both chose and kept Shaka for myself. Dad immediately resented my sudden and new found popularity with Ter and Pam. He told me we could only keep one Kitten and that the other two would have to be drowned. Slyly he put the ball in my court. I was supposed to choose one Kitten to live. If I wanted to keep Shaka it would be my fault that Pam and Ter's Kittens would both be killed. Even if I had been willing to sacrifice Shaka, I would still have to choose between my Brother and Sister. I really didn't believe he would harm any of those beautiful, little furry creatures. Even though he dug a big hole at the bottom of the garden and warned me I had better make my choice soon or he would drown all of them. I remembered how that shithead Brian Gore had vilified himself forever by drowning my first Kitten years before. We had all hated him for what he had done. So, I was confident that this whole frustrating episode was just a big bluff. Especially as the days past when he'd only ask me if I'd made my choice yet, when I'd annoyed him and he wanted to piss me off. I came home from school one day to find Dad home alone. He didn't acknowledge my arrival when I walked into the room, but just stood silently looking through the window into the back garden. I walked up to the window and looked out. It was in that curious, subconscious way that people do when they find someone who seems to be looking at something. I probably stood there for 5 minutes or more, mindlessly gazing over the fields. All of a sudden I became conscious of something missing and realized it was the big mound of earth that had been beside the hole that Dad had dug. I shot a quick glance over at Dad, who hadn't moved. I shot out of the house and into the cot to check on the Kittens. They were gone and so was the blanket lined box they'd slept in. I raced back indoors to find Dad facing me when I entered.

"Where's the Kittens?!" I demanded, dreading, but not

believing what the answer might be.

"I told you to make your mind up which one you wanted to keep didn't I?" he replied; "Now they've all been drowned and buried at the bottom of the garden." I hated the gleam of triumph and satisfaction on his face. I could see he was squaring himself up almost into a fighting stance in anticipation to my response. I would love to have disappointed him but I couldn't help myself.

"Who the Hell do you think you are, King Bloody Solomon?!" I yelled as I glared at him. I braced myself and turned to receive the rain of blows he aimed at my head.

"What's going on now?!" Mam shouted, as she came in from shopping.

"He's killed the Kittens!" I croaked, trying my best not to cry.

"It's his own fault!" Dad shouted, giving me another slap. "I warned him."

"Well, leave him alone." Mam told him.

"Oh yes, that's right, go on, pick his sleeves up!" he yelled at Mam, "He'll grow up like your Brother Jimmy, wait till he leaves school, I'll have him down the pit with me, see how he'll like that!"

"I'm not going down the pit!" I thundered as I slammed the door behind me.

HELL FIRE

"'Ave you ever cut your finger?" Bellowed Blodwyn.

"Yes, we 'ave!" We all chanted, looking at our fingers for scars and triumphantly displaying the evidence. We were all sitting in a group facing Blodwyn, whose turn it was to teach us kids this week in our Sunday school lesson. We had already listened to the opening prayer and sang hymns and were now about to get the main course.

"'Ave you ever burned your finger?" Continued Blodwyn.

"Yes we have!" We all answered. I wanted to go into detail and tell how I'd got my latest burn scar melting lead to make toy soldiers but Blodwyn ploughed right on.

"It do 'urt don' it, even worse than cutting it?" She stated.

"Yes!" we all agreed.

"Well, can you imagine a burn an 'undred million times worse? And not just on your finger, but all over your body!" She shrieked.

"Yes!" We all lied.

"An' not just a quick burn that'll get better, but a terrible, 'orrible burn that will last forever an' ever an' the most 'orrible pain that will never end. 'Ave you ever 'ad toothache? Well this pain is ten million times worse. The Devil will be there with 'is pitchfork an' 'e'll be just laughin' at you while you're burnin' an' screamin' in terrible agony. It will last forever an' ever, for all eternity, can you imagine what's that gonna be like?" She gloated, with relish, eyes glittering with certifiable satisfaction.

"Yes!" We all lied again.

Well we'd been warned. We'd heard all about the wailing and gnashing of dentures. We had no one to blame but ourselves, if our all forgiving, heavenly Father condemned us, his earthly children to burn forever in a lake of fire. We would suffer the tortures and agonies of eternal damnation for telling lies. Or for trying to see what color knickers Sylvia was, or was not wearing. Personally, I wouldn't do that to my children, never mind what sins they may be guilty of, but then I'm only human. Sometimes, especially if there were not many kids in attendance we would sit in an adult's bible discussion. I t could be interesting but mostly it would go way over our heads. It's no wonder there is so much intolerance between the variety of great religions in the world. Members, not only of the same religion, but of the same church would snarl and squabble over the meaning of the message. Just like a pack of Jackals over the last scrap of flesh on a Zebra's arse bone. Dad was always foremost in the fray. Once he got his teeth into something he would lean forward in his seat towards whoever he was addressing. Then with the forefinger of his right hand begin stabbing back and forth in emphasis, as though he was pitching invisible darts into an invisible dartboard. It was on one such occasion, Dad, as dogmatic and as unyielding in his belief as the best of them, was emphasizing his point of view. Stabbing away furiously he carried on past the point of boredom by his own imagined righteousness and eloquence. His much suffering peers had long ago ran out of argument and interest in the subject being discussed. In contrast to Dad they were laying back in their benches with the look of martyrs on their faces and trying politely not to yawn. The younger Mr. Noble, was sitting next to Dad but also sitting back and therefore out of Dad's line of vision, but in the rest of the congregation's view. He gave Dad an exaggerated look of pity. Encouraged by the resulting snigger from some of the others, he began sticking out his tongue, crossing his eyes and revolved his finger around the side of his head. He nodded it left and right in the manner of an imbecile. Then he emphasized his performance with a pained roll of his eyes and a stab of his own finger towards Dad. I saw both Megan and Blodwyn cover their smirks with their hands and Mr. Noble smugly fold his arms across his chest and gaze up at the ceiling in a huge display of resignation. As young as I was I realized that his performance was designed to belittle Dad. As soon as we got home I spilled the beans. I was questioned and cross examined for an hour and Dad was livid. Not with me for a change, but by his sense of outrage, betrayal and belittlement by his Christian Brothers and Sisters. He was so angry I thought him capable of returning to the Tabernacle and burning it down. But he didn't return, and when I say he didn't return, - that was it, - he didn't return. Normally Dad went to chapel four times a week, three times on Sunday, then again on Wednesday night. From the time I let the cat out of the bag he just stopped attending the Tabernacle and waited patiently for a response. They didn't keep him waiting long.

"I've come to see if Brother Emrys is alright?" Inquired Old Mr. Noble, as Mam answered his knock on the door. "We haven't seen Him in chapel since last week."

"You'd better come in." Mam said with a sigh. When he was enlightened as to the reason for Dad's absence he was totally unconvinced as to the validity of my story. He declared that his relative, young, fat Mr. Noble was incapable of the antics I'd described. Dad maintained that I was too young to have made up such a story. No motive existed for its invention, even if I hadn't been too young. I was made to repeat my story for Mr. Noble's benefit. He glared at me with unfeigned hostility. I stared back with fearless, defiance. I thought to myself 'the last time I saw a face like that was on top of a Totem pole.' That was the beginning of a whole procession of Tabernacle member's pilgrimage to meet with Dad. Young, fat Mr. Noble, with his excuses and finally an apology. Megan and Blodwyn with their 'turn the other cheek'. 'Blessed is he who forgives those who trespasses against him' and so on and so forth. Dad was in his element and he wasn't going to relinquish the attention easily. Hurt and martyred he relished the attention and subsequent groveling by his Brothers and Sisters in the Lord, as much as I relished one of Mam's home cooked Sunday dinners. Instead of going to The Tabernacle on a Sunday morning Dad would take Terence and me on long walks to 'The Devils Bridge'. Kind of appropriate under the circumstances. We'd gaze in awe from the side of the bridge down in to the swirling, cascading, crashing waterfalls and whirlpools. I'd think to myself, if Dad ever taught me to dive, or swim, this would be the place. This must have gone on for at least a couple of months. It was the only time, apart from holidays that Dad actually did anything with us, but as they say, all good things must come to an end. Eventually Dad relented, repented and allowed himself to be coaxed back to The Tabernacle. He hadn't done anything really sinful that would condemn him to everlasting torture in the lake of eternal fire, like go to a movie theatre or even worse a pub. All he did was not go to the Tabernacle. Anyway he went back, - and there was much rejoicing in the land as the multitude welcomed the prodigal Sheep Emrys, back into the fold. All the prayers were for Dad. Thanking God in his mercy for softening the heart of our forgiving Brother Emrys. Returning him back to the loving arms of his Savior. Even the 'squawking in tongues' had words that sounded eerily like Emrys. It was Dad's finest hour, the undisputed man of the moment. The dramatic display certainly suggested that everyone present was happy to be reunited with something that had been missing. But - was it 'Dogmatic Dad' or his weekly monetary offering? - One day, - or should I say one 'glorious' day, all will be revealed.

For as long as I can remember, I have always liked girls and by now, I was well aware of the difference between them and myself. A difference which I wholeheartedly approved of. Childish games of 'Doctors and Nurses' and the mutual flashing games, of 'I'll show you mine if you show me yours,' was great. As long as I was a spectator and not a participant. I'd look and fiddle whenever it was offered, but a pretty little girl would only have to say 'Show me yours' or try to touch and I'd remember immediately the imaginary chores I had to do for Mam. Then I'd be off in a flash, - no pun intended. When the other boys and I were alone, I could lie and boast with the best of them. Fantastic stories of our imaginary sexual encounters and mythical conquests. The most tragic part of it all, wasn't the lies, but the fact that we believed each other. The oppressive teachings of the Tabernacle on that subject. An indefinable, forbidden atmosphere I felt at home. When anything of that nature came up it made me totally shy in the company of adults. The slightest hint of sex in their conversation and I would melt into a ball of embarrassment. I would strive to become invisible. I became so adapt in the art of disappearing in full view, that I reluctantly got to hear every piece of gossip and dirty doings, which was circulating around Brynmawr. The people of Wales have to be the undisputed Champions of the World when it comes to gossip and not just the women, the men are just as bad. They are all wonderful minders of other people's affairs. Mam along with neighbors, Mrs. Woodyat and Mrs. Griffin were like the 'Three Gossipiers'. When they were joined by Mrs. Lake and Mrs. Cox the chops would really start to fly. I would usually be on the floor modeling with plastercine or arranging my toy soldiers. The topic might change from the state of the weather and of the price of bacon to lingerie. Which I found embarrassing enough, then it would degenerate to, -

"Oh, did you hear about Rhonda Morgan?"

"No, what's she been up to now?"

"Well it's not 'er that's been up to anythin' this time, as far as I know, no, it's her old man Percy, bin carryin' on with that Wendy Williams from Nantyglo."

"Oh, that's Rhonda's own cousin too, in' it? Underage she is too!"

"No, she's over sixteen now but she's been at it since she was twelve!"

"No never, well yes, but then Rhonda was like that too, 'fore she was married, only wore knickers to keep 'er ankles warm!"

"I don't think being married 'as slowed 'er down!"

"Runs in the family, if you ask me, I 'eard that Wendy's Mother Pat, got pregnant with little Ed with one of them Yankee GI's when 'er 'usband was off fightin' the Japs!"

"Really, who told you that?"

"Mrs. Roberts, you know she only lives up the road from Pat, nosey bugger she is, knows everybody's business!" "

"Oh yes, she's a real gossip her, you can't tell her anything unless it's all over Brynmawr! And she's a fine one to talk, did you hear about old man Price runnin' out 'er back door when 'er 'usband came home early from the pub, wearin' nothin' but his shirt and boots he was with his big thing swingin' all over the place!"

"Who, 'er 'usband?"

"No, old man Price, you silly bugger!"

From the corner of my eye I saw Mrs. Cox look at Mam and shift her eyes in my direction reminding Mam of my presence, as the subject was getting racier by the minute.

"Oh, don't worry about him," Mam responded, "He's too dull to understand what we're talking about." In contrast to being insulted by Mam's remark, I felt relieved that Mam was so naïve as to believe I was innocent and totally unconscious of anything carnal. On the contrary, thanks to their informative and educational discussions, I was to learn that almost everybody in Brynmawr was a hypocritical Bible thumper, a drunk, or a pervert, or a whore, or a slut, or a nymphomaniac.

****

Peter Wilson was a new kid in school, he had recently moved from London. Being the new kid his novelty naturally drew a disproportionate amount of attention from the girls. In so doing drew a disproportionate amount of hostility from the boys, who were jealous of what they considered his unwarranted popularity.

"We don't want any bloody English kids in our school, stealing our Welsh girls!" Terry Lake stated indignantly. Not that any of our Welsh girls would have been seen dead with a shitty little runt like Terry Lake anyway. Egged on by shitty Lake a few of the other boys began to pummel poor Peter. Terry Lake picked up a stone and threw it at Peter hitting him on the ear. Blood ran all down his neck. Being a part of my nature to zigg while everyone else is zagging, I leapt into the fray and in spite of being proudly Welsh, I shouted,

"I'm English too, who wants to fight me?" I shared a few punches amongst them and that was it. After that incident, Peter became my shadow whenever we were in the schoolyard. On one occasion we were both picking up stones and throwing them as hard as we could at the ground or the school wall. One of the other kids had recently made a discovery. When a certain type of stone was split open they were a shiny, veined glass inside. There were quite a few of us spread all over the schoolyard thus occupied. I was bending over picking over what looked like likely candidates, when Peter suddenly began to giggle. He nudged me in the hip with his elbow to gain my attention and pointed at what was amusing him. I looked and saw the backend of another boy standing in a huge pair of rubber boots. As he bent down to pick up a stone, the largest set of genitals that I had ever seen on a two legged animal dropped out of his trousers. They were split in the seam from arsehole to breakfast time. He'd straighten up they'd disappear. He'd bend and wallop! – There they were again, 'just a swingin'.' Well I laughed so much I thought I'd explode, Peter and I had to hold each other up. The owner of the prize package seemed to sense our amusement as he turned his head and gave a puzzled frown in our direction. We quickly looked down and pretended to be preoccupied with the stones, both of us still shaking with laughter. Once again he bent down and plop! – Out it all came again, like a rabbit out of a magicians hat. I mean it wasn't just funny, it was also bloody embarrassing which made it even funnier. By now we were almost helpless. He turned his head and glowered at us. We both looked at the ground again, really enjoying this silly game. When he turned back and bent over again and Wham! that giant salami dropped back into view. I knew it was too good to keep to ourselves and was in the process of waving my arms at some of the other boys. I pointed at the object of our amusement but turned back to find myself looking straight into two furious eyes. He glared at me from beneath his thunderous beetling frown. Woe is me, all I could do is laugh. I covered my mouth with my hand and hoped he wouldn't see me doing it. The monster with the monster lurched towards me with hostile intentions etched all over his face. He didn't know exactly what we were laughing at, but he looked as though he knew exactly what he was going to do about it. Peter Wilson's giggles turned into a whimper as he dove behind me to take cover. It turned out to be bad strategy. When Big Raymond reached me, he gave me the most almighty shove in the chest with both his hands. I was lifted completely off my feet and propelled backwards into Peter. When we hit the stony ground I was sitting on Peter's lap. Raymond Bailey was only a little more than a couple of years my senior but he was enormous. He actually looked like a seasoned body-builder, - from the waist up. I said he lurched towards me and that's exactly how he moved. He would throw his weight forward, catch his weight on one foot and the impetus would carry him on barely keeping his balance. Sometimes he wouldn't be able to stop his forward momentum unless he could grab hold of something like a wall or a fence. We thought his ambling gait was caused by the huge, hand me down, rubber boots he wore. He had been wearing them for most of the few years I'd known him. In order to walk home he had to more or less swing himself from one handhold to the next. He favored a route that was fenced and he'd move forward almost hand over hand like Tarzan swinging through the jungle.

We also thought that the upper body exercise entailed gave him his huge muscles and Superman strength. Raymond was one of about seventeen Brothers and Sisters. Any item of clothing was destined to pass from one to another irrespective of the size or the sex until it finally faded away. Unfortunately Raymond's affliction wasn't caused, as we all thought by his outsize boots. The terrible truth was that he had a form of Muscular Dystrophy that caused his legs to steadily degenerate. Even so his upper body seemed to swell with more muscle every time I saw him.

I barely made it to my feet, leaving poor Peter still sitting on his arse, blinking like an owl. Big Raymond lurched at me again. I threw a wild punch that caught him on the side of his neck. It seemed to have the stopping power of a Butterfly. He staggered on relentlessly swinging haymakers at my head as he came. If he'd caught me with just one of his mighty fists I think I would have gone straight to 'The Happy Hunting Ground.' His strength and power, lucky for me was only surpassed by his awkward clumsiness. I managed to dodge his fists and connect with a few good punches of my own that almost checked him in mid lurch. But, I could only back away so far so fast and I ran out of luck when I ran out of room. I found myself boxed in with the boy's toilet wall directly behind me. Big Raymond grabbed me in a bear hug and whipped me off my feet. He hurled himself, with me still in his arms at the toilet wall. After my back smashed into it with lung crushing force, we both slid sideways onto the ground. Wrapped in Raymond's big crushing arms with my back wedged against the bottom of the wall and all his weight on top of me, I was as helpless as a kitten. Struggle as I may I wasn't going anywhere.

"Come on Ade, get up!" - I wasn't sure if I was hearing things, - I managed painfully to twist my head slightly to one side as I heard it again, "Come on Ade; get up, you're not doing any good down there!" I could barely see the face of my Uncle Fred. He was peering down at me over the high wall that towered over the schoolyard from the road above our school. "Come on Ade, get up and fight!" demanded Uncle Fred yet again. I've got to be as honest now, as I was with myself back then and admit that I was beaten. I hadn't actually said 'I give up' but I would have been happy to. If I could have got enough breath in my lungs to do so. Here came that voice again, "Get up Ade, come on get up and fight!" I did, don't ask me how, because I don't know. I didn't know then, I don't know now, but I did – and I fought and I fought. Every time I threw a punch it connected and almost every time I connected Big Raymond went down. Every time Big Raymond threw a punch he missed and when he missed the impetus lost him his balance. His poor semi crippled legs let him down. I have no illusions now as I had none then. If Raymond had caught me with just a few of those mighty blows he would have smashed my face. If there had been nothing wrong with his legs he would have pulverized me. But, he didn't catch me and his legs were too weak. Soon Big Raymond was staggering around clumsily with blood pouring from his nose and his badly split and swollen lips. The right side of his face was skinned and swollen bellow a left eye that was black and all but closed. The knuckles on both my fists were also swollen and bloody as I measured him and punched his face at will. I asked Raymond at length if he had had enough and much to my relief he nodded his head. We walked silently together towards the wash room to clean ourselves up. I didn't realize it, until it was pointed out to me a little later. But, I had just learned one of the biggest, and for me one of the most important lessons of my life. Uncle Fred was my favorite Uncle and was down from London on holiday. When I got home from school that day Uncle Fred seemed to be waiting for me. Without giving anyone else an explanation he invited me to take a stroll with him. We made our way along a country lane leading into the hills. He told me he wanted to talk to me. This immediately made me feel important. It also had an intriguing air of mystery about it. I had never had a private man to man talk with an adult before in my life. He told me he didn't have a lot to say but it needed to be said in private. He knew Mam would possibly not approve and Dad definitely wouldn't. It had to do with the fight he had witnessed earlier. First he asked me how I felt about winning. Not really knowing what else to say, I just said "Good." Although he must have been as aware as I was, that it was only Big Raymond's awful disability that afforded me my dubious victory. That was not what he was leading up to,

"How would you have felt if you'd lost?" he asked, I simply shrugged as I hadn't really thought about that aspect until now.

"You wouldn't have won if you hadn't got up would you?" He continued. I shook my head.

"OK, listen to what I'm going to tell you and you'll never lose." He told me. Naturally I was intrigued as I had always wanted to be the best fighter in the World.

"Never, ever give up!" He stated, "It's as simple as that, then the only way they can beat you is to knock you out or kill you. If you won't give up they can't beat you. Keep coming back, never mind what they do. Just keep coming back even if they're better than you. Eventually they'll lose heart, they'll lose confidence. They'll start to lose, you'll start to win. Make your mind up that you're going to win. Whatever it takes, or how long it takes and in the end you'll always win." And he was right, that is the way it is. Also, when that theory had been tried and tested again and again the amount of confidence it brings with it is magical. The confidence that spills over into your body language is not lost on an opponent either. Even if you're receiving a severe beating you know without a doubt that eventually the shoe is going to be on the other foot. You can only appreciate what a powerful weapon Uncle Fred had given me, when you consider the time, place and the mentality that presided in my environment. I would think that the same could be said of most small towns. But from personal experience I can only speak of Brynmawr and all the small towns that surrounded it. Tough reputations were admired, emulated and striven for. If ever achieved, nurtured. It was 'I'm the fastest gun in the West' mentality. They wanted to be King of the Castle and thought of as the toughest of the tough and the meanest of the mean. The peak of pugilism could only be attained by beating anyone or everyone who may have fancied their chances. Once the summit had been surmounted there was usually no lack of challenges from those who coveted your celebrity. My Brother's reputation in this regard had been growing steadily for some time. Already famous for his violent temperament, the viciousness he displayed to all he vanquished and a left fist that was legend. My double role as Brother and reluctant punch bag can attest to that. By now Ter had left school and was working in Beynon's the same Colliery as Dad. Ter was always considered to be the brainy one in the family and met with unanimous opposition from our whole family, to his decision to leave school to work down the pit.

"Why don't you stay on in school?" Pleaded Dad, "You could go on to College, get yourself a real education and make something of your life."

"All my friends have left and earning money down the pit." Ter argued.

"You won't like it, I started work in the pit when I was only 14, I never had the chance that you've got, to get an education and better myself." Dad stated.

"I'm sick of school!" Ter persisted.

"The coal mine is hard work, dirty, unhealthy, poorly paid and dangerous!" Dad continued, "I only wish I'd had the chance that you've got, I would never have gone down the pit, it's a terrible life. Your only 15, at least stay in school for another year and then see how you feel, if you've any sense you'll change your mind."

"I want to work in the pit." Ter sulked. So he left school and worked in the pit and he hated it, as it was hard work, dirty, unhealthy, poorly paid and dangerous.

"Can I go down the Valley Road to play with Sheila and Valerie Mam?" I interrupted, thoroughly sick of hearing about school.

"No, you can't," Dad growled at me, "Get in the garden, there's plenty of weeding for you to do yet. Just you wait till you leave school; I'll have you working down the pit with me!"

Uncle Fred, Auntie Pat and their two younger Daughters, Joan and Margaret had already returned to London. Sheila and Valerie stayed for the whole Summer and were my constant summer companions. During that time, if my parents were out in the evening Sister Pam and I were looked after by Sheila and Valerie both 3 years my senior. Bedtime was a delight as Sheila and Valerie would often come into my bedroom wearing their little short nightdresses and bounce all over the bed. They would wrestle each other, wrestle me and practicing kissing, using me as the practice dummy. They turned me into a junky, all I wanted to do was kiss. Sheila and I would spend hours every day perfecting it. I constructed a kissing palace out of bales of hay in the field beyond our back garden. That's where we'd make for whenever I could dodge Dad and his constant chores. I didn't see Uncle Fred again until the following Summer Holiday, when Mam, Dad, Ter, Pam and I, went to stay with them in London. I had never been to London before and there was so much to see in that great Historic City. After visiting the London museums I was asked by Uncle Fred what else I wanted to see in London, more than anything else. 'Piccadilly Circus' I answered, without one second's hesitation, so off we went to Piccadilly Circus. When we arrived, the family and I stood looking at the statue of 'Eros' in the centre of the circus and Uncle Fred asked me,

"Well Ade, what do you think of Piccadilly Circus, do you like it?"

"It's very nice," I answered politely, "but where are all the Lions and Elephants and Clowns?" The highlight of that day was a shop called 'German's', all it sold was Arms and Armor. It was fantastic, I have had so many dreams concerning that shop, from that time to the present. Another favorite of mine was The Tower of London, there's lots of interesting things from torture chambers, head chopping blocks. Crown Jewels, giant cannons, but best of all was in the White Tower, armor-armor-armor. There were suits of armor made for Medieval Princes, some smaller than me. There was a suit of armor made for a very heavily built man who stood over 6-feet-10-inches tall. Two suits of armor that had been made for Henry VIII, one must have been made for him when he was young and athletic, the other when he was gross and fat, but both equipped with an embarrassingly enormous 'Codpiece' that resembled a Sherman Tank.

Uncle Fred and his Family lived in Kensal Green. That was where I first met Bobby Selsden. It was mutual hatred at first sight. The kids were playing in the street and seemed to be enjoying themselves, so I ran out to join them. Bobby, who had his back to me, turned around to face me as I approached. The look he gave me would have withered an Oak tree. I suppose that such a look from him would usually send an unwelcome stranger into a fast retreat. Instead I allowed my features to mirror his. This meant that voicing threats of aggression were completely superfluous. Without a single word we launched ourselves at each other's throats. Bobby was a very tough kid, but it seemed I had his number. It did cross my mind more than once that he must have had an Uncle Fred type talk with someone. The way he kept coming back for the punishment I was more than happy to serve him. He finally caved in, but not before he gave me one hell of a scrap. I got the usual telling off from Mam and Dad when I walked indoors to wash off some blood. But the wink and sly smile I received over their heads, from my Favorite Uncle, more than made up for the scolding. Ter got himself a very pretty girl friend and was getting ready to take her out on their first date. After preening himself, self-consciously as Mam and Dad looked on. Suffering the ribald jibes and innuendoes of our bawdy Uncle Fred, he went off on his date to the Cinema. When he returned few hours later, he was asked by Uncle Fred if he had enjoyed himself. Ter assured him that he had, as Mam, Dad and the rest of the Family looked on approvingly. Ter must have turned every rosy shade in the spectrum when Uncle Fred added, "Ok then, if it was that good let me smell your fingers!"

****

Our Jewish Greengrocer Mickey Jacobs was a very good friend of mine; his Brother Benny was a Boxing Manager who handled the very skillful Heavyweight from Cardiff's Tiger Bay, Joe Erskine, who was to become British Champion. Mickey had advised me how to restore my latest acquisition from Aladdin's Cave. A Zulu Assegai with a shaft which was broken a few inches shy of its long, broad bladed head. I'd added it to my collection for only 5 shillings because of the damage to the shaft. Mickey himself was very interested in my hobby. He told me he had a source from which he could supply me with some good deals. True to his word a few days later he presented me with a sinister looking weapon, which he described as an Arab Dirk. For the3 shillings Mickey charged me for it I was extremely happy with the deal. A week or so later he sold me a 16th Century Portuguese Rapier for just 5 shillings, I was ecstatic. He told me he had access to something really special but I would have to be prepared to part with at least 2 pounds to own it. The suspense was killing me as I had no idea of what this something special was going to be. My imagination ran riot as a list of wildly exotic possibilities kept revolving through my brain. Every day I'd make a B line to Mickey's shop on my way home from school.

"Have you got it yet, Mickey?" I'd ask hopefully.

"Not yet Ade, maybe tomorrow." He'd answer. You can't imagine my disappointment on the day I walked into his store and Mickey proudly presented me with the much awaited mystery weapon, - a bloody fencing foil.

"I don't want that soding thing Mickey!" I groaned, without the slightest cushion of diplomacy in my voice.

"Why not, what's wrong with it?" asked Mickey. The shock and disappointment on his face that must have mirrored my own, "It's almost brand new!"

"Yes, it is bloody brand new and that's not all that's wrong with it!" I shouted, "I collect exotic and antique weapons, not modern sports equipment!"

Mickey and I almost had a serious fallout over that little episode. He was disappointed not to make a good return on his investment. I was just disappointed. I soon began traveling back to 'Aladdin's Cave.' In anticipation of having to find some extra money to subsidize my floor polishing wages to be able to afford Mickey's mysterious disappointment. I had wandered around the Saturday morning market which was held at Market Square. I asked some of the stall holders if they needed any help. I struck gold.

"Yes son, could you pop over to the corner café and get me a couple of cheese sandwiches and a cup of tea?" One would reply. "I'm on my own and I can't leave the stall unattended." Off I'd rush and when I'd return it was. "Thanks Kid, here's 6 pence for yourself." 6 pence! That was a day's floor polishing wages.

"Hey sonny, could you get me something from the café?" another stall holder called, "See if they've got a Welshcake or some kind of muffin and a cup of coffee."

"Get me a cup of tea while you're there." Shouted a third vendor, "Milky please, with one spoonful of sugar." Within a few weeks I would be waiting in the dark, early in the morning for the first of the vans and trucks to arrive. I would help with the unloading of every kind of produce imaginable. By the time the last vehicle had arrived and set up I would be running about taking refreshment orders. When the market was closing I'd be there helping with the reloading.

Sabers, Cutlasses, Field Swords and that Japanese Samurai

Sword, that I would have cheerfully traded my Brother for, were soon added to my collection. The only problem and for me a small price to pay was the occasional truant I had to play from school. Saturday used to be the only day I had time to put a minimum of eight hours into a trip to Hereford. Now I was working from 5 am to 5 pm every single Saturday so the weekend was out of the question.

My Birthdays were always a big disappointment to me when I was a kid. There always seemed to be so much fuss made of anyone else when ever their Birthdays came around. So naturally, I expected school to close for the day to celebrate my Birth. Even if they didn't go so far as declaring a National holiday. Also, I expected an abundance of wonderful presents such as Ter and Pam received for their Birthdays. I would be asked what I wanted for my Birthday, I would make my choices, only to be told,

"Oh no, your Birthday is too close to Christmas. Maybe you can have something like that then, but we'll just get you something small for now." I didn't want something small for now. It was my Birthday, no one else's Birthday and I wanted something big, the same as Ter and Pam.

"No you can't have that now; your Birthday is too close to Christmas."

My Birthday was the 5th of December, twenty days before Christmas. Ter's Birthday was on January the 3^{rd,} 9 days after Christmas, I pointed this out but was told, "Oh, Christmas is gone by then, so it doesn't count." – WHAT?!!!! No, I didn't understand that one either. Maybe they counted it as being 356 days before the next Christmas? Being the extra kid in the middle of a 6 year older Brother and a 6 year younger Sister, made me feel like a spare prick at a wedding. My wild schemes hatched for the attention I craved always seemed to blow up in my face. Literally sometimes. Like on the occasion of my re-enactment of Guy Fawkes attempt to blow up the Houses of Parliament in 1605. I had made plastercine models of Guy Fawkes and his fellow conspirators. Then dismantled a pile of fireworks in order to utilize the explosives. I carefully arranged the whole scene, struck a match and blew my hair and eyebrows off. Standing in the swirling smoke with my black face and wide frightened eyes shouting "Mammy" I must have looked more as though I was performing a re-enactment of Al Jolson's Minstrel show.

My next scheme was intended to kill two birds with one stone. You may recall earlier that I said I was only afraid of two things One being my fear of heights and the other I'd promised to refer to later in my story. Well, now it's later in my story. - SEX was the other culprit. It wasn't that I didn't approve of sex, on the contrary. I did approve and was extremely interested. As long as I didn't have to participate. All my posing, posturing and bragging was total bullshit. I had never done anything and I was certain that I would grow old and die before I ever did. So I thought of adopting a persona that would portray me as an interesting and lovable rascal. It would also bolster my bullshit in the eyes of my equally full of crap friends at the same time. I thought of Cousin Desmond who was about 8 years older than me and his startling, blatant preoccupation with the female form. One of the Truck drivers who regularly stayed at Queen Street for 'Bed and Breakfast' used to leave magazines for Desmond that he'd brought back from his trips to Paris. Anything from 'Les Follies Bergere' was Desmond's favorite. Strippers, Exotic Dancers, Fan Dancers. As long as they were in a state of undress Desmond loved them all. Even then I had found it embarrassing. I remember Mam and Auntie Vira being highly amused by his exaggerated, lecherous gloating. They teased him unmercifully while he'd just giggle and revel in his notoriety. That was going to be my new gimmick. It would take a lot of courage to surmount the initial embarrassment but once I'd mastered that it would be easy sailing. So I began my new hobby, collecting pictures of glamour girls. I needed a scrapbook in which to mount my intended collection, but didn't want to spend my hard earned wages on one. I converted an old Christmas Annual into a scrapbook. I pasted any girlie photos that I'd cut out of newspapers or magazines onto the pages with a mixture of flour and water. I soon amassed quite an impressive collection. My favorite being a photo of the gorgeous, exotic, Laya Raki, almost wearing something leopardish. The time had come for the grand unveiling ceremony. It would elevate my standing from a snotty nosed little kid to 'The Guy with the Flair for the Ladies' and 'Girlie Coinsure.' The only snag in my plan was I didn't have the guts to show it to anybody, especially Mam. I hid my sexy scrapbook in plain view in the bedroom I shared with Ter. I knew he would have no interest in looking at a kid's Christmas Annual, especially an old one. I soon lost count of the times I would judge the time right to show off my new hobby. After collecting my scrapbook from my bedroom, I'd take a deep breath, walk into the sitting room with it under my arm. I'd look around at everyone, with butterflies in my stomach and my heart in my mouth. Then turn on my heel and take my scrapbook back to the anonymity of my bedroom. I just couldn't bring myself to unveil the new me. I also had a feeling of self loathing as I had to admit to myself I was a coward in this regard. I could force myself to climb a cliff that terrified me but not emerge from the 'I love sexy girls' closet. Time after time I'd steel my resolve only to buckle and run when the proof needed to be in the pudding. So back to the drawing board to re-plan my strategy. My new gutless plan was simple, I would use the unwitting talents of Sister Pamela, who could be totally relied upon, not, to keep a secret. Like the time I was sitting indoors, minding Pam and practicing smoking a cigarette. Pamela watched me; suitably impressed by the sophisticated figure I posed. In spite of the watering eyes and hacking cough. Pam realized that smoking was at least a bit naughty. asked me,

"Do you want me to tell Mam you were smoking when she comes home?"

"No, I don't think that would be a good idea." I replied.

"Alright, I won't tell her." She smiled sweetly. Fifteen minutes later Mam walked in and Pam proclaimed, "Mam, Adrian wasn't smoking while you were out."

So it was obvious, if you wanted to share news with the world, just tell Pam a 'secret'. So next time I was minding Pam I brought my scrapbook from my bedroom, made a big deal of looking around shiftily. I scanned the pages, and closed the book when ever curious Pam tried to look over my shoulder. Finally I walked around the room in search of a good hiding place, as Pam, as curious as ever watched my performance. After deciding to conceal my treasure in a low and very accessible cupboard I left the room. When I returned a little later I could tell by the speculative and guilty expression on Pam's face that so far, my plan was working. The rest was easy, Pam wouldn't be able to resist showing Mam 'Adrian's secret.' Mam's eyebrows would rise up to her hairline with surprise. She'd look at me in a new light, a smile would break out around her mouth. I'd reluctantly plead guilty to the ownership of the 'naughty' scrapbook. I'd get a gentle ribbing to which I'd respond with the appropriate amount of partly fiend embarrassment. Then bask in my new found notoriety. Dad and Ter were already home before Mam arrived. As soon as she walked through the door, Pam sped like a whippet to my hiding place and produced my scrapbook with a flourish,

"Look what Adrian has stuck in this book, Mam." 'Well it's done now.' I thought, with a feeling of both relief and apprehension. My apprehension turned to concern, my concern to panic. Instead of the surprised Motherly smile, a look total disgust and then fury transformed Mam's face. She flung the book from her and descended on me like an avalanche. She grabbed me by the hair and swung me completely off my feet. I was punched, pinched, scratched and kicked unmercifully until Mam completely ran out of steam. Fortunately, just before I ran out of teeth. She left me cringing in the corner as she tore page after page out of my scrapbook and hurled them into the fire. I peaked all around with one eye through the fingers of my hands that I still held up to protect my face. Both Ter and Pam were wide eyed and slack jawed with shock. Even Dad looked dumbfounded. What sparked such a violent reaction from Mam I still don't know. It isn't as though the photos were pornographic or even crude. Most of them I'd clipped out of newspapers that had been read by Mam and Dad. Just pretty ladies wearing bikinis or lingerie. There were a few naked girls I'd cut out of pinup magazines but no more than a bare arse and a few exposed tits. Certainly nothing stronger than 'naughty' Cousin Desmond used to gloat over. As you can well imagine, that was an episode that did wonders for my nonexistent confidence in my pursuit of sexual experience. At home I felt like a disgusting leper, no one spoke to me indoors for a week or more. Except Ter, who would sidle up to me when no one else was in earshot and whisper, "I know the dirty, filthy things you do."

Dad's remedy was making me go to 'The Tabernacle' three times on a Sunday and on a Wednesday evening, instead of just Sunday school.

A few weeks later I finally managed to break the ice with Mam by inviting her to accompany me on one of my trips to 'Aladdin's Cave' my treat. I knew she had a weakness for boiled ham sandwiches, made with newly baked bread. Still warm from the oven, spread with lashings of fresh country butter. Then a thick slice of cream sponge with a nice hot, steaming cup of tea. I told Mam about the Market place where the aforementioned delicacies were acquired and could tell by her drooling chops I had a deal. Even before I went into detail about what a great Antique shop Aladdin's Cave was.

It started out to be a great day. I felt entirely grown up as I purchased our bus tickets. Then we actually talked and listened to each other all the way there on our 2 hour bus ride. Once arrived I was beside myself with importance, as I conducted our tour around the beautiful City of Hereford. We made a b-line for the eatery I ordered for both of us and then paid the bill with a flourish. Mam enjoyed our repast every bit as much as I knew she would. I endured a long boring trek around women's clothes shops. Another of Mam's weaknesses, before I presented my piece-de-résistance, the famous Aladdin's Cave. Aladdin's Cave also proved to be a great success, not only did Mam love it, but I got a couple of great bargains. An 18th Century East Indian Push-Dagger and a German Storm trooper's Dagger. I was thoroughly contented, on our return bus ride, as Mam recounted how impressed she'd been with Aladdin's Cave and its interesting and exotic wares. How enjoyable lunch was and how surprised she'd been by the amount of money I'd been proudly flashing around.

"How much money do you earn, working on the Market?" Mam asked. I was still riding high with my own importance, so I came out with some vastly exaggerated figure. Then much to my horror Mam said, "Well you don't really need that much. From now on you can keep whatever else you earn but you must bring 10 shillings a week home to me." SHIT! If I'd only told the truth. Sometimes I didn't even earn as much as 10 shillings! I wonder if you can imagine how miserable life can be for a 10 year old kid working his arse off in all weathers. Sunshine, pouring rain and freezing snow to earn wages that now would often have to be subsidized by the pocket money I earned by polishing floors all week. Just to be able to bring home 10 shillings a week to Mam.

That was bad enough. But due to my big mouth to which everyone I've ever known can attest to. I'd also boasted to my friends about my market day earnings and now I had to deal with some serious competition. Another nail in the coffin of my earning power, was when the café vendors themselves became aware of the potential profits to be gained. They simply sent one of their employees over to the market and take the appropriate orders, which ensured them, and not a rival café of the custom. I'd hit a major setback, which I had to grin and bear, as my armament program ground down to a crawl.

****

A few of my friends and I were playing in 'The Prickly Field.' Actually we didn't know what the field was called, or who it belonged to. We called it the prickly field because it was absolutely chocked full of enormous, thorny gorse bushes. It was a terrific place to play our war games or hide and seek. Or just chasing each other through the gaps, pathways and avenues that wound in and out of that spiky jungle. I was a heroic, Barbarian, Welsh Prince driving Cousin Raymond, Malcolm Bailey, Raymond Woodyat and Dai Hughes, who I visualized as Julius Caesar's invading Roman Legionaries out of my mountain Kingdom. I was stopped short by one of my favorite sounds, - Girls giggling. There were 4 of them, all about our age, all pretty and best of all, all of them looking at me. Which was the way it ought to be. I was the Patriotic Welsh Prince and hero of the moment, as I drove the villainous Roman invaders before me. Oh, wait a minute they've spotted the girls and are rallying their forces. I must strike before they form their impenetrable tortoise formation. I steadied my imaginary white stallion as it reared in anticipation of my reckless do or die glorious charge. I was gratified to see that the girls were riveted with the excitement my dashing figure inspired.

"Charge!" I screamed and thundered at the enemy with all the force I could muster. I smashed right through their ranks sending them flying in all directions.

"Look what you've made me do!" squawked Dai Hughes as he tried to scramble out of the middle of a gorse bush, "You made me scratch all my fuckin' legs!" I turned quickly back to the girls, embarrassed by Dai's bad language. But, instead of the shock I had expected from them they began giggling with a vengeance.

"You'll go to the Devil if you say words like that!" I warned Dai. Partly afraid for his soul, but mostly jealous of the attention he was getting from the girls.

"You play too fuckin' rough!" Said Raymond, agreeing, with Dai, "I've got thorns in my fuckin' arse!" The girls exploded, and that was just the beginning. It was f this and f that, it was like an effing competition. Encouraged by the increasing reaction their swearing induced from the females, the boys language got even worse.

"You'll all go to the Devil, if you say words like that!" I persisted pathetically, but no one was listening. I was mortified. I'd gone from centre stage, Warrior Prince to the invisible man in 2 minutes. The girls only had eyes for the blasphemers, I couldn't stand it. I took a deep breath, swallowed hard, barged into the middle of them and said, "Are we fuckin' playin' or what?!" The girls giggled furiously for my benefit, as I drew a breath and waited for the thunderbolt. I gazed skywards and the towering electric pylons in the next field caught my eye. I wondered if God would send it flashing from there. Or would it come zipping at me independently from the Almighty's own electric power supply in the wide blue yonder. The apprehension almost turned to disappointment as I waited and nothing happened. I wasn't struck by a thunderbolt, but then I was struck by a thought instead. It seemed I had just bartered my eternal soul for a couple of minutes attention from a few giggling girls. 'Fuck it' I thought, just like Esau, or Aesop, or whatever his name was. Selling his birthright for a mess of potage -? Or was it Amos 'n' Andy selling their afterbirth for a pot of porridge?! As you can well appreciate, if I was willing to risk my mortal soul for attention from a few silly giggling Girls as a young kid. Just imagine the length I was prepared to go to a few years later when gaining attention was a very vital part of my making a living.

The prickly field also set the scene of our next adventure. It began the winter before. I'd fallen through the ice on the Waun Pond and got drenched to the skin with ice cold water. Not wanting to go home and get into a row for playing on the ice after I'd been told not to, I had to find somewhere else to dry off. I found that the furnace in the garage for the double-decker buses was tailor made. Whilst drying off my clothes and warming my wet frozen body back to life I'd noticed a few attractive looking fire extinguishers lined up on the wall. I marked it down in my memory for future reference. So going back to the prickly field. It was now well into a very rare, dry, hot summer. I was amazing my gang by starting little fires with a magnifying glass. I was surprised that none of them had seen it done before. They'd all gasp with astonishment every time the little pinprick of sunlight would smolder and then suddenly leap into flame as I adjusted the glass. We'd stamp it out and then do it again. Eventually I got fed up playing the sorcerer and a new game crossed my mind. I remembered the fire extinguishers I'd seen 6 months before in the garage. So off we went to 'borrow' them and to buy a box of matches. When we returned to the field we started off gradually and set fire to a small bush. Once we had a good blaze going we put it out with the fire extinguishers, it was great fun so we set fire to a few more and put those out too. The smoke or fire must have disturbed a few rabbits that suddenly broke their cover out of the gorse bushes and zigzagged about us looking for a new hiding place. We all instinctively leapt after them squirting great jets of white foam in their wake. Confused, the rabbits dodged from bush to bush and we ran around and around barely missing each other with our wild firing. When the rabbits had finally disappeared it seemed to be an anticlimax to go back to what we were doing before. Instead we decided to set one of the larger bushes alight. Then station ourselves all round it let blast at a mutual signal and have one grand finale before calling it quits. All seemed to go to plan as the heat from the giant gorse bush almost sent us reeling backwards,

"OK!" We all screamed, "Let her blast!" and nothing happened, none of us had any more than a pathetic dribble left in our extinguishers. We ran around like blue-arsed flies, trying to get close enough to hit the scorching flames with branches. We were driven back by the searing heat, as the fire raged and spread like measles. There was only one thing left to do, - RUN LIKE HELL! We didn't look back until we were all standing outside my garden gate. We saw the most indescribably huge fire we could ever have imagined, it was absolutely incomprehensible. I swear we could still feel the heat up on that hill more than a mile away from the closest flame. Fire engine sirens began to wail as they sped to the scene from Brynmawr and a half a dozen neighboring towns. All our neighbors came out and gazed with disbelief at the fiery inferno. I became aware that Mam and Dad were standing inside our garden gate awestruck by the sight of all the fire and smoke.

"Well at least we know where Adrian is," Mam said to Dad, as she nodded her head in my direction, "So we know he had nothing to do with that, for a change."

Apart from our yearly Holidays when we usually spent a couple of weeks with Gran in Bristol, there would be day trips to the seaside. Porthcawl, but more often Barry Island. That being the most popular resort for all of the mining families from the Valleys. There was the beach, the Fair ground and the Famous Knickerbocker Glory, which was a tall glass goblet, alternately filled with fruit, cream, jelly and topped with a huge mound of ice-cream. The Knickerbocker Glory would be the main topic of conversation with us kids on our bus ride to Barry Island. Also the main ingredient in the gallons of vomit we all produced on our bus ride back. Nevertheless it was all great fun.

When it was announced that the family would be going to Blackpool this year for a change I was ecstatic. Instant visions of the famous 'Blackpool Tower,' a copy of France's Eiffel Tower. The Beach, the Fairground with its giant Ferris Wheel and Rollercoaster, but most of all 'The Fabled Blackpool Illuminations.' Millions of flashing, sparkling, glittering, multi-colored bulbs that encrusted everything along the beachfront streets, to the Tower itself, Boy, I couldn't wait. Until Dad told me I wouldn't be going.

"What do you mean I'm not going?!" I asked in disbelief, thinking this was one of Dad's jokes and appreciating, that this was about as good as Dad's sense of humor got.

"What I said," he answered, "we're going to Blackpool, you're not."

"Why can't I come?!" I whined, "I haven't done anything wrong have I?"

"Blackpool is a lot further than Barry Island." Mam answered, "It'll be better if there's just four of us to worry about."

"Well why has it got to be me who has to stay home?" I argued.

"Pamela is too young to leave at home," Mam replied, "And Terence is old enough to look after himself."

"I'm old enough to look after myself!" I countered.

"No, you're not!" Dad shouted, "Even in Barry Island your always getting lost!"

"I never get lost! I yelled, "I know where I am, I just don't know where you are!"

"Well you'll know where we are this time!" Dad gloated, "We'll be in Blackpool and you won't!" I hated the glint of triumph in Dad's eyes and the satisfied smirk on Ter's face, as I ran out of argument. I was the only one who wouldn't be going to Blackpool. I had some fun while they were away but unfortunately got caught. I released the brakes on a truck and caused it to crash over the edge of a quarry. But I know that wasn't as good as Blackpool. I cringed every time I heard Dad telling friends or family about some incredible aspect of their Blackpool trip. How much they'd all enjoyed themselves. His voice would increase considerably in volume, whenever he noticed I was in hearing range. I hated being a kid; I just couldn't wait to grow up.

I used to spend as little time as possible at home; if I wasn't in school I'd be wandering the hills, woods or valleys, usually searching for Hedgehogs, Lizards or Snakes. I had realized by now that there were no Red Indians living in them thar' hills. I was wandering them thar' hills one day, intending to pick a jar of succulent purple Wimberries. Suddenly I came face to face with an old nemesis and Vera Lynn's War time song sprang right back into my head, 'We'll meet again.'

It seemed as though time was suspended as I gazed into the familiar evil, yellow eyes of The Giant Grey Raggedy Ram. The same rotten bastard that did not respect the law of the wild. It had almost broken my leg and my back after tossing me into the air like a pancake. It had Demonstrated its ingratitude after I had saved it from torture and humiliation at the hands of two spiteful boys. Cautiously I backed away to where I felt I wouldn't fall foul of another sudden charge. When I gauged the moment was right I spun around and sped home. No, I wasn't afraid of my old enemy, far from it. The Ram was armed and so would I be, the Ram had huge, heavy curly horns, I would get an equalizer, my Assegai. When I returned to the scene of my encounter, the Ram was nowhere to be found. I searched the hills, gullies, valleys and riverbanks for hours. Wary and cautious of every step I took, in case the evil beast was lurking in ambush to take advantage of any careless move I might make. Eventually as time went on, I came to the conclusion that we wouldn't meet again today. With a deep sigh of resignation I started to walk back home. I had hardly began my journey, when there standing on a small hillock beside my path was the Ram surrounded by a few equally raggedy Sheep. I could feel my adrenaline surge as I crouched into a fighting stance and advanced bravely but warily towards my mortal enemy. It eyed my approach with its expressionless, yellow eyes. Step by step I crept closer, judging the best time to charge and strike. Then the Ram, who suddenly seemed to tire of my presence, turned and trotted off, followed by his scruffy harem. I broke into a charge but the Ram and its ugly retinue simply increased their speed and left me in their wake. I circled around the hills to cut them off and to their surprise emerged on their right flank. I took immediate advantage of the closeness of my position and hurled my Assegai at the Ram with all my strength. It missed by inches and try as I may I never got the same chance again. I realized also that the Assegai, which had been invented by Shaka the great Zulu Napoleon, was not designed for throwing. It was strictly a stabbing spear and was used in the same way an Ancient Roman Legionary used his Gladius. Over the next few weeks I stalked my old enemy but couldn't get close enough to avenge the assault it had perpetrated a few years earlier. Each time I failed, my resolve for vengeance grew stronger. The Ram seemed to be toying with me, I needed to make a plan. I searched the hills until I'd find what I was looking for. A gully with sides so steep that even an agile mountain Goat couldn't scale it. Preferably a box canyon that I could chase my enemy into and it could only escape by coming through me. I found a gully with shear sides but it had an exit as well as an entrance, but immediately I found an answer to that problem. I made my way to the Sports ground to the building where the sports equipment was stored. I 'borrowed' both the soccer goal nets, which I transported one at a time up into the hills to my chosen gully. First I found a suitable site near the exit of the gully where the sides were narrow enough to be spanned by one of the nets. I secured it with pegs and rocks so that it completely blocked any escape. Then I retraced my steps until I found a similar site close to the other end. I arranged my remaining net flat against the ground so that it could easily be used to block the entrance in the same fashion as the exit, after I had driven my quarry into the trap. My trap was complete, now all I had to do was spring it. As you may imagine that was much easier said than done. For weeks I patrolled the hills. More often than not I wouldn't even find my intended prey. When I did, it was usually too far away from where I wanted it to be. Other times it tormented me by going right when I wanted it to go left and left if I wanted it to go right. I soon learned that if I moved very, very slowly I could control the direction in which I wanted it to go. This was more effective than the mad, frantic rush straight at it that had turned my earlier stalking into a total disaster. I always made a B line for my trap for some reason when ever I'd start a new search. Hoping optimistically that the Ram might have just obliged me by wandering into it of its own accord. Believe it or not one day – or should I say? 'One Glorious day', this line of reasoning paid off. As I had done dozens of times before I was pacing my gully from the entrance to the blocked exit. Dreaming the same dream of my eventual Battle with my bitter enemy. Fighting to the death for hour after violent hour the Bloody turmoil would surge and ebb. From exit to entrance, from side to side the Battle would rage. The giant Ram would charge with an almighty crash against my shield and send me reeling, but I would stand fast and then charge myself. Ha! The Ram wouldn't expect that and I'd stab and – "Baaah-Baah-Baaaaaah!" No, it wasn't Stevie Nicks singing. It was the Sheepish chorus of the giant raggedy Ram's harem. In their midst cropping and chewing at the sparse grass was the raggedy Ram himself. 'Great,' I thought, gazing in disgust through the football net, 'trust the stupid idiot to be outside the exit, instead of the entrance. With trembling hands and thumping heart I began to move the rocks and stakes from the net and lay it flat. I raced back down the gully and put the other net in place. I hoped it was secure enough to do its job. Once satisfied with my efforts, I raced like a Cheetah around the hills in order to come up on the Ram from the best angle to aim it into my trap. I soon arrived in position with lungs burning, head spinning and adrenaline pumping like mad. It took a superhuman effort to stop, calm down and slowly survey the situation. I didn't want to blow my advantage by making any sudden moves, which might send the Ram galloping off in the wrong direction. I crept forward stealthily, as the Ram still chewing grass, balefully eyed me. I felt as though I was getting dangerously close as the huge Ram, seemingly unconcerned by my presence stood its ground, I cursed myself for not bringing some kind of weapon with me. Suddenly three of the sheep that had been grazing close by trotted away from me straight towards the gully. As I watched their progress the Ram turned and trotted after them and all four went straight into the gully. With a feeling of elated unreality I raced after them and immediately began to put the net back in place. I had rehearsed this scenario so many times in my mind's eye. I paused as I remembered that three Sheep were also in my trap and they were never part of my plan. DAMN IT! Now what? I didn't want those bloody sheep in the gully. This was between the Ram and me, but if I drive the Sheep out I also risk losing the Ram with them. That didn't bare thinking about. 'I've got the Ram,' I thought, 'I've actually got it, but I don't want the Sheep. With a deep sigh of resignation I chose the largest of the stakes I had used to secure the net and trudged down the gully with a heavy heart. Naturally, as I had expected when I reached them they were all the wrong way around, the Ram being closer to me and the Sheep beyond and less accessible. Waving the stake like a sword, ducking and diving, I finally managed to maneuver the Ram and Sheep into the positions necessary to drive the three Sheep back out the way they came in. That left the Ram behind where I wanted it. By the time the three Sheep had rejoined the rest of their flock I was back securing the net. When finished I sat half dazed and contemplated my next move. I was well aware of the formidable weapons my opponent possessed from a personal and very painful past experience. Now was the time to choose mine. All the way home I played a variety of scenarios over in my mind. Would I be a Red Indian Brave in hand to hand combat with a massive Bear or a Puma? What about Theseus fighting the nightmarish Minotaur in the Labyrinth? Or I could be a Zulu Warrior and the Ram could be an African Water Buffalo, after all I did have my Zulu Assegai. By the time I arrived home I had decided. I was going to be an Ancient Roman Gladiator, the gully would be the Arena. Yes that's it. The Majestic Coliseum. Now to choose the appropriate weapons. I chose a large shield that I had made out of a wooden coffee table top, on which I'd painted a white and gold Eagle as my crest. For my Gladiator Sword I chose my Indian Push-Dagger. The Push-Dagger has a very thick straight blade about nine inches long. It differs from other Daggers in the design of the handle which is parallel to the base of the blade. It is joined to the hilt by two gold inlaid iron spars on either side of your fist. When you hold the handle, the blade becomes an extension of your fist and you strike by punching instead of stabbing. Much to my relief the Ram was still secure when I got back. By the time I had climbed down into the gully everything felt right. I was at one end of the Arena my ferocious nemesis was at the other end. I gave myself just long enough to let the immortal words of Uncle Fred run through my mind, 'Never give up and I'll never lose.' I was now set to do Battle. I strode bravely forward, the huge Coliseum was packed to capacity, the cruel Roman crowd screamed for blood as I saluted and chanted,

"Hail Caesar, those who are about to die salute thee!" The crowd in my head roared, I looked at the sky where I had pointed my Dagger and mentally saluted Mithras, god of Warriors. "Adrian-Adrian-Adrian!" I was obviously named after Hadrian the famous Roman general, who had built the wall that spanned the North of England, to keep the wild blue-painted Barbarian Picts and Scots out of the South and up in Scotland where they belonged. On to glory I marched. As I rounded the bend and caught sight of my mortal enemy I hummed the old Wartime song, 'We'll meet again' and here you are, you bastard. I stopped and crouched behind my wooden war shield about five paces from the Ram and waited for its charge. The evil, yellow eyes stared unblinkingly, we both stood frozen in time. I braced myself for the crashing impact that would smash into my shield any second. Would I have the strength to withstand its brutal charge, how long could I endure the repeated battering? The Ram lowered its huge, horned head menacingly, 'Here it comes.' I thought, but instead the Ram began nibbling away at the grass before returning its baleful, yellow gaze back in my direction, chewing away and seeming totally unaware that World War three was about to break out.

"Fuckin' do something! I screamed at it, losing my patience. It stared and chewed.

That was it! I yelled my War cry and charged, shield first straight at the Ram's huge head hoping to trigger a response. Bang! – Ouch! I got my response. The Ram's powerful butt immediately reminded of me of the last time I'd tangled with it. Even through my heavy shield the impact sent shock waves all the way down to my heels. I felt pain in every joint and my stomach felt as though it had exploded. I expected a continual battering but I had to induce its attack once more. It seemed reluctant to charge without being provoked. This time instead of holding the shield so tight against my body and absorbing the whole force and weight of the Ram. I let the impact take the shield to my left and I slashed down with the edge of the Push-Dagger and caught the Ram on the head between its horns. As we paused and eyed each other again I could see a pink bloodless gash on the Ram's head. I didn't try to provoke another charge from the Ram, instead I charged myself. I hit the Ram with the shield in the face as before. Then turned into the right and punched with my Dagger at the Rams left side. My guts churned with horror. My right hand felt red-hot as my whole fist and even my wrist followed the Push-Dagger right inside the Ram's huge, grey, shaggy body. I withdrew my dripping Dagger and my blood soaked arm from the huge gaping wound, with a lightning fast reflex of shock. It was as though I had placed my hand into a fiery furnace, or touched a live electric cable. That was it, the Battle was over. The huge, shaggy, grey Ram lay dead at my feet as easily as that. It died without making a sound. I couldn't believe what had just happened. I didn't know how I felt. I was still buzzing with adrenalin with no way to expend it. I felt almost as deflated as the Raggedy Ram now looked. I'm not really sure what I'd expected, an epic Battle, a momentous struggle? If I'd been asked before if I intended killing the Ram to satisfy my lust for revenge, I think I would have said yes. But now this sudden feeling of finality left me feeling bewildered and lost. I'd contemplated the Battle itself but not the conclusion. It had been too easy to kill. I hadn't really looked beyond the actual Battle and now I had a dead body, which I hadn't previously taken into account. In spite of the situation's dream like quality, I appreciated what a horribly vicious and efficient weapon a Push-Dagger is. Almost in a trance, I wandered off towards the nearby reservoir to wash the blood off my hand, arm and Dagger. On the way, I tried to figure out my options. It didn't take me long to decide. Having cleaned myself up, I trotted off home filling in the details to my latest idea as I went. As I had hoped I met some of the gang. I told them to go to their homes and nick as much butter as they could, without their Mums noticing the loss. I went myself to knock on the door of Dai Hughes and invite him to join us. None of us liked Dai very much, as, - well how can I put this politely? – He was a fucking idiot. Nevertheless he was the only person I knew who had the stomach for the task I had in mind. I called into my own house and picked up a half a pound of butter, my Arabian Dirk, a box of matches and a large empty biscuit tin. Then our little party began our trek back into the hills. On our journey I recounted the whole story, - well more than the whole story to be accurate. By the time I had finished, the mighty Battle had, in the telling surpassed all my own original expectations. Unlike my giant Bear story, this time I had a carcass to prove it. Dai Hughes earned his dinner as I thought he might. He slashed away with my Arabian Dirk happily while he skinned and butchered our meal. As no one wanted to watch his gruesome progress, the rest of us busied ourselves gathering arms full of wood and started a fire. As Dai hurried back and forth with huge chunks of Ram meat. I soon had the butter sizzling in the biscuit tin in which to cook it. Later I sat there contented, as I chewed happily on one half cooked and very tough leg of Ram; I thought all that's missing now is our kitchen table to sit under.

****

I had never seen so many people in our house before, about half of them I'd met before, the other half I hadn't. They were all relatives from far and near. The reason for the gathering of our clan was that my Great-Grandfather, Grancher Gould lay on his deathbed and relatives from everywhere had come to pay their last respects. They left our house and returned in small groups, after spending their allotted time with Grancher Gould. They asked and answered questions concerning his condition in whispers, as though we were all in a strange Cathedral. It was a terribly depressing experience and there were long faces everywhere I looked. Sighing and sobbing that made a lump rise in my throat. I needed air to breath, as I felt stifled. I went outside and walked around the garden, startled that the birds were still singing on such a solemn occasion. They circled in the sky above me before starting their migration to warmer climes. I don't know how long I stood in the garden. I had let my mind wander and was looking with eyes half closed, squeezing them and purposely blurring the colors of the last of flowers, that hadn't yet succumbed to winter's advance. One of our second, or third Auntie-in-Laws returned from Grancher and came sobbing down the steps. She was supported on each side by two other strange family members. I watched them pass and then gave them time to re-enter the house before I slowly followed. When I entered the somber atmosphere had intensified, dozens of pairs of eyes seemed to regard me, as Dad said to me,

"Adrian, I have got some awful news, your Grancher Gould is dead." The solemn expression on Dad's face turned to horror, then embarrassment as a smile cracked my face and God help me I laughed until my sides hurt. If looks could kill I would have been twice as dead as Grancher Gould. I appreciated the fact Dad didn't seem to like me very much, but the look of hatred on his face would have turned Medusa to stone. I only laughed more. I was sure everyone in the room was looking at me with a mixture of bafflement and disgust and all I could do is laugh. I just couldn't help myself. I was as fond of Grancher Gould as anyone in that room. I didn't find anything funny in news of his demise but my nerves were ragged. I'd had no experience in how to express such sorrow. Only those who have had the misfortune to have reacted as I did, in such unhappy circumstances, can appreciate how terrible I felt. Tears are running down my cheeks as I write these words now, but unfortunately they are over a half a century too late. Grancher Gould was buried on November the 5th which is Guy Fawkes' Day. Naughty little boys who had been chased repeatedly out of his fruit garden by Grancher in the past let fireworks off behind his gravestone that night.

****

"Would you go to the Grammar School if you pass the exam?" asked Mam.

"No." I answered, "I don't like school."

"He's too dull to pass anyway!" Dad chipped in, "The pit is the best place for him." I didn't rise to the bait, I was sick of hearing him yapping on about the pit.

"Well if you don't want to go to the Grammar School, you'll have to go to the Secondary Modern," Mam said, "would you prefer that?"

"No," I replied, "I don't want to go to school, any school, I'm not interested."

"He hasn't got the brains to go to the Grammar School anyway!" Dad interrupted

"Oh yeah!" I answered him, "I suppose I've got enough brains to work down the pit, seeing you and Terence work down there!" Smack! His hand bounced off my head,

"Leave him alone Em,'" Mam said, "No wonder he's got no brains when you keep hitting him on the head."

"Yes, that's right; you're always picking up his sleeves!" Dad grumbled, "He'll end up like your Brother Jimmy!"

"That's good!" I replied, "Uncle Jimmy doesn't work down the pit!"

Each year, students above the age of eleven from a number of schools in the area took the eleven-plus exam in the hope of being admitted to the Grammar School. My totally uneducated guess is, that up to 200 students would try the exam each year, - and what I know for a fact is that only the top 60 are admitted. When they attend, they are then split into two more manageable sized classes. 30 students per class and in order to keep each class as academically equal as possible, are divided by numbers. Odd numbers in one class, even in the other and are referred to as the O's and the E's, odds and evens. First year students were 1-E, or 1-O, second year students were 2-E, or 2-O and so on. A further division was that an equal number of students from each grade were split into 4 'houses' the Red house, the Blue, the Green and the Yellow. Merits and de-merits were tallied each month for every student and the results would be announced at each of the house's monthly meetings. Fierce inter-house competition was encouraged.

An air of tension gripped our entire classroom. Today we were going to hear the results of the eleven-plus exam we had all taken about a month before. The results were read out in alphabetical order, punctuated by screams of joy by winners and cries of despair by the losers. The winners were allowed to leave the classroom immediately in order to return home and inform their parents of the good news. Many of the losers trembled or sobbed and proclaimed that they dare not go home at all to face their parents. I'm sure that many of these would have done much better in the exam if they hadn't been so terribly anxious in the first place. My name beginning with S was way down the list and I was thinking more of the upcoming summer holidays than worrying about the results of any stupid exams. Then it was announced I had passed to the Grammar School. 'WOW!" I thought, 'Great, I can go home and tell Mam.' I couldn't have cared less about passing the exam. I only liked the idea of leaving school for the day. I still wasn't interested in attending the Grammar School, or any other school for that matter. I could read, write, count, add, subtract, multiply and divide. What else did I need? If ever I needed to know anything in the future that I didn't know now, it, left me with two options, I would either ask someone who did know, or look it up in an appropriate book.

"Adrian has passed his exam to the Grammar School." Mam announced to Dad as he arrived home from work. He glared at me as though I had just been caught shoplifting.

"What did he come, last?" He asked.

"No, I came twelfth, out of over a thousand!" I lied haughtily.

"If he goes, you'll have to buy him a new school uniform." Dad warned Mam, ignoring both me and my vastly exaggerated claim. I didn't like the idea of school, or having to wear a uniform. I think what may have decided me to attend the Grammar School was Dad's obvious lack of enthusiasm and his disbelief in my ability to have passed in the first place. I hated wearing a cap and continually got into trouble for refusing to do so, we also had to buy a school satchel in which to carry our pens, pencils, school books and homework.

The Grammar School was very close to where I lived and it only took a few minutes to walk there. The school yard at the back of the school was bordered by a wooded area. There was just two fences that separated from it from our back garden. I was horrified the first day I attended and we were also assigned to our respective 'Houses,' I was assigned to 'The Yellow House,' can you imagine that? The bloody Yellow house. Yellow would have been the last color I would have chosen. If I'd been given the choice it would have been the 'Red House.' Red was my favorite color and who knows, I might have even taken a bit more interest. I had come twelfth in the exam so I was in the E's and as I sat at my desk, that first day in class the last thing on my mind was grades. I scrutinized each of the other pupils in turn, 'I'd give her one.' I told myself if the girl in question was attractive, 'not her, or her.' 'I can beat him, for sure.' I'd tell myself. I looked at the first boy then each of them in turn assessing their fighting potential. Maybe a few question marks in my class I decided. I hadn't checked out the O's yet, but time would tell. A few fights later, I was, without a doubt the undisputed 'King of the E's.' I was soon to find out there was a very formidable question mark in the O's named Jenkins. Jenkins was an ugly bastard, tall, with very large hands and feet. He had carrot colored hair on a really odd shaped head. A nasty freckled face and horrible red eyes that were constantly watering. Jenkins was a very notorious and pugnacious bully. He soon had all the other kids running scared and to be honest, even I gave him wide berth initially. But, just like my fear of heights he played on my mind until I found I couldn't live with myself until I'd settled it. I knew it would be an easy matter to provoke Jenkins. He was wild and aggressive and would lash out violently at anyone who even looked at him the wrong way. He had never threatened me personally so far, in fact I don't even remember talking to him. I still thought it was only a matter of time before he got around to me and now I'd made up my mind, I became impatient. Hardly a day went by without Jenkins bullying or harassing someone. I decided to jump the queue and bring the matter to a head. I went looking for him during lunch break and when I found him the location couldn't have suited me better. At the back corner of the school gym was a small triangular area hidden from the rest of the playgrounds by the school buildings. As I came around the corner, there was Jenkins repeatedly slamming some kid against the back wall of the gym. I stood and leaned back against the corner of the wall with my hands in my pockets and just looked stonily at Jenkins. He paused, still holding the other boy by a fist full of shirt and glared at me with his red watering eyes.

"What do you think you're looking at?!" He growled.

"Something that's escaped from a Zoo, by the look of you." I answered. He immediately let loose the other boy and strode towards me threateningly. I slid my hands out of my pockets stood my ground and that was enough to stop him in his tracks.

"I'd be very careful if I were you!" He snarled.

"WOW - A talking Chimp!" I replied, in feigned amazement.

He growled with impatience and attempted to walk past me, but I stepped sideways and blocked the narrow space between the building and a ditch.

"Get out of my way!" He demanded, "If you know what's good for you!"

I still hadn't raised my hands from my sides and as he barged forward to push his way past I kicked him viciously in the shins.

"Hit him back Jenkins!" The voice came from a very, unexpected source The boy who had just been on the receiving end of Jenkins' bullying probably had his money on Jenkins. He must have thought that this show of support may have been an opportunity to ingratiate himself with his tormentor. In the meantime Jenkins was doing a little war-dance while he nursed his bruised shin.

"Go on Jenkins, hit him back!" came the other boys voice once more. Heeding his advisor, Jenkins drew back his large fist to strike. So I punched him in the nose, then I turned into a windmill. My initial assault backed Jenkins into the corner, he was a punch bag, I was a human threshing machine. My opponent was a great bully but when put to the test, turned out to be a very poor fighter. Badly injured Jenkins had to be taken home, as I, escorted by two Prefects walked proudly to the Headmasters office .I was gratified that by now the whole school knew why I was to be punished. That walk to the Headmasters office soon became an all too familiar journey.

We were expected to remain after school a few times a week for Choir practice - I don't do after school. On days when we were required to attend Choir practice I would go to the toilets at the back of the school. I'd sneak from the toilets through the wooded area, over the fence and across the field over another fence into my own back garden. It was left to the Prefects in charge to ensure that we attended Choir practice. They would collect the reluctant singers as though they were Bounty hunters and we were criminals. It wasn't long before an informant grassed my escape route to the Prefects and on one occasion I was almost caught in an ambush. I ran instead out of the front gate but was spotted by one Prefect who chased me all the way home. I was always a fast runner and although he was much older than myself he was unable to catch me. But, he was very persistent. I knew I wouldn't be able to reach my garden gate, open it and get inside before he caught up to me. I tried, but as I reached the gate and made a grab for it, he made a grab for me. I spun around and threw a punch that caught him flush on the jaw and knocked him completely out. I was thrilled as that was the first time in my life that I had ever knocked someone unconscious with one punch.

There was only two things I liked about school it introduced me to stamp collecting that was pretty cool. Oh! and how could I forget Sandra? Sandra Ford had to have been the prettiest girl in my class, so it's obvious that I fell in love. She was a little taller than me; she had dark eyes and shoulder length, jet black hair. I remember one day our Welsh language Teacher asked if any of us would like to join a Welsh Folk Dancing class. She and some of her Welsh Nationalist associates were organizing it. Very few hands were raised and those who did I scrutinized with unfeigned disgust, until I saw Sandra raise her hand and mine went up like a shot. The classes were held twice a week, in the home of some old Welsh poet, or Bard, or Druid. Whatever he was, he was extremely eccentric. He had a long flowing mane of pure white hair and a nose to match. He wore nothing but black to emphasize his whiter than white hair. I had seen him walking around Brynmawr and he never looked at, or talked to anyone. He seemed to love windy days when the breeze would blow his long hair, nose and long black cloak out horizontally as he strode swiftly about his business. If it wasn't windy he usually wore a large black cavalier style hat. His house looked quaintly Welsh from outside, inside it looked like a library with books everywhere. the whole house smelled of old books, sweaty socks and cat's piss. We were taught some steps and we hopped about like electric Goblins, while he fiddled with his violin and tossed his snowy white mane in time to the music. Sandra looked stunning, as she hopped and swirled, her short gymslip flying around her and exposing much more of her shapely bare legs than I ever saw in school. I even got to touch her soft warm hand, as we'd dance, swapping partners continually. Unfortunately Sandra was as aware of me, as I was of anyone else in the house, but I was smitten. I even resorted to stalking her after school and even then she seemed totally unaware of my existence. As a result of my schoolboy obsession I soon learned where she lived. I found a secret vantage spot from where I could remain hidden and spy on her while she sat reading in her garden. The bubble burst and somehow the magic faded, one day as I was watching her alone in her garden. Unaware that she was being watched she suddenly pulled up her skirt pulled down her draws and took a piss on the Daffodils.

House meetings were held on the first Monday of every month, the 'Yellow House,' held their's in the Science room. I hated them, first all the merits would be read out, who'd won them, who got the most. Then everyone would cheer and congratulate the scholars concerned. Then they'd read out who'd received the de-merits, who got them. Who got the most and everyone would boo, jeer and despise the villains concerned. I must admit I had very few rivals who threatened to dethrone me in that department.

"Once again, thanks to Street, the Yellow house has come in last out of the four houses," announced Brian Berks, the Prefect, "we would have come second, if we weren't blessed with mister Adrian Street!" He suddenly hesitated, his eyes narrowed and his big sloppy mouth pouted,

"Street,-Street? He mused, "Did you have a relative named Street attend this school a few years ago?"

"Yes!" I replied proudly and happy to change the subject, "Terence Street, - my Brother." His eyes disappeared, only to be replaced with two sharp, ugly daggers.

SAVED BY THE BELL

Paul James was a strange boy, he had dark red hair and his eyes matched the color of his hair exactly. He was extremely good looking, far too good looking I thought for a boy. He was friendly had a good sense of humor. Fun to be around when we were alone and I could have liked him. But, he had a knack of saying the wrong thing whenever he had an audience that it was impossible to ignore. We would have to fight and I would beat the crap out of him. He didn't seem to bare a grudge and we soon became friends again, until once again he'd say something dumb and get another thrashing. I didn't enjoy fighting him as I always beat him without too much trouble and he was no challenge. But, never mind how often I beat him up, he would never back down. He obviously wasn't afraid to keep trying. In the end I made a joke out of his lack of diplomacy. From then on, whenever he overstepped the mark, I'd laugh and rough him up in a less brutal manner. This actually became a good exercise for me, as I had bought a book on Judo and Paul was perfect to practice it on. I mastered a few throws which impressed Paul so much he begged me to teach them to him. We always drew a large audience of students who would enjoy watching and would cheer our efforts. So far I hadn't thought of our combat as wrestling. I had seen films of Commandos training in hand to hand combat and thought that any form of martial combat other than boxing was, were called Commando Tricks. I knew what wrestling was, but just like Boxing it had never crossed my mind that a person could make a living from it. I had never heard of professional wrestling matches. I thought that a wrestler would either belong to a Turkish Sultan, a Persian Shah, or else perform in a Circus, in the manner of a Circus Strongman. I saw the movie 'Mighty Joe Young' and knew that the ten giants in the line-up, who contested Mighty Joe in the famous tug-of-war were wrestlers. I was immensely impressed by their size and the Herculean feats of strength they performed. They bent steel bars as though they were licorice sticks and snapped iron chains and horseshoes like cotton, but I never wondered what they did to pay for the groceries. Strangely enough, it was a wrestling hold applied by me, which led to the only time I ever came close, to coming unstuck at the hands of Paul. We had been sparing around for a few minutes, with Paul as usual, coming up short. Suddenly he made a grab for my left leg and placed himself neatly into a side headlock. I squeezed his head hard but he lifted my leg and twisted around and into me threatening my balance. I was aware of a low wall behind me, so instead of fighting to maintain my balance, I purposely laid back on the wall. I still secured the headlock on Paul and for the amusement of the onlookers, made a show of casually making myself comfortable. That was a bad mistake. In so doing I had lost the contact of the ground with my feet and had no anchor, which is needed, to really apply my strength. All in a second, I had conceded full control to Paul. I struggled with all my might, which now felt puny. Just to get back off the wall seemed impossible. Even though I still held Paul's head securely in a headlock, there was no power left in it. Paul was able to bare all his weight down on me and control my movements as though I were a Baby. It was only the school bell that sounded to beckon all the students back to their classrooms that rescued me from a major embarrassment. I was secretly livid at myself for making such a stupid mistake. It wasn't until much later that I came to appreciate what a great lesson I had learned, or should I say lessons. Number one, after thinking it through again and again I came to the conclusion, that if I was ever going to make that mistake, I had found the best time to make it. What if I had made that same mistake when I was fighting someone more formidable during a real conflict, rather than merely rough practice with a friend? Number two; - if your tactics always work for you, you never learn anything new, why would you need to? If you don't learn, you'll never improve, - again, why would you need to? I am certain that many of you have found yourself suffering in some disadvantageous position during a fight. Then later after analysis, admonishing yourself with 'when he did that, why didn't I do this?' or, 'when I was in that position why didn't I do that?' I eventually came to the conclusion that I hadn't missed any chances at all. Because if you had fights as often as I did, you are eventually going to find yourself in those positions again. Next time you're going to know how to deal with it.

Paul and I were practicing in the school yard one day. I was allowing him to throw me, using maneuvers I had taught him, with one throw after another in quick succession. A crowd of boys stood around cheering our efforts enthusiastically. As I stood up from a stomach throw, I staggered theatrically for the amusement of the onlookers. The Prefect, Brian Berks stepped out from amongst them and grunted,

"Have you seen this one?!" As he stomped on my foot and shoved me hard in the chest with both his hands. I hit the deck but my foot stayed where it was, there was an excruciating pain in my ankle which I thought was broken. I had to hop back to class when lunch break was over and I could feel my ankle swelling as I sat at my desk. I suppose I must have looked more distracted than usual and the teacher asked me what was wrong. My answer, that I had broken my ankle, caused a hilarious commotion from most of the pupils who hadn't been present when I'd been injured. The teacher like them thought, that I was, as usual offering a ludicrous reply at her expense. She ordered me to go and report myself to the Headmaster for insolence. It was only when I began to hop to the door in obvious pain that she realized that I wasn't acting the fool, which for me was not normal. I was sent home and Dr Chopra, our family Doctor came and examined my injury. He said it wasn't broken but very badly sprained and said it would be best to keep me home from school, as I shouldn't put any weight on it for a while. I was delighted and I hopped merrily, until over a week later the Doctor came to see how I had healed. He was appalled to see me still hopping about.

"Nora why is he still hopping?" Dr C asked Mam, "He should be walking by now. He needs to put some weight on it, otherwise it won't heal properly." Not wanting to go to school, I milked the ankle for all it was worth but my subterfuge came at a price. Even now after all these years, I still sometimes get the old pain, if I happen to find myself in a very cold and damp climate.

Even before the 'ankle' incident Prefect Brian Berks had cleared up the 'Daggers from the eyes' Mystery. - According to him, he used to beat my Brother up on a regular basis. I found out that it was the other way around, hence his interest in me.

The boys in our class were having a free period one day, while the girls were engaged with a P.T. lesson. We were in the assembly hall with three Prefects in charge of us. Unfortunately for me, one of them was Berks the Berk. I had my sketch pad on the table in front of me and was happily drawing away. A free period was the only time I could indulge in one of my favorite pastimes, as Art, was not taught at this shit-hole they called a school.

"Street!" Barked Berks, "Up here!" Berks and the other two Prefects were lounging about, seated in chairs on the stage on which the Teachers perched during morning assembly. After climbing the steps to the stage as ordered, Berks made me stand to the side of him while he held one of my wrists. "You can stand here for the whole of free period," he told me, "that way you'll be sure of getting into no more trouble and bringing down 'The Yellow House' with more de-merits. – I used to beat the shit out of this little Monkey's Brother when he was in school." He informed the other two Prefects. Smirking Berks leaned his chair onto its two back legs as he casually crossed his feet on the top of the table that separated him from the other Prefects.

"No you didn't!" I snarled, "Nobody can beat my Brother, he used to beat you up, he told me!" Even though I had been on the receiving end of Ter's beatings more often than anyone else, I was still proud of my Brother's fighting prowess. One of the easiest ways to raise my ire was to besmirch Ter's violent reputation. Berks rocked himself back and forth, obviously getting agitated at my verbal retaliation. I noticed that the back legs of his chair were dangerously near the edge of the stage. He squeezed my wrist has hard as he was able and his face registered a look of disappointment after seeing no resulting sign of distress on mine. He continued,

"He was nothing but a little coward. I had him crying like a baby ever-AAAHH!" I kicked one of the back legs of his chair right off the stage and launched the first Ape into space. Berks went crashing down off the stage and landed on the back of his head on the hard floor of the assembly hall. The resulting commotion diverted the attention from me so I slipped unchallenged back to my seat and carried on with my drawing.

Every student in the school gathered each day in the hallway, outside the assembly hall. The reason for the gathering was milk break. Each student would take a glass bottle that contained one third of a pint of milk from one of the dozens of metal crates that would be stacked just inside the door. The door led from the front entrance down to the level of the front yard via a flight of stone steps. I would always run to the milk supply as fast as I could every day. I would try to drink at least two or three bottles in the time reserved for our break. We were only entitled to one each, but try telling that to a greedy, growing boy. There would always be Prefects in attendance, so you can guess what happens next, YES! Berks, I was just reaching for my first bottle when I was grabbed by the scruff of the neck and thrown back against the wall. This, I was sure wasn't in retaliation for the 'Kamikaze stage dive' he'd performed, as he didn't seem to be aware that I was the one who'd caused it.

"Let's just wait here until everyone else has had a chance with the milk shall we!" Berks barked, and that was it, what came over me I don't know. Berks was twice my size and at least five years my senior, but I felt my boot crash into his shins. Then in one movement used the rebounding boot to launch me away from the wall with a mighty push to his chest. I followed it with powerful blows to his face with my fists pumping like pistons. He was hurled backwards and sat arse first in a big metal trashcan that had been placed beside the milk crates. As I continued to rain punches onto his unprotected face, it became even more unprotected. He slid further into the trash can hampering the movement of his arms and legs and I continued to punish him with all my might.

"STOP THAT AT ONCE!" Came a shout from outside and here comes 'Rolly' Jones the gym Teacher galloping up the steps from the front yard. I just had time to give the trashcan a mighty kick that sent it crashing past 'Rolly' and down the steps into the yard bellow with the screaming Berks still inside it. I've often wondered since, if the Berk may have had the feeling of Déjà vu as he and the can hit the hard yard below. I missed the final impact as rampant 'Rolly' Jones had whisked me up and was shaking me like a Go-Go Dancer would shake her arse. I was marched on that all familiar trip to visit the Headmaster, but got off surprisingly lightly. I can only imagine that the age and size difference between Berks the jerk and I, plus my claim of self defense, worked in my favor for once. I'm certain that 'Rolly' Jones would liked to have seen me more severely punished. I'd never really got on with him from the start. He must have sensed the natural aggression in me and thought that it would prove very useful on the Rugby field. I must have been a disappointment to him, because I never was and I never will be a team player. In my lifetime, I have rarely found one person I could really rely on, let alone a whole team of them. I have always been too much of a Prima-Donna to want to share my victory and subsequent glory with anyone. I did find Rugby good practice for fighting and was prone to tackle other players, whether they had the ball or not. Or whether they were on the opposing team or my own. It was for this very reason that 'Rockin'-Rolly' demonstrating supreme wisdom had suspended me from playing half way through my first season. At the beginning of my second season, Rolly gave me the big lecture on team spirit and getting another chance to show what I was made of. Then finding that I'd grown out of my Rugby boots that had been Terence's hand me downs. Mam refused to waste money on a new pair and that finished my less than illustrious Rugby career for good. The only team games I may have enjoyed, were Base-ball and Basket-ball which were called Rounders and Net-ball in Britain. They were only played by Girls, not that the games themselves would have interested me. But - I have always been a sucker for athletic Girls in action, if you'll pardon the pun.

****

Dad bought our first Television set. It was a thirteen inch, black and white set and he had bought it just in time for our family to watch Queen Elizabeth $2^{nd's}$ Coronation. June 2nd 1953. The day of the Coronation our house was packed Every available seat, chair or sofa was occupied by an adult. All us kids sat on the floor. Everyone in the room glued to the TV. We were not the only family captivated that day. Every household in Britain, with an H shaped aerial fastened to the chimney on their roofs must have been invaded by their TV-less families and friends. Out of an adult population of 36,500,000 at that time the Coronation was viewed by 20,400,000. Approximately fifty-six percent. Sylvia Peters did the commentary and introduced the procession which was every bit as Regal and spectacular as befits Britain's Royalty. The Golden Coach, and the flashy uniforms of Soldiers representing every corner of the British Empire.

In its infancy British television was a sad affair. The single channel was only on for a few hours a day, but whatever was on we'd watch it. Even the test card. Dad must have been its biggest fan. On the rare occasions that a movie was shown, it would be the town's main topic,

"There's a film on the tele' tonight!" we'd hear,

"What's it called?" would come, the question. Actually it didn't really matter what the film was, because everyone who had access to a TV would be watching it. If a movie was on TV, Dad would be riveted to it. I could never understand why it was such a terrible sin to go to a movie theatre to watch a film, but ok to watch the same film on TV. On Sunday Dad wouldn't watch TV. Nor would anyone else, TV was banned on the Sabbath, as in our house Sunday was set aside to be miserable. Whether at home or in Sunday school.

Mr. Birchmore was our new Headmaster. I'm not kidding, that was his name and it couldn't have been more appropriate. Birchmore by name birch more by nature. He must have worn out more canes than any other Teacher in Britain going as far back as something out of a Charles Dickens novel. He was tall, big boned, dark haired and a total brute. My first encounter with him, he told me right away that he had been warned about me, in particular, by the previous Headmaster. I didn't doubt his word. During my last encounter with the previous Headmaster he had informed me that it was only due to the fact that he was retiring that he didn't expel me. He added that he would give his replacement that dubious pleasure. I can't pretend that I didn't deserve expulsion. I fitted into the Grammar School like a hand in a boot, a clowns boot at that. I was constantly late. Wouldn't do my homework. Wouldn't attend choir practice. Constantly played truant. Was very disruptive in the classroom and most of all, I was always fighting. Apart from that I was a model student. Miss Jenkins was our French and Latin Teacher. I could never make the old Bat out. One minute she was screaming at me and calling me a filthy little Taureg and the next she was trying to bribe my good behavior with foreign stamps. Of which she seemed to acquire in a vast abundance. I asked her one time if she'd got a set of stamps she gave me off a 'French Letter' - a British slang term for a Male contraceptive. I think it may have gone over her head, if some of the more astute pupils in the class hadn't began screaming with laughter. Another time, I had only just settled in my desk right after our milk break. I had managed to down three or four bottles in record time. Miss Jenkins was in the process of calling the class to order, when I exploded with a great classroom shaking burp!

"Street, stop that at once!" She screamed at the top of her voice.

"Ok, Miss!" I answered bravely, "Which way did it go?!" The whole class laughed so hard. In fact, I was still giggling myself until I felt the excruciating sting of the first of the six stripes I received from Birchmore. Just for my attempt at trying to spread a little happiness in those otherwise grey, dreary halls.

Mr. Price, our Biology Teacher looked like Benny Hill on steroids, but the comedy ended there. He would pace stealthily behind you as you sat on your stool bent over your work. We could never understand how he knew exactly who was responsible for any slight disruption that may have occurred behind his back as he wrote on the blackboard. It may have been the trembling with fear, or the sweating with terrified anticipation, that gave you away. But, when you felt him stop behind you, you'd know you'd been nabbed and he'd punish you by grabbing your ear and twisting it spitefully.

"Call me 'Buzz' when we're not in school." Mr.Price invited us, about twenty School boys including me had joined the troupe of Scouts under Scoutmaster Buzz Price. We could call him Brian instead if we wanted, but he preferred Buzz, so Buzz it was. He was great, like a great big roly-poly overgrown schoolboy. He was interesting and good fun, nothing like the cruel ogre who ruled the Biology room with an iron tweak of the ear. We were divided into two groups the Buzzards and the Badgers. I was in the Badgers as it was me who had chosen our name. I got my Scout badge for learning how to tie knots with great difficulty. Tracking couldn't have been easier as it had snowed the night before our test. So, instead of searching for subtle little signs and clues set by the Buzzards, we simply followed their footprints in the snow. Buzz introduced us to what he called 'Blanket stew.' It was everything edible you could find brought to the boil in an enormous saucepan. It was then taken off the fire, wrapped in a thick blanket and allowed to finish cooking in its own heat. We would all go off trekking or tracking. Then when we returned hours later we'd find a steaming stew piping hot and ready to eat.

Buzz also introduced us to the subterranean world of potholing or caving. Our Scout hut was located in Llangattock, just a mile or so from the first of the caves known as Eglwys Faen [Stone Church] and a little further on, the big one Agen Allwedd which we called Aggy-Aggy. I loved caving and spent hours at a time, crawling on my belly through tunnels hardly big enough to squeeze through. Then suddenly emerge into a cavern that looked as though it could easily contain Buckingham Palace. I collected Bats from the caves and took them home for pets. Llangattock is absolutely beautiful, the views of cliffs above the pathway that leads to the caves. The tiny river hundreds of feet below, surrounded by a Bird infested, Silver Birch dominant forest. It would take my breath away every time I saw it. It was definitely one of my favorite places in Wales.

****

"Hello, would either of you like a fuck?" I inquired politely.

With a look of shock, both girls, who had been playing happily in the field, until we came along, turned and scuttled away as fast as dignity would allow. Often when I asked the same question it might be much faster than dignity would allow. I was always guaranteed the same response from the girls and more importantly from my gang. They loved to witness the reaction that my naughty inquiry would provoke. Since I had become such a 'smooth talker,' I had been regarded by the other boys as Casanova, Don Juan and Errol Flynn, all rolled into one.

"Oh Ade, you're terrible!" They'd giggle, their eyes brimming with admiration. "Let's go over the Park and see if there are any girls over there." So, off we'd go and if there were

I'd repeat my performance. As the girls blushed or ran, my little group would slap my back and do a little dance of glee. It was a great gimmick; I was regarded as a super-stud. It confirmed, or at least added considerable credibility, to the fanaticized tales of my insatiable, sexual prowess. It didn't seem to occur to any of my gullible gang that none of them had actually ever seen me score. Hey, but they believed my ruse and I even began to believe it myself. A perfect opportunity presented itself one evening, when playing around a lamppost we were approached by Hillary.

"Hello Hillary, you look lovely tonight!" I recited, "Would you like a fuck?"

"Yes please!" She replied, "If it's with you!" I froze, - we all froze, you could have heard a pin drop, but the only thing that did drop was the silent descent of our jaws.

"Ha-Ha-a!" I laughed, unconvincingly, "Did you hear that boys? That was a good one, Ha-Ha, she said yes!" - 'Please let her be joking,' I prayed.

"Where shall we do it?" She asked sweetly, as she slipped her arm around mine.

"I don't know anywhere!" I stammered, feeling an electric shock run right through my arm and down to my heels.

"Yes you do!" contradicted one of my 'friends,' who had recovered from the shock, "What about the place where you always take them, - the barn in the field!"

The barn had set the scene, for most of my imaginary encounters.

"What barn?!" I croaked, "Oh-er-a that barn!" I added as I saw a gleam of disappointed enlightenment begin to form in his eyes.

"C'mon!" Said Hillary, tugging me along, "I know, which barn, I've been there before." I was petrified; my heart began beating like a war-drum.

"Yahoo!" Cheered my gang, as I disappeared into the darkness with Hillary. While they cheered, I felt as though I was walking to the Guillotine. As we approached the barn the whole building seemed to creak eerily in the evening breeze,

"Listen!" I said to Hillary, hoping to frighten her, "There's someone in there!"

"No there isn't!" She contradicted impatiently, "It always

sounds like that!"

"No it doesn't!" I argued, "Oh I forgot!" I blurted, as a little inspiration sprung out of my befuddled brain. "I forgot, Mam wanted me for something!" I was gone like a Bat out of Hell. I was ashamed to leave my house for a month after that episode. Even the drudgery of weeding the garden under the savage scrutiny of the Super Slave-master seemed preferable to facing my disillusioned gang. They must have heard the tale of my cowardice, in the face of Fanny, from a disappointed Hillary. Then to top it off, another episode arose, that shattered my delicate sensibilities to smithereens. I often wondered if my sudden metamorphosis from a scruffy little dirt-bag, who would only wash his filthy neck, under the threat of death, provoked any suspicion when I began to spend more and more time bathing. From filthy to spotless, I couldn't get enough bath-time. One day I was engaged in my new favorite pastime, completely absorbed and completely erect. I heard a giggle coming from the open bathroom window. I looked up and saw Ann and Shirley looking through the window grinning like two Hyenas. I screamed,

"Go away, get lost-aaAHH!!!" I plunged down and tried to drown myself in ten inches of water the startled girls ran off giggling like the little Hyenas they were. I grabbed a towel; fell out of the bath slithered over to the window and slammed it shut. I thought I must be having an awful dream, this didn't happen, it couldn't, it was just too unthinkable. Now I became a recluse. There was no way I could ever show my face outside again, but as with anything else, time gradually healed the pain and I began to forget. I wandered about the garden one day and heard the laughing and shouts of the kids playing in the field. I was soon racing over the grass to join them after leaping over our garden fence. I was happy to see all the girls and none of the boys at play. As I drew closer I was horrified as I recognized Shirley. She was talking excitedly and holding the forefingers, on both her hands an exaggerated twelve inches apart. Then Ann began miming a rhythmic pumping action with her left hand as the other girls watched her actions in wide eyed appreciation. I was halted in my tracks as though I had ran into a solid glass wall, as the girls screamed,,

"Hey Adrian, come and show us what you were doing in the

bath!" My face burst into flame and I ran like a Bat out of Hell.

The Sunlight was almost blinding as it sparkled brilliantly through the constantly dripping water that fell from the ceiling of the cave. It exploded into a million tiny pinprick jewels as it struck the rocks that surrounded me on the cave floor. Steam rose in delicate waves from the weak heat of the early morning Sun as it shone into the entrance of my dank sanctuary. I had been watching a pair of pink breasted Chaffinches. The female dull, while the male gaudy in the throes of the new breeding season flaunted itself shamelessly. They were hard at work building their nest on a ledge just inside the entrance of the cave. There, even in my young life I had seen generations of Chaffinches build before. Soon they will be laying their eggs, four, sometimes five, tiny bluish eggs, decorated with purple-brown speckles or splashes. Then, when hatched, open bottomless beaks and ugly blind eyes would fill the little nest, but day by day the ugly hatchlings would grow more beautiful. We had an agreement, if I kept quiet and made no sudden moves, they in turn would entertain me for hours with their chip-chip-chipping song. They flew back and forth with the wiggling living protein that would nourish their ravenous chicks and reward me with the pleasure of their company. Company that I could only enjoy for a few weeks this time every year. In the absence of my Chaffinches I would just sit and think. This was much better than being in school, where I was supposed to be. Or too close to Dad and his constant chores, grizzeling, grumbling and 'just wait until you leave school, you're going down the pit.' Later in the day, weather permitting, I would leave my dark hideout and walk for hours. Into the mountains, along the river, or Bluebell Wood, enjoying the prolific fauna and flora. That's how I found 'Saladin' my Jackdaw. He became so tame, that I could trust it to come back to me and land onto my outstretched hand, after being allowed to fly to the top of a house, or even a tree. That came to an unfortunate end, when a Girlfriend I had at the time, wanted to have Saladin sit on her hand, even though she was frightened to death of it. The girl's name was Marilyn Timmins. She was a couple of years older than me and about half a foot taller and we had been petting heavily for three weeks. For that reason it would have been hard to deny her request to carry my Jackdaw. Marilyn held her hand as far away from the rest of her as she could stretch it. Her head, likewise in the opposite direction. Her eyes were wide and blinking furiously as I attempted to transfer Saladin off my hand and onto hers. Marilyn began to panic. Saladin flapped his great black wings to aid his balance as he stepped cautiously onto Marilyn's hand. That was enough for her to begin screaming and make a grab with her other hand and grasp Saladin around both his legs. Now it was Saladin's turn to panic as both his legs were being crushed together. Wings beat the air furiously; Marilyn screamed and ran around in circles waving my Jackdaw violently like a flag. Feathers flew all around her, she was too terrified to release her grip on poor Saladin. It wasn't until Marilyn had taken off running down the road that she released the Jackdaw's legs. He rose up into the dingy grey sky and flew out of my life forever. Marilyn was also out of my life forever. I don't think I ever spoke to her again.

After leaving my cave another morning, where I'd been busy playing truant, as usual. I wandered through the mountains in the direction of the town's reservoir. I was following a zigzag stream that emptied into the reservoir and amusing myself by leaping from one side of the stream to the other every few steps as I drew closer to my goal. I looked down and saw a Seagull sitting on a ledge above the stream. I was surprised that it didn't fly away at the sight of me. I crouched on the bank above the ledge and slowly reached down to it The Seagull snapped viciously at my hand as I attempted to touch it but didn't try to escape from the ledge. I wondered if it was hurt or sick. It was only recently that I had seen increasing numbers of Seagulls arriving and flying around the reservoir, or scavenging on rubbish dumps. Before that, I had only ever seen Seagulls at the seaside. Try as I did, I couldn't get hold of the Seagull without risking a nasty bite from its powerful, sharp beak. I pulled a shoe lace out of one of my shoes and tied a loose loop in the middle of it. With one end of my lace in each hand I lay on the bank and attempted to swing the loop over the Seagulls beak in order to tie it closed. After a dozen attempts my plan worked. I tightened the loop grabbed the Seagull and struggled to my feet. Unfortunately the loop slid down to the base of its beak and lost its power of restraint. The Seagull gave me a savage bite under my armpit as I folded my arm around it and prevented it from biting again. Blood from the bite soaked my shirt and stained the Seagull's back as I made my way home, with 'Sinbad' my homicidal pet Seagull. I never carried a watch and never knew the time, but I had judged my arrival just right. I reached home as all the kids were coming home from school. I walked triumphantly down the road like 'The Pied Piper of Hamlin' at the head of a crowd of kids all trying to get a closer look at my new friend. But, standing outside our garden gate, ready as usual to spoil my parade and glowering like a constipated Gargoyle, was dear old Dad.

"What have you got there?!" He growled, nastily. 'Shit! Even he could recognize a bloody Seagull when he saw one,' I thought.

"Sinbad the Seagull!" I announced proudly, as I introduced my fair feathered friend, to my furious, flustered Father.

"Put it down this minute!" Dad ordered. 'Are you out of your mind?' I thought, 'after what I've been through to catch it.'

"No!" I replied, "It's a pet." If I put it down one of the other kids would claim it.

"Don't you tell me no!" He roared, "Put it down at once!" He had made a grab for me, but let go quickly as the Seagull made a bite for him. Then he got hold of the left sleeve of my school blazer and pulled my school cap out of my blazer pocket and started whacking me on the head with the hard peak as though it was a club.

"Let that Seagull go!" He demanded, sounding like Moses addressing Pharaoh.

"I will not, leave me alone!" I replied, sounding like me. My head was stinging as though it was covered with Bees as Dad battered my head repeatedly with my cap. I retaliated by thrusting the snapping Seagull at him. Soon we must have resembled a re-enactment of Robin Hood, sword fencing with the Sheriff of Nottingham. Dad slashed at me with my cap and I countered, as I thrust and jabbed with my Seagull. Back and forth we fought and Dad began to give ground as I hacked at him skillfully with my Seagull. Just when it looked like the Seagull and I would win the day, I saw Dad loosen his belt. I knew right then, that even if my Seagull and I attempted to double-team him we would still be no match against the dreaded belt-buckle. So, I threw the Seagull in Dad's face as I tried to dodge past him. Fate seemed to be against me and he caught a handful of the shoulder area of my blazer. That, combined with the impetus of my charge swung me behind him. I immediately took advantage of my unexpected position. I grabbed the back of Dad's thick leather belt, in order to prevent him sliding it through the loops in his trousers. We both began spinning around in circles, Sinbad snapped at our legs to avoid being trampled to death. Dad attempted to turn around and grab me and I clung on to the back of his belt like grim death. Dad slowed to a halt as he began to lose his wind, his grip and his trousers. Again I took advantage by shooting off like a rocket for our garden gate, with Dad close on my heels. I hadn't stayed around long enough to see if Dad was still wearing trousers, or if he'd got his belt clear. My worst fears were soon confirmed. I felt the wind from it whistling past the back of my neck. My brain was working overtime as I tried to plan my escape on the run. My first hope was that Mam was home, provided I could open the door to the house, before he caught me. If I did get in and Mam wasn't home, would I have time to run through the house, out of the back door where I was sure to be able to outrun him? Halleluiah, praise the Lord, I burst into the house with such a sudden explosion, that Mam who was sitting at the kitchen table threw the cup of tea she had been drinking over her shoulder. It soaked the wall behind her. If I'd got behind her any faster I would have been wearing the tea.

"What's going on now?!" Demanded Mam, as Dad, looking wild and totally demented, burst in after me.

"Dad made me throw my Seagull away!" I accused, over her shoulder.

"The little blighter threw it in my face!" Dad countered.

"Now leave him alone, Emrys!" Mam told him, as though throwing Seagulls at Dad was an everyday occurrence.

"That's right! Wailed my Father, "Pick his sleeves up, he'll turn out just like your Brother Jimmy! And Blah- Blah, wait till I get him down the pit, Blah-Blah-Blah" – Well you know the rest.

For me, school, as always, was mind numbingly boring, although with the chronic increase with the amount of truant I was playing I was experiencing less and less of it. I had sang with the school choir in two consecutive Eisteddfods in spite of my aversion to choir practice. I was also capable of acquiring decent marks in English, History, Geography, Mathematics and Biology. If I 'applied' myself, but in the words of the Headmaster Mr. Birchmore, when he told me that I was to be expelled,

"You lack interest and you refuse to apply yourself. You're always fighting, will not submit to authority and you are the most disruptive creature in the classroom that I have ever had the misfortune of experiencing."

'WOW!' I thought, 'And with such little effort.' What had really brought the 'expulsion' situation to a head, was, my refusal, to submit to him caning me anymore. When Birchmore laid one on you, the cane left a welt on your arse as thick as a pencil and as black as ink. Once more I had been found guilty of fighting and sentenced. "Bend!" Birchmore ordered after reciting the charges.

"No." I replied, "I'm not doing that anymore." his expression changed to one of bewilderment, he looked as though a Blacksmith had dropped an anvil on his balls.

"WHAT, - WHAT DID YOU SAY?!" He roared.

"I said, I'm not bending and you're not caning me like that anymore." I replied.

"Are you mad, have you completely lost your mind?!" He inquired. I just shrugged my shoulders, Birchmore looked baffled. "Do you think I should just allow you to get up to your constant, disobedient antics without punishing you?!" He demanded.

"If you want to cane me, you can cane my hands," I answered, "I'm not going to bend down again."

"Why not, are you injured in that area, or is Mr. Adrian Street so special that he has to be treated differently than anyone else?!" He argued.

"I'm not injured in that area and I don't intend to be, I don't care about anyone else, I only know I'm not bending down." I said.

"I'll phone your Parents and see what they think about this!" He threatened.

"We don't have a phone." I answered.

"That's beside the point!" He roared, "I'll send for your Parents!"

"If my Mother ever saw the marks that you've made on my

arse with your bloody cane, she'd smash your face in with her fist!" I shouted, "Bring her down if you want to but I think you'll be sorrier than I will!"

"GET OUT, YOU LITTLE LOUT! He screamed. "GET OUT OF MY SIGHT THIS MINUTE!" As I made my way towards the office door he took an almighty slash at me with his cane. It caught me partly on the backside but not before it sliced across a world globe which took the main force of the blow as it sent it spinning around like a top. I slammed the door behind me and marched home. Next time I was sent to Birchmore for punishment he acted as though nothing undue had transpired between us on our last meeting. After he finished reciting my list of transgressions he said,

"Hold your hand out Street!" I complied and he slashed at them as hard and as viciously as he was able."Was that any better for you Street?" He inquired, sarcastically.

"Yes, thank you, Sir." I replied with a forced smile as I left his office.

****

That summer, the family and I spent our holidays in London again, with Uncle Fred. I was warned on the day we arrived by all the kids I met to watch out for Bobby Selden. He had vowed to avenge the beating I had given him a couple of years earlier. They told me that after our fight Bobby had immediately joined a Boxing club. He had earned himself a reputation as a very tough and able Amateur Boxer. I could well believe it, as I remembered him as a very tough kid when I'd fought with him before. Even Uncle Fred told me to keep out of his way. As days turned into a week and there was no sign of Bobby Selsden, it became obvious to me he was keeping out of my way. I began accusing him of being scared and boasting what would happen to him if he ever had the guts to show his yellow face. I even went around singing, 'I ain't got no Bobby!' but to no avail, everything was quiet on the western front. Well there was always plenty to do in London, so I didn't pine away. There was Guy the Gorilla to get re-acquainted with in Regents Park Zoo and the most fantastic Antique Market open every Saturday in Portobello Road. We only had a couple days of our Holiday left, when I heard that Bobby Selsden was looking for me. I hurried through the house and out into the street, so as not to keep him waiting. Apparently Bobby hadn't gone into hiding but had just returned from a vacation himself. He had just learned I was back in town and by the look on his face had been told by the other kids what I had been saying about him. We went straight at it. I caught one stunning blow from Bobby right between the eyes and Bobby went sailing through the air from a very neat little hip toss. I kept my hold on him, so we both hit the road with Bobby underneath. I was on top of him controlling him handily in a side headlock. He must have been shaken but struggled furiously to free himself, but he wasn't going anywhere. He began punching me in the side of my ribs. It wasn't doing much damage as he wasn't in a position where he could get any force behind it. I wasn't really doing him much damage either, but he was as mad as hell. As a result he was struggling with all his might. That was what I wanted him to do. It couldn't have been a very exciting fight from the spectator's point of view, but I was happy, playing the waiting game. Bobby was fighting hard and using energy trying to break free. I was almost relaxed and only using sufficient strength to keep him where I wanted him. On the ground where he couldn't fight his fight. When I felt the time was right and he was sufficiently tired I'd let him up and see if he could still outbox me. If he could, we'd go back on the ground again as hard as I could put him there and I'd punish him some more. I would patiently repeat this as many times as necessary till I had exhausted him. When he could no longer defend himself. I would punch his lights out and finally beat him with his own game, - Boxing, and so far everything was going to plan.

That's when my Brother came out to see what all the commotion was about.

"What are you doing down there?" He asked me, "Get up and fight properly!"

"I'm doing ok." I told him.

"No, you're not!" He insisted, "He's punching you in the ribs, get up!"

"I'm doing ok!" I repeated, "I'll get up when I'm ready!" I didn't want to lay there while squeezing Bobby's head and explain my strategy to my Ter. There was a fair possibility it wouldn't work with Bobby listening in. I was really wishing Ter would piss off and leave me alone. Instead of going away, he grabbed me and forced me to stand up and relinquish the hold on my prey.

"RIGHT, now fight properly!" He ordered, and I thought, 'funny, I didn't know they celebrated the 4th of July in Britain?' Bobby hit me so hard, that I saw a fireworks display, that I've seldom seen surpassed and blood ran from both barrels of my nose. 'You bastard.' I thought, but as I lunged for him I got smacked on the hooter again. I puffed the blood running from my nose and mouth out in a scarlet spray. Then set myself to the task of turning this affair around. Bobby bobbed and weaved around me like a blue-arsed fly while I flailed air, he punched my head off. Bobby came in for the kill but I got a hold on his head again. I tried to run it into the steel railings that surmounted a garden wall. But, Ter was there again to advise me how to fight. He broke us up, so we could square off again. Bang! I caught a left on the jaw and a right in the mouth that split both my top and bottom lips. I stopped to spit some more blood and caught two more in the mouth in quick succession. 'Defend yourself at all times you bloody idiot!' I reminded myself. Well this went on, me missing. Bobby scoring. Until Ter, decided prematurely that I'd had enough. He dragged me back indoors leaving Bobby the undisputed winner and me as mad as hell. I don't give up and I knew that Bobby Selsden's fists couldn't have taken much more punishment, after the tremendous force with which they had been hitting my face.

****

First impressions are very important and what a great impression I must have made when I started attending my new school, Brynmawr Secondary Modern. Even though I have always been a fast healer my face still resembled a rotten pumpkin and my swollen lips looked as though they belonged to Donald Duck. I was standing with two other boys who had also been expelled from the Grammar School. We were separated from the other students. I felt all that was missing were the shackles and leg irons which would prevent us, 'the tried and condemned,' from escaping. Sentenced to transportation to Botany Bay for the next twenty years. Our introduction to the rest of the School by Mr. Jones, the Headmaster seemed to be the main event, of the morning assembly,

"Ah yes, and before the assembly is dismissed to your separate classes. I want to stress, to these three new pupils in particular," he said, indicating us with a nod and a glare. His nose wrinkled as though someone had dropped a stink bomb, "that this, is not a school that will tolerate any nonsense, or misbehavior of any kind, - is that clear?!" .

"Yes, Sir." We all mumbled.

"What's your name?" Mr. Jones asked the first boy, "Come on boy, speak up!"

"Clive Phillips, Sir." He replied.

"I don't think you like me very much, do you Phillips?!" He demanded.

"Oh yes I do Sir!" Corrected Phillips, hastily.

Mr. Jones let a little smile of satisfaction raise the edges of his mouth.

"What's your name?! He asked the next boy.

"Eric Barnes, Sir!" Chanted Eric.

"I don't think you like me very much either, do you Barnes?!"

"Yes, I do sir!" Eric assured him. Another little smirk from Mr. Jones.

"What about you, what's your name?!" He demanded, glaring at me.

"Adrian Street, Sir!" I answered.

"I'm sure you don't like me do you Street?!" He snapped.

"No, I don't, Sir!" I spit, grateful for the opportunity of clearing the air. Much to my surprise Mr. Jones burst out laughing.

"Oh and why is that Street?" He managed to squeeze out between chuckles.

"You caned my Uncle Jimmy!" I exploded. His eyes narrowed and his mouth pouted, but I doubt that he realized what I was talking about after so many years.

"Hmmm! I'm sure I'll be caning you too, Street! He said still trying to suppress his mirth. 'Yeah Right!' I thought, 'We'll see about that!' Yes, my new Headmaster was the same Mr. Jones, who had caned Uncle Jimmy. The same Mr. Jones, who got a bloody good pasting from Gran as a result.

****

I don't remember if I was aware of Bodybuilding, or even weightlifting, in those days. I knew what barbells and dumbbells were, but associated them more with Circus Strongmen. I had seen the Charles Atlas ads in magazines and newspapers, but even at that age, I didn't believe a person could turn himself from a weakling into a Superman, 'in just seven days.' What really brought my attention to it was Ter, went to 'The Sophia Gardens Pavilion' in Cardiff to watch a Physique Contest which featured Mr. Universe, Reg Park as special guest poser. He also demonstrated various Bodybuilding exercises. I had never seen Ter more enthused about anything and he told me everything he had seen. Reg Park had absolutely blown my Brother's mind.

"When Reg Park picked up a barbell and began demonstrating his 'bent forward rowing' technique," Ter explained, "he was nothing but a huge mass of muscle, and when he did his posing routine ---!" Here his power of description failed him, but he had a program and a couple of Bodybuilding magazines that he gave me and I was hooked. I almost wore out every photograph with the power of sheer scrutiny. I read every word till I could have recited the stories off by heart. I knew nothing about Bodybuilding but from that time I began to make up exercises hoping they would work. They did, in two months my chest measurement increased from thirty-four to thirty-six inches. Dad's chest measured a muscular forty-three inches and I made it my goal, to someday equal, if not surpass him in that department.

Ter had been complaining about working down the pit for over a year, he hated it. He'd had enough and wanted to leave and go into the Army as many of his friends had done already. Some of our Family members, had tried to persuade him to stay in school and not to go down the coal mine four years before. Now the same Family members were trying to persuade him to stay in the pit and forget about the Army. As it had been in wartime, anyone working underground, was immune from being called up for National Service. Ter wanted to leave the pit and make himself eligible. Dad, Dado and Uncle Alf, had all served their time in the armed service and warned Ter that it was a horrible life. In the end Ter had his way and left the pit. He got himself a job as an apprentice Bricklayer and seemed much happier in that line of work. He soon forgot his desire for the Army. One day I came home from school and was told by Mam that his call up papers had been delivered. I knew where Ter was working and I couldn't wait to tell him the good news so I raced there and told him. His face went absolutely white and completely horror stricken and I wondered what was wrong with him. I knew, or in this case thought I knew how much he wanted to go into the Army. Mam wasn't happy either, nobody normal wants their Son in the Armed Forces. The day he left he shook hands with Dad, even shook hands with me, Kissed Pam and Mam goodbye. He walked out of the door and up the steps to our garden gate, then come running back crying, hugged Mam and said he didn't want to go. So we all cried, but he had to go anyway and that was that. I had lost a Brother for a couple of years, but now I had gained a bedroom to myself. Then we moved house into a newly built estate called Bryn-Awel. Bryn-Awel was the highest point in Brynmawr. Bryn-Awel means Breezy hill, Brynmawr means Big Hill, so we were moving to a breezy hill on top of a big hill which was about a mile above sea level. No wonder I have a strong heart and lungs. Our new garden was a shapeless mountain of hard clay, embedded with huge, heavy rocks. Dad was in his glory, as a merciless slave driver, he had learned from the best when he was a prisoner of war and he obviously didn't want his training to go to waste. Under Dad's watchful eye, I shoveled clay and dug out rocks, which I used to build a restraining wall. As the new kids, in the new houses, explored their new environment it drove me mad with jealousy as they played, screamed and laughed in the fields above our garden.

Although I was no longer attending the Grammar School I was still a member of the Boy Scouts. That came to an end one rainy weekend, when we were camping under canvas which wasn't even slightly waterproof. We were sitting miserably trying to dry ourselves after being dripped on all night around a fire that we were trying to keep alight, with whatever wet wood we were able to gather. We had ran out of food the day before and after a sleepless night, some of the boys had gone home and had scrounged enough grub to serve us all a reasonable Breakfast. Now we were all starving again and it was my turn to go home and forage. By the time I got home in the pouring rain, I was like a drowned Rat. I explained the situation to Mam but she absolutely refused to give me any food to take back to the camp. I didn't have a single penny of my own to buy any, as there weren't any floors to polish in our new house. The money from the market had slowed to a trickle and it wasn't worth the effort anymore. Mam was mad, because she thought I didn't want to work the market anymore as she was taking ten shillings off the top. The thing was, there wasn't much chance of earning as much as ten shillings, in the market anymore to come off the top. The fact that I was with the Scouts this weekend and not even trying to get work in the market, for Mam was the final straw. So that was it. I explained to her that I had eaten other people's food, that they had shared with me yesterday and again this morning, but she had made her mind up, no food! So rather than face the other Scouts with no food, I never went back, it was just too embarrassing. I really looked forward to growing up and getting the hell out of here.

****

I applied for and secured a job as a paperboy, at Cable's News-agents, I was to work seven days a week. Dad turned a blind eye to the fact that that included the Sabbath, as long as I completed my paper-round, in plenty of time for Sunday-School. I had to be at the News-agents by between 6am and 6-30am every morning, to finish my delivery before School time. I was paid ten shillings a week, which I had to split equally with Mam. I began to work about fifteen to eighteen hours a week, so I could give Mam five shillings and keep five shillings for my pocket money. I had the longest, hardest route that Cable's had to offer. The winter time was especially hard, struggling through drifts of snow, which was sometimes deeper than I was tall. It's no wonder that I was soon playing truant from school again as 'truant time' was sometimes the only time I had to myself. Otherwise it was paper-round till school, or Sunday school, then when school was over, work in the garden and bring in the coal for Dad. Do my homework, - yeah, right! Then go to bed. Damn! Even working down the pit couldn't be that bad. I wanted to earn more money, which would also give me a legitimate excuse to keep away from Dad and his bloody garden. When the Fair came to town, I shot down to the fairground to see if the boss, Mr. Deakin would give me some work. When I arrived I was told that Mr. Deakin wasn't there at the moment but should be back soon. The Fair wasn't open yet and was still in the process of being erected by the fairground hands. I was hoping that they wouldn't complete their work too quickly, as that would give me a better chance of getting a job. There were a few of my friends hanging about watching the progress, including my Cousin Maldwyn. I walked over and joined them while I waited. We were chatting away, when we were interrupted by a group of boys. The leader was shouting at the top of his voice to his companions. He had the coarsest, crudest accent I had ever heard. I turned and looked with disgust at the author. "Don't look at him!" One of my friends warned me, "That's 'Hairy the Gypo!" - "C'mon, quick, let's get outta here!" Said another one. I had heard of Hairy the Gypo, of how tough and violent he was supposed to be, but I had never ever seen him before. I checked him out, I was anything but impressed. Anyone who saw the movie 'Snatch' starring Brad Pitt will know what a 'Pikey' is, Brad Pitt's rendition of the Pikey accent and attitude, was nothing less than incredible. Hairy was a Pikey, but in Wales we called them Gypos. The tales I had heard of the infamous Hairy's legendary fighting ability, conjured a picture in my minds-eye of a huge, hairy, hulking brute, with muscles bulging everywhere. Here glaring at me with hate and disbelief, that there was anyone alive, who would be reckless enough to make eye contact with him. He was the sorriest, scrawniest, puniest most pathetic looking little runt I had ever seen. He was probably about seventeen or eighteen years old but looked more like twelve. For someone who spent most of his life out of doors he was extremely pale. I was barely fourteen at the time and although not very tall, I towered over Hairy. He looked to me more like an emaciated, emasculated Jockey than a Fighter. But if there's anyone who appreciates the saying 'never judge a book by its cover,' it's yours truly. It's just as well because that little bastard was a human dynamo. Lucky for me I had already learned, that you don't try to punch a Boxer. If you do, you're going to get hurt, unless you're a superior Boxer, which I wasn't. But, a Boxer can't hurt you unless he punches you and can't punch you without touching you. If he comes close enough to touch you, you can touch him too. With the result, Hairy was soon in what must have been for him, very unfamiliar territory. On the ground, tightly secured in a headlock and unable to do what he did best, - punch. Fortunately Ter wasn't present to sabotage my strategy but the Fairground seemed to be alive with his disciples. They seemed to believe that fights were something to do with some twat named the Marquis of Queensbury, who had probably never had a fight in his life. To me, a 'fight,' unlike a sporting contest, is fought under the 'Law of the jungle rules.' If you're getting your head punched off, why not use a kick, a thumb in the eye, a bite, a chokehold or any other kind of hold to turn the tide in your favor? As a result of this way of thinking, I have often been called 'a bad looser' but loosing, is something I was determined, not to become good at. I've always replied to my critics, 'I'd rather be a bad winner, than a good looser.' If someone picks a FIGHT that's what they should get. Not a Boxing match, or a Wrestling match, but a FIGHT! Why should a person who is good at fighting be hampered with discrepancies over the way the fight should be fought? So if someone has a grievance against me and wants to hurt me. Should I submit to engaging in some form of combat, where I get the shit punched out of me. Just because my enemy wants me to forgo what works for me, in favor of what works for him? Well thanks - but no thanks! As far as I'm concerned, you do what you wanna do, - I'll do what I wanna do, – and we'll see what happens. now I've got that off my chest, I'll get back to the story.

The Fairground laborers had stopped work to watch the fight. As it wasn't exciting enough for them, with both combatants struggling on the ground. I was forced by them to let Hairy up. Then we would start again. This happened more times than I care to remember. Hairy would throw a few punches then I'd throw him down again as soon as our fight recommenced. While this was going on Mr. Deakin returned to the Fair, he ordered his workers back to work and all us kids off his Fairground. I had been waiting to see him, but thought this might not be the best time to ask him for a job. Instead we all walked off the Fairgrounds and around the corner to a big truck parking area and resumed our conflict from the beginning. Soon Truck drivers were getting out of their trucks and out of the nearby trucker's greasy spoon café, to watch our violent antics. It wasn't long before the Truck-drivers took over from the fairground laborers in their annoying self appointed duty, of getting us back up off the ground, 'to fight properly.' Both Hairy and I were determined to stick to our own game plans, So far our uneventful battle, according to the unofficial timekeeper Maldwyn it had lasted an hour and fifty minutes. Most of that time had been spent on the ground and neither of us much the worse for wear. Who knows if we'd been left to it, we may have even broken Great-Grandfather Big Jim Arnold's marathon fight record. But that was not to be. A couple of the Truck drivers, thinking it was an adult duty, to break up a kid's fight finally stopped the action. We were both, dragged to our feet, and pried apart, separated and pushed away from each other and advised to go home.

"Ok Mister, I'm goin' home now!" I heard and surprisingly understood Hairy say, that was a split second before Maldwyn shouted a warning,

"Look out Ade!" And splash, - FIREWORK HEAVEN AGAIN! Maldwyn had shouted his warning, as he saw Hairy slip one of the studded leather wrist bands he wore from his wrist and around his fist. As he spun around the Trucker he carried the full impetus of his spin, into one almighty punch. It exploded right into my nose and mouth. It didn't knock me down, which must have been disconcerting for Hairy, but I had never been punched as hard as that in my life before. I don't think a blow from Thor's Hammer could have hurt more, or have been more stunning. A couple of truck drivers grabbed me to stop me from retaliating. That supplied me with an after the fight alibi of 'if they hadn't grabbed hold of me – I would have----! Yeah right! By the time I had been fit to retaliate, Hairy would have died of old age. I had a face that bled over everything and everyone that was anywhere near. I thought my neck had broken and Vesuvius was erupting through my head and both ears simultaneously. It had taken me almost two hours to put a huge dent in Hairy's ultra-violent reputation. It only took that one last punch to restore it. By the time I got home I was soaked from head to foot with more blood than I thought I possessed. I was hoping that there would be no one home and I could set about cleaning myself up, without causing any fuss. Dad as obliging as ever was there. His reaction to the condition I was in, was as surprising as it was distressing,

"What in blazes, has happened to you?!" He demanded, with shock and horror registering on his face.

"I had a fight," I admitted, 'But he was a lot older than me!" I added, hoping that that fact would excuse the state I was in.

"Who did you fight with, - who did this to you?!" He wanted to know.

"I don't know who it was." I lied, "I only know he was about eighteen." I insisted. I kept on emphasizing his age rather than his size. Not willing to admit, that someone closer to my own age, would have been capable of making such a mess of my face.

"It was Hairy the Gypo!" Volunteered Maldwyn, much to my disgust, "He hit him with a leather knuckleduster with metal studs in it!" Dad wasn't aware of whom Hairy the Gypo was, but he aimed to find out.

"C'mon!" He ordered, "I'm taking you to the Police Station!" So off we went. Me looking like something out of the 'Chamber of Horrors.' Escorted by Dad and followed by Maldwyn down to the Police Station, where a Police Constable behind a desk took our statements. I was as vague as I could possibly be. Maldwyn never stopped yapping. The Policeman asked us if we knew where the Gypo lived; I didn't know and thank goodness, neither did Maldwyn,

"Try and get him cleaned up a bit," suggested the Policeman, "we'll send one of our Constables with you and see whether we can spot him anywhere in town. There's a washbasin you can use through there." He added, indicating a passageway. I took as much time as I could. Hoping that everyone would lose interest and we could forget about the whole incident. We were soon walking towards the Town square, with the Blue uniformed

Bobby in tow. As we neared the square we could hear the loud, garish music blasting from the Fairground and crowds of people were moving in that direction. I tried to dawdle as much as possible, as we fell in automatically with them. I was convinced that if we were unlucky enough to find Hairy, the Fairground would definitely be the most likely location. Maldwyn, much to my dismay was marching ahead of us like a Bloodhound. Almost as soon as we entered the Fair, I heard Hairy's horrible voice. I looked away from the direction of the voice and tried to walk away from his vicinity as quickly as possible and lead my party with me, but much to my chagrin Maldwyn's voice rang loud and clear, "There he is!" There he was indeed. As the eyes of the Policeman and Dad focused on Hairy, he seemed to shrink before my eyes to an even more diminutive size than ever. I felt as ashamed and embarrassed that someone so small was capable of making such a mess of me. If the ground had opened up, I wouldn't have fell into it, I would have dived in head first. When the Policeman apprehended Hairy, I was hoping that he would belt the Copper, just for Dad to witness what the little Rat-bag was capable of. He submitted as gentle as a Lamb and as ordered, led all of us to where he lived. It was near a pond close to the base of the Milfraen Mountain. There was a dirty tarpaulin sheet, that had been propped up to make a low tent, maybe about four and a half feet high. Sitting just inside, smoking a pipe was Hairy the Gypo's Mother. She looked like a filthy hot air balloon, which had been deflated to the degree that it resembled a big blob. Her body spread out in all directions and completely hid her feet from view, even though she was sitting down. The only garment she was wearing was a dirty, silky under-slip. It did nothing to hide two massive, spotty, bra-less breasts. They spread out over her Buddha like gut like a pair of giant hot-water bottles. She looked like Jabba the Hutt in drag. She squinted suspiciously through the smoke of her pipe and the fire of sticks, burning at the entrance to her makeshift tent. The Policeman explained to her the reason for our visit.

"You're a naughty Boy, 'airy!" She said, "Tell 'em yuh won' do it agi'n!" The Policeman turned to Dad and asked him if he intended pressing charges, he had to repeat the question, as Dad was staring mesmerized with horror and disbelief at the dirty, fat blob that was Hairy's Mother.

"Er no," Dad answered, as the question at last penetrated, "Not this time."

"Say thank ew 'airy!" Prompted his Mother, through another puff of smoke.

"Thank 'ew," said Hairy to Dad, "I'm sorry I 'it yer boy, Mister."

The fury and shame that went through my whole body, as he said those words were indescribable. I felt as though my brain, throat and heart, dropped into the pit of my guts. 'Oh, we'll meet again, you bastard' I thought. When we got home I had to sit through Dad's monotonous rendition, as he described to Mam all the trouble I'd caused him that day. And yes, I do believe 'Uncle Jimmy' and 'just wait until I get him down the pit' was mentioned once or twice. I was however, grateful that he never once mentioned Hairy the Gypo's physical attributes. I chomped at the bit, when I was ordered, by both Mam and Dad to keep away from the Fair from now on. I couldn't wait to get back down to the Fair and this time I wouldn't be looking for a job. The Fair was there, but Hairy wasn't. 'Never mind,' I thought, 'even better, I know where he lives.' The next morning I arrived at the Gypo campsite before I began my paper-round. Even though it was still dark, I could see that it was deserted. All that remained, was the usual mountain of rubbish they had left behind them and their smell. Gypos don't usually stay in one place for very long, they often go looking for greener pastures of their own accord, before they are moved along by the appropriate authorities, it could be months or even years before they may come your way again.

****

Bodybuilding magazines were my present passion. Answering an advert I found in one of them, I sent off for a 16 week bodybuilding course, by George Greenwood. The course was illustrated and explained various exercises that could be performed with Barbells and Dumbbells. It also included a rubber cable, that could be used instead of weights if you weren't lucky enough to possess any, which I wasn't. I made a homemade

Barbell, out of a five-foot iron railing, with two buckets fastened to each end, which I filled with rocks out of the garden. I put another four inches on my chest, breaking the 40 inch barrier which had been my next target by the time I completed the course. I later joined a Gym in Ebbw Vale that boasted a few mats for gymnastics and a single 150 pound Barbell. The gym was open twice a week and I used to walk the three and a half miles each way, over the mountains just to save myself the bus fare. That was better spent on more bodybuilding magazines. I attempted to interest my best friend Peter Inge in Bodybuilding, but Peter's passion was Professional Wrestling. I would show Peter photos of Steve Reeves and Spencer Churchill. Peter would tell me tales of his favorite Mat Stars like 'Nature Boy' Buddy Rogers and Antinino Rocca. At the time of my preoccupation with bodybuilding, it went in one of my ears and out of the other. I had got over to Ebbw Vale early one day to do a little magazine shopping, before going to the gym for my workout. I spotted a 'Boxing and Wrestling' magazine and thought I'd buy it for Peter but read it myself that night after I got home from the gym. That was it! For the first time since wanting to be a Red Indian, I knew for sure what I wanted to do with my life. That was to become a Professional Wrestler. I was so impressed with the super athletes, the colorful, brash characters of the modern day Gladiators, Don Leo Jonathan, Gene Stanley, 'Nature-Boy' Buddy Rogers and Dr. Jerry Graham. It all fitted together, Mam had asked me many times since I became interested in Bodybuilding, "What are you going to do with all your muscles when you get them?" Now I had the perfect answer, 'Use them to help me become a great Wrestler.' The Boxing and Wrestling magazines were always American. We never saw any magazines on British Wrestling. They were 80 percent Boxing and just two, three, or if you were really lucky, four stories on Wrestling. Even though I wanted more Wrestling, I very much enjoyed reading about Boxing too. The fighters of the present day and the historical legends of the Sport made great reading. Mam always used to complain about my obsession with Red Indians, every time I'd open my mouth to speak, she used to say, "If it's about Indians, I don't want to know!" Now it was "if it's about Wrestling or Bodybuilding, I don't want to know!" Peter was the only person I could really talk to about Wrestling and now I really listened. We could hardly wait until the next edition of Boxing and Wrestling was on the news-stands. We began practicing together, but Peter rarely gave me any competition, I had always been a strong kid, but now I had become very strong, as a result of my Bodybuilding.

Dad complained about my Bodybuilding, especially when I exercised with my Barbell made of rocks he used to say,

"There are plenty of rocks in the garden for you to lift, instead of wasting your time and energy on that nonsense!" I was digging rocks out of the rock hard clay, one day after Dad had dragged me away from my weight-lifting. That in itself didn't please me very much. An hour or so later, I heard the excited squeals and laughter of the girls in mock protest and outrage as they were chased and mildly molested by the boys. They were just out of sight, but tantalizingly in earshot from the fields above our garden. Dad was hard at work, lifting heavy seeds out of a paper packet and popping them one by one into the earth. I dug out rocks, loaded them into a wheel barrow and took them around the house and down to the bottom of the back garden. I tipped them onto the ever growing pile that would be used at a later date for building rockeries. I knew Dad was aware of my agitation and my awareness of the fun the other kids were having in the nearby field. I also knew he was patiently waiting for me to say something about it.

"Dad, I'm going to play up in the field." I told him at last.

"You're not going anywhere!" He told me, "You've plenty of work to do here."

"I'll take another three barrow loads, then I'm going out." I told him, hoping the compromise would satisfy him. Dad didn't answer me, so I carried on. When I had completed my third trip I came back around the front of the house and asked him,

"Dad where do you want me to put the barrow, do you want it here so you can carry on with the rocks, or shall I put it away?" Dad glared at me and replied,

"Put the barrow there and get it filled, I told you, you're not going anywhere!" I was completely immune to his glaring by now and refused to be intimidated.

"Well if you won't tell me where to put it I'll leave it where it is," I replied, I'm going out." As I made a move to walk away from the barrow and up the steps to our garden gate, Dad stepped into my path.

"Get that flaming barrow filled and empty it down the garden!" He growled viciously. I knew he was getting rattled, as the word 'flaming' was like swearing to him.

"And, I said I was going to take another three loads and then I was going out!" I told him, "I've taken three loads, now I'm going out!" Dad undid his thick leather belt and slid it out of the loops on his trousers.

"Get back to work right now!" He ordered, swinging the belt.

"No, I won't!" I defied him, "I said I'm going out, so get out of my way!"

WHOOSH-SMACK! Dad lashed out with the belt with all his strength and it caught me right across my back. The buckle hit my right shoulder blade and for a second almost paralyzed me with the pain.

"Now get back to work right now, unless you want another one!" He screamed, swinging the belt around threateningly. I stood my ground and said to him as calmly and as quietly I could,

"Get out of my way, I'm going out." Dad swung the belt,

"Pick up those rocks, and get that barrow filled now or I'll beat the Hell out of you!" He roared, I bent down and picked up a rock and examined it calmly, before I said,

"If you hit me one more time with that belt I'll smash your bloody face with this rock." Dad's face turned pale and he crouched into a fighting stance, arm up, and belt ready to strike. I adopted my own stance ready to launch my rock.

"You'd better leave him alone, Em,'" Mam's voice came from the window half way up our stairs and facing the garden, "He'll do it!"

Dad brought his belt arm out to his side and tried to make it crack as he snapped it, it failed to crack.

"He'll do what I tell him to do while he's living in my house!" Dad roared.

"Leave him alone Emrys, 'he'll do it!" Mam warned him again as she watched me ready to strike. As Dad straightened up I walked past him keeping the rock handy.

"Yes, that's right, get out and don't bother to come back!" Dad shouted in my face. I turned and hurled the rock in the direction of his feet making him jump back to avoid being injured.

"I'll be back when I feel like coming back and not before." I told him.

"This is my house and you'll ---!" He spluttered at my back as I walked up the steps. I turned to him and interrupted.

"It's our house not yours, I work the same as you do and while we're on the subject, I've just lifted my last rock in this bloody garden." I said indicating the one I'd hurled at his feet, "any more gardening to do, - do it yourself. I'll never work in the garden for you again and the only rocks I'll lift is when I'm Bodybuilding."

"Bodybuilding, HUH! Just you wait till I get you down the pit!" He screamed at my back. I didn't turn or answer him as I slammed the garden gate behind me. And I never did work for him in the garden again.

School as ever was a total waste of time. We had art lessons which I was thrilled to discover, only to be disappointed with the arsehole who taught us. I can't remember his name so I'll refer to him as Mr. Twat. Mr. Twat's idea of art began and ended with everyone in the class drawing a group of fruit, jars, vases or bottles, or an occasional landscape, which I found boring-boring-boring! If it isn't Warriors, Girls, Bodybuilders, Wrestlers or Animals, I'm not interested. One day Mr. Twat declared that we could all draw whatever we wanted to draw. He had probably eaten the usual models he used to arrange for us to copy. I drew a fantasy garden, crammed with Exotic Birds of Paradise, Flowers and Butterflies and then painted it all with watercolors. Even though I say so myself, it was gorgeous, but when Mr. Twat saw it he said,

"I'm not even going to grade that, you've obviously traced it!"

"How could I have traced it?" I asked him, "I've been sitting five feet in front of your desk since I started it and what could I have traced it from anyway?"

"I am an Art teacher!" He lied, "I recognize tracing when I see it!"

"Well, I'll paint another one right now and you can watch me do it from the beginning to the end!" I suggested, "Then you can see for yourself that it wasn't traced!"

"Do you think you're the only pupil in this class Street?" He shouted, "You'll do nothing but still life from now on, you won't find that so easy to trace!"

"Stick your bloody apples up your arse!" I suggested, "Huh, Art teacher, my foot. You're jealous 'cos I can draw better than you!"

"Hold your hand out Street!" Mr. Crewe, our new Headmaster ordered, we will not put up with your insolence in the classroom. I had already had my big argument with Mr. Crewe as to my rules, when it came to me being caned on his second day as Headmaster. "Bend over Street!" He had ordered, "You're going to get six of the best!"

"If you want to cane me, it will be on the hand, I don't bend for anyone." I answered arrogantly. We had the same argument I'd had a year and a half earlier with Birchmore. With the same threats and in the end, with the same result.

Billy Griffiths was our PT teacher. He was always very aloof if you weren't one of his favorites. He was with one of his favorites one day. A prefect about 18 years old who I called Pratt. Billy was coaching him for the upcoming inter-school sports day, when Pratt would be competing in the Shot-put event. Pratt was tall, long limbed, well built, blond and arrogant. In fact he would have made a perfect candidate for the 'Hitler Youth' in both appearance and attitude. The rest of us were standing around watching his progress. Then run pick up the shot and bring it back to Pratt, so that Pratt could throw it again. When I say the rest of us were watching him, - the rest of us excluding me would be more accurate. My attention was riveted to the netball area where the girls in their short shorts were halfway through their practice session. Pratt was obviously enjoying the attention he was receiving. Playing centre stage and lapping up the hero worship and praise he got every time he made a good shot. I was in my own world, Pratt couldn't compete for my attention when there were nubile young girls in action.

"Street, wake up and bring that shot over here!" Billy's shout brought me out of my reverie. I resented my abrupt plunge back into reality, so I picked up the shot and threw it back to where it landed at their feet. I received a double bladed stare from Pratt, while Billy Griffiths' mouth dropped open and for once no sound came out of it. When he recovered from his surprise he called, "Street, come over here and do that again!" So over I went and without any previous training in shot putting, I matched Pratt shot for shot. Pratt was livid that I'd stolen his thunder. So was Billy Griffiths, when I told him forty-five minutes later that I wasn't interested in competing for our school. Especially after he had split his time coaching Pratt with me. Pratt hadn't been aware that I even existed until that incident, now he had an axe to grind that he would have liked to bury in my head. Our conflict was short lived. He'd tried to keep me in after school a couple of times. In the Secondary Modern School Prefects were authorized to order detention, well we all know how that one goes. - I don't do windows and I definitely don't do detention! He confronted me one day, as I arrived in the school yard with,

"Where were you yesterday, did you forget that I told you to stay after school?!"

"No, I didn't forget." I answered him, "But I don't stay after school." I tried to walk by him as I spoke, but he crowded me into a Hawthorne hedge. The hedge divided the schoolyard from a five foot drop to Clydach Street, which ran along one side of the school. I tried to force my way past him but he grabbed the lapels of my jacket and pushed me backwards into the hedge. I felt the sharp thorns scratch and stick into my legs, arse, back and shoulders. I pushed back but was off balance and the fact that he was very much taller than me helped keep me that way. It became a contest of strength with me losing the battle. I tried to push my way out of the thorny hedge but Pratt forced me further into it. It soon became evident that there was no chance of my escape from my painful predicament by trying to get out of the hedge the way I'd got in. I also came to the conclusion that whatever I did now the thorns that were already sticking in me weren't going to get any more painful than they already were. So as soon as my new strategy formed in my mind I pretended to panic and pushed back at Pratt as hard as I could. I took a tight hold of his jacket and as soon as I felt him push back with all his force I placed one of my feet against the thick base of a Hawthorn bush and suddenly reversed my push. With an almighty pull towards me I dragged the Pratt in the direction he had been pushing, face first right through the lethal Hawthorn hedge. The expression on Pratt's face was a treat to behold. The force of my pull had brought me right to the edge of the wall on the street side of the hedge. Before Pratt could recover I took a quick look up and down the road to make sure there weren't any cars coming along. Then I tightened my grip on Pratt's jacket and launched myself backwards into space. Pratt got ripped the rest of the way through the hedge. As I landed lightly on my feet, Pratt came down heavily on his head. I don't think there was much fight left in him but to be on the safe side I spent the next five to ten minutes kicking the shit out of him.

The Secondary Modern Girl's Hockey team had an inter-school match against a school in Crumlin one weekend. It was announced that anyone from our school who wanted to go and support our team would be welcome to accompany them in a chartered bus. I was the only boy in the whole school to board the bus for Crumlin that Saturday morning. Much to the utter amazement of all the girls and teachers who were also going on the trip. Everyone knew how much I disliked school. I've never cared for team sports. So why had I got up extra early in order to finish my paper-round in time to travel all the way to a piss-hole like Crumlin on a freezing cold morning? If you were to see some of our girls, running and leaping about in their little short gymslips with a strong Welsh wind whistling up their Khyber's you wouldn't need to ask. AND the very thought of a whole flock of strange, but similarly clad girls, in the Crumlin girls team was motive enough for me. After arriving at the Crumlin Sports Field it seemed like a frozen eternity of walking up and down the sidelines numbed by the icy wind before the girls got changed and the match commenced. I thought it well worth the effort and discomfort when I beheld the two opposing teams of stalwart Amazons going into action. The hateful wind became my ally as it blew their skirts up as they raced each other after the ball up and down the field. I Positioned myself near one of the goalposts so as to get a full frontal as the girls ran towards me and a full moon when they ran towards the opposite goal. The only thing that threatened to mar my horny day out was the Goosebumps on the bare legs and bums. Suddenly a cannonball like shot from a powerful strike that narrowly missed the goal and smacked me in the balls did a lot of marring. In fact it entirely kicked the horny aspect right out of the ballgame, - pun intended. Some of the girls tried to cover their embarrassed smiles, the rest of them laughed out loud. Only a few, including a couple of the teachers seemed sympathetic. They rushed up to me to inquire if I was ok, or if I needed any assistance. They were the ones who actually embarrassed me the most. I tried to smile disarmingly and appear unconcerned. I tried even harder not to scream and fall down. I suffered further embarrassment as I tried to convince everyone that I was fine with an unconvincing squeak of assurance. My face and ears began to burn in spite of the freezing wind. I retreated from the hockey field, walking like a castrated Duck with the sound of the tittering girls fading behind me. I didn't know and cared even less, who had won or lost the match.

The stick of chalk looked too delicate and out of place in Mr. Jenkins' huge, hairy, paddle like hand. Just as the huge, hairy, paddle like hands looked out of place on Mr. Jenkins, who was otherwise tall and scrawny. The only thing that was distinguishing about his gaunt, grizzly face was the big pebble thick, lenses on his glasses. The chalk screeched as he wrote on the blackboard and I noticed how skinny his hairy forearms were as the cuffs of both his shirt and jacket rode almost down to his elbow. My attention was easily diverted from Jenkins to one of my class favorites. The tall and very pretty Dawn Woods as she began distributing books to each of the students in the row of desks next to mine. Dawn was a quiet girl, but would smile shyly even when I recited my bawdy poem, 'Dawn, Dawn, you give me the horn,' and never took offence when ever I'd cop a feel. She smiled down at me as she passed my desk. I turned just in time to watch her bend over as she placed a book on the next desk in her row and whispered something to the girl sitting in it. Dawn had the longest, prettiest legs and always the opportunist I lifted the back of her skirt with my ruler in order to admire her knickers. It was then that the roof fell in. At least that was what I imagined. Jenkins, unbeknown to me until that second, had spotted what I was up to and smashed me on the head with a pile of books. The force, the pain, the shock, the humiliation and the embarrassment he caused me, with his sudden 'Pearl Harbor' attack, sent me into a fit of rage,

"Don't you ever do that again, you arsehole!" I roared.

"Oh, and who's going to stop me?!" He roared back.

"I will, a' OUCH!" I yelled as the books bounced off my head once again. I shot out of my desk and punched Jenkins, SMACK! In the jaw and all I remember is the shock and horror on his face, as he reeled backwards sat on the desk behind him. He teetered on it for a full second before he and the desk crashed back onto the classroom floor. I didn't check to see whether he was conscious or not, I stepped over him and walked out of the classroom. Which I noticed as I slammed the door was as silent as a grave. I always had the ability to make a grand entrance, but WOW! What an exit! I didn't return to the school for about two weeks, but the day I did, just as I feared,

"The headmaster would like to see you in his office, immediately!" I was told on arrival. 'Shit!' I thought, 'This is going to be good.'

"I assume you know why you were sent for?" Asked Mr. Crewe, the Headmaster.

"Yes, I do." I replied.

"I am not ordering you to do anything." he told me, "In fact, I am not even going to check, to find out, if you do, what I'm going to ask you to do. I would like you to apologize to Mr. Jenkins, for what occurred in his classroom a couple of weeks ago."

"No, I won't apologize!" I stated, "He hit me with a pile of books, I hit him back and - -!" Mr. Crewe held up his hand against my outburst.

"I already have the gist of what happened," he interrupted, "as far as I'm concerned the matter is over and done with. I would prefer you to apologize, but I'll leave it up to you. As I said before, I am not even going to check with Mr. Jenkins."

"Well thank you, Mr. Crewe," I answered, "but even though you're not going to check, I'll tell you anyway, that I would never apologize."

"It's your choice." He replied with a sigh, "Please close the door, on your way out." I couldn't believe that that was it. I considered I'd done a lot less than that on other occasions and been beaten black and blue as a result. I did feel a little guilty, but only because Mr. Crewe had been so unexpectedly nice about it. I was still comfortable with myself that Jenkins got what he deserved and I wasn't about to hand a victory back to him by lying that I was sorry. I was left pretty well to my own devices after that. If I didn't want to go to school, I simply didn't go and a truant officer was never sent to inquire why. I was asked by Mr. Craven, the History teacher if I would repair and complete an Indian ink drawing of a Roman Legionary to hang on the wall in his class. I did it for him. He then asked me if I would draw some more Historical pictures for his class. Next I drew 'Alfred the Great and then a clash of 14th Century Knights in Armor. If that had been what school was all about I wouldn't have minded it so much. Instead of taking my regular lessons with the rest of my class, I would sit on my own in an empty classroom and draw whatever Historical pictures I wanted to draw. That way the rest of my class could get on with their lessons without any disruption from me. I was happy alone, doing what I liked to do. I would go home, or for a walk, or read my Body-Building or Boxing and Wrestling magazines in class while the rest of the students did their regular lessons. I was reading one day in the Math's room when the teacher walked up to where I was sitting. He asked me what I was reading, while the rest of the class was busy with their math's. I showed him the latest issue of 'Man's World.' He studied it for a minute or two then walked back to his desk at the head of the classroom. Then he displayed my magazine to the rest of the class and pointed to the muscular Body-Builder adorning the front cover

"Look at this!' He invited my classmates, "Adrian Street in ten years time!"

"He-he-he!" Everyone chortled obligingly. 'Wrong,' I thought, 'it's not going to take me that long.' As usual I was correct, I appeared on the front cover of 'Man's World' three years later. That proved to me that my math's were more accurate than his. Although I have to admit, that for me two and two equaled wrestling.

About this time we got a visit from a careers officer. After introducing himself he started at one end of the classroom and asked every student his or her name and what they intended doing for a living when they left school. I could hardly wait until it was my turn. Now I was going to get my chance to announce my chosen profession Share my dreams with an interested adult. Have the opportunity to discuss two of my favorite topics, 'Professional Wrestling' and me. I fidgeted with impatience. The other kids seemed to drone on and on about working in the pit, becoming nurses, joining one of the services, when they were a bit older. How utterly boring I thought, feeling sympathy for the careers officer. Who, I realized probably had to listen to this mundane drivel every day of his working life. 'Never mind,' I thought, 'I'll make his job a lot more interesting when I let him know he has a future 'World Champion Wrestler' in his midst. I squared my shoulders and expanded my chest in anticipation, determined to look the part.

"And what's your name?" He asked me eventually, "And what do you intend doing when you leave school?"

"Adrian Street and I'm going to be a professional Wrestler!" I declared. The careers officer's eyes narrowed and his mouth pouted out as though he was about to blow me a kiss. He stared at me for no more than five seconds while I waited in anticipation for his response. He drew in a short breath and said to the next student,

"What's your name and what are you going to do when you leave school?" That was it. I was feeling more than a little miffed as I felt I'd been snubbed and wondered what I could do to get back at him, when he asked Eric Barnes,

"What's your name and what are you going to do when you leave school?"

"Eric Barnes, sir and I'm going to work in the slaughter house." A look of sheer horror came over the face of the careers officer.

"The slaughter house! Why would you want to work in the slaughter house?" He spluttered. - "Because I like animals sir." Answered Eric.

****

I didn't like Mamo's cooking, There was always so much salt. The only way I could tell the difference between salad and stew was that the one was served cold and the other was hot. The only redemption was her desserts that completed the meal which was usually pretty good. On this particular night, dinner had been salt, flavored with more salt and a dash of white pepper. It was hot so it must have been stew and quite horrid. Dessert had been Bread Pudding and was quite excellent. I had been getting on everyone's nerves all night as usual. I was pestering Dado to show me everything he remembered about wrestling. Dado had apparently been a very good amateur wrestler in his younger days. But his Father like mine was very religious and thought that wrestling was barbarous and unchristian. He finally succeeded in forbidding Dado to continue with it. One of Dado's notable victories was over an opponent who went on to become the Light-weight Champion of Great Britain. Dad had advised Dado to ignore me and to my disgust Dado was succeeding in doing an excellent job of it. I was determined to make Dado take me seriously. If I could make him appreciate how strong I was for my age maybe he would reconsider and show me something useful. I was still pleading and coaxing as we were getting ready to leave Mamo's house and go home. I asked Dado if he would allow me to pick him up just to show him that I could. Instead he grabbed the last slice of bread pudding and before ramming it into his mouth said,

"If I can put this bloody bread pudding down, I can put you down!" In so doing he shot forward and made a grab for both of my legs. I grabbed his head as a counter move to prevent me from being taken off my feet. Dado struggled furiously to put me down. I tightened my grip around his neck and we staggered all around the room. I was delighted, not only was I wrestling with an ex-amateur wrestler, who happened to be my Grand-Father, but I was controlling him handily. I felt as though I was in no danger of being taken down, the more Dado struggled the harder I squeezed. Then Dado collapsed! I released him immediately. It turned out that the bread pudding had got trapped in Dado's throat. With the hold I had on his neck he couldn't swallow the bread pudding or spit it out. Dado had no longer been trying to take me down, but trying to survive. I was unwittingly choking him to death. After coughing bread pudding all over the room and everyone in it Dado went berserk. He came for me like a rabid dog, eyes blazing, mouth foaming and spitting bread pudding like a Demon. Mam, Dad and even Mamo had to dive in between us to prevent Dado from trying to do me some grievous bodily harm. It took a superhuman effort from everyone and a repeated apology from me before his rage finally subsided. We are a very foul tempered family. As soon as we were outside Mamo's house and on our way home Dad started in on me. Mam nipped it in the bud before his temper could hit a crescendo and said that she thought that what had happened was more Dado's fault than mine. Dad's monotonous grizzeling continued, "That's right, pick his sleeves up, - he's going to turn out just like your Brother Jimmy, I'll have him working down the pit ---- etc and so on." He was interrupted. Mam suddenly burst into fits of laughter. I don't know if it was a release of tension caused by what could have been a very tragic incident, or if she thought what had happened was that funny. Whatever it was Mam just couldn't stop laughing. Dad's flapping mouth snapped shut like a bear trap and he didn't speak all the way home. Even if he had I don't think anyone would have heard him as Mam was laughing so hard. I was bursting to join her, even though I still didn't know why she was so amused, but Dad's stony countenance made me choke on my laughter almost as much as Dado had choked on his bread pudding.

That summer we visited Barry Island for the day. I had been visualizing a knicker-bocker-glory since Breakfast time. On arrival I decided to get myself an ice-cream immediately as a quick fix. Then I could spend more of the day anticipating the icy treat before finally satisfying my taste buds. I had been saving my money for months and was all set for a good day out. At the first ice-cream vendor I came to I purchased five ice-creams One each for my Mam, Dad, Pam and two for myself, but no one else wanted an ice-cream that early in the day. Rather than waste them I ate them all myself - quickly before they melted. I went off alone to Barry Island Fairground. While walking around I spotted a photographic studio and decided to get my first physique photo taken in a proper studio. The photographer seemed suitably impressed with the shape I was in for a 14 year old kid. I told him I had just eaten five ice-creams for the protein. He suggested I should eat a lot of seafood and drink plenty of milk. He told me my photo would be ready to pick up in about an hour, so I decided to take his advice and find some seafood while I was waiting. I had noticed a stall as I was entering the Fairground that sold all kinds of Shellfish and thought that would probably do. I had never eaten Shellfish before so I asked the vendor which variety contained the most protein. He told me it all did, so I told him I would try a portion of everything to see what I liked. I almost gagged on my first attempt at swallowing raw oysters but masochistically managed to get them down. Then a dish of whelks, which was no trouble at all after the oysters. Neither was the cockles, winkles, or the mussels. The vendor told me that mussels built muscles and that's where they got their name so I ordered another two helpings. I took a large bag of boiled shrimp with me to eat while I explored more of the Fairground. They looked like large pink insects to me and as I had never eaten them before, didn't really know how to. The whole shrimp got stuffed into my mouth, head tail, legs, guts and all. I didn't like them very much, but hey! If they were going to build up my muscles, what the hell! When I finished the shrimp I noticed I still had enough time to go and get something to drink to take away the unpleasant taste all the shellfish had left in my mouth. A couple of large milkshakes later I was brimming with so much muscle building protein I had a job to walk. I told the photographer that I had taken his advice and itemized everything I had eaten and drank within the short period it had taken him to prepare my photo. He told me that I must have a cast-iron guts, which I remembered taking as a compliment. I was very pleased with my first physique photo at the time, even though it comprised of me performing the most awkward looking lat-spread. I was already trying to think of a suitable excuse to show it off to any girls I might be lucky enough to encounter that day.

I rode on a number of the old usual Fairground rides when I suddenly came upon one I had never seen before. It was called 'The Rota' and it comprised of a gigantic drum shaped contraption that was entered by a door in one side. The door was closed before the ride started. Everyone would stand against the walls and it would spin at an incredible speed which would pin everyone in it to the wall. Then the floor would drop away and leave everybody stuck to the wall by the sheer force that the speed created. As the Rota gradually slowed down gravity would once again prevail and everyone would slowly slide down the wall to the floor. After it stopped the floor would rise again to the level of the door. It would open for new riders to enter and anyone who wanted to get off could do so. The riders had the option to stay on for as many free rides as they wanted. There was also an observation balcony around the entire top of the drum where other paying customers could watch the spectacle. The ride seemed to be a magnet for girls, so I couldn't buy my ticket quick enough. At first I watched a few rides from the observation gallery and then decided to try it out for myself. It was great! When the wheel spun, the faster it went the more it molded the women's and girl's clothes to their bodies. When it began to slow and they started to slide down the walls their skirts and dresses would be dragged up to their eyebrows. WOW! I thought I'd gone to heaven. The Ladies would of course feign extreme embarrassment. At the same time love every second of the naughty attention they were getting by showing off the pretty knickers. Knickers that they had probably put on especially for the occasion. They were really enjoying the sexy game almost as much as I was. They would shriek and scream, pretend to struggle with their hiked up skirts and dresses. Making sure they didn't succeed before they enjoyed the whoops and wolf-whistles from many of the male spectators. I was too overawed to whoop or whistle and I rode the Rota for ride after ride. As much as I was enjoying my new experience I began to feel a little queasy and thought it would be a good idea to get off when the Rota stopped. But every time it did some new lady would get on and I found I just couldn't bring myself to leave before I got a chance to see what I was going to see. I'll stay on for just one more ride I kept telling myself as a naughty new candidate entered the ride. I really would mean it until the ride was over, the door would open and another pretty girl would get on. I wasn't feeling queasy anymore, I was feeling horrible. I needed to get off but I couldn't resist each successive pretty face, bust or legs. As the Rota stopped this time I was ready to dash out of it as quickly as I could. Then the prettiest girl yet entered and smiled right at me. Now was decision time I knew I desperately needed to leave but I was rooted by her gorgeous smile. Blast! The door closed and the Rota began to spin again So did my head, so did my guts, so did the ice-cream, the whelks, the cockles, the winkles, the mussels, the oysters, the whole shrimp, heads, tails, legs, the milk shakes. The Rota spun faster and faster, so did my head, so did my guts. - I won't mention the rest of it, as with an explosion it all left my guts and whooshed around that Rota like a techno colored Tornado. There was lots of protein for everyone. Pints of milk and enough fish to feed the five thousand. I even got splattered myself as I shot around and got some coming in the opposite direction. What you may call getting my own back. No one was denied a goodly portion, even the spectator's cheers for the sexy girls turned to one of disbelief, dismay and horror. I saw one man whipping his glasses. When the Rota slowed everyone slid back to the ground much faster than usual with the help of the newly lubricated walls. I shot a quick glance at the very pretty girl as I dashed across the floor of the Rota to be the first one out of the opening door. She was still looking at me, but no longer smiling, I suppose too much protein can do that to some people.

****

The beginning of September 1955 was to be my last term in school. In December I would be 15 and school would be part of one of my favorite subjects, - History! I felt I had been waiting all my life for this time to come, "Then." I told everyone, "I'm going to London to become a Professional Wrestler." No one was surprised or impressed by my declaration. Almost every young kid born in every small town or village in South Wales made the same declaration. Not about wrestling but about getting out of those wild and wooly Welsh hills and doing something more positive with their lives. The only thing is, no one ever made good on their dream and everyone had heard it all before. Parents, grand-parents and even great-grand-parents had all, in their time said the same thing. But here they all were living the same dreary life, in the same dreary town, dreary decades later. Mocking the aspirations of each new generation who were naïve enough to think they would ever leave the Welsh hills and live happily ever after in London. If they thought my ambition to go and live in London was ludicrous, can you imagine what they thought of my dream of becoming a wrestler when I got there.

"A little snot nosed kid like you could never be a wrestler!"

they'd tell me, "You're too small, have you seen the size of those Professional Wrestlers?!" I hadn't actually, but I had never been afraid of anyone and I'd refuse to let size become an obstacle. Plus I was still body-building and I was still getting bigger. "Have you seen the size of Bert Assirati? He's over nineteen stone!" They'd add. No, I'd never heard of Bert Assirati at that time, even though he was one of the biggest names in Europe. Certainly the biggest name in British Wrestling, but they never had Wrestling on TV in those days and I'd never seen a British Wrestling magazine. All my Wrestling Heroes were from the American 'Boxing and Wrestling' magazines. I think Mam was the only one who thought that I might make good on my threat. She knew how determined and single minded I could be when I became obsessed with anything. She knew also that I was very fond of Uncle Fred and he was one of the very few people that I would take any advice from. The next time Uncle Fred visited us, Mam asked him to talk to me,

"You want to be a Wrestler," He said, "but what are you going to do for a job?"

"Wrestling will be my job," I replied, "I'm not interested in anything else."

"There's no such thing as a full time Professional Wrestler," he told me, "they all have regular jobs, like everyone else and they only wrestle in their spare time. Usually on the weekends, they probably make a few quid but it's more of a hobby, it's not a job."

"Well it's going to be my job," I argued, "it's all I want to do and I'm going to be good and I'll make a lot of money."

"Most of the Wrestlers I've seen are fat old men, about forty years old who take turns at winning or losing for about five quid a match." He stated. Now even Uncle Fred was skating on thin ice. I'd heard so many people insinuating that wrestling was fake it made me want to puke. It was often just the excuse I needed to show them how wrong they were. It pissed me off, but tying them in knots was just the practice I needed and an appropriate compensation for them to pay, for annoying me in the first place. But, as it turned out, Uncle Fred was quite right. In those days there was no such thing as a full time Professional Wrestler in Britain. He wasn't far out in his estimation of the financial

175

rewards they received for their efforts either. I wasn't convinced and I didn't want to be. "I'm going to be a full time Professional Wrestler and that's all I'm going to be, I don't want a job. - J-O-B stands for Just-Over-Broke and that's not going to be my style. All I'm going to do is wrestle and make a lot of money doing it!" Uncle Fred's eyebrows rose and I heard his huge sigh of exasperation as I turned on my heel and walked off.

"See what I mean? You can't tell him anything!" I heard Dad chip in, as I slammed the door behind me.

In spite of, or maybe because of Dad's conviction that pubs were houses of sin I would occasionally pop in for a pint or two, or sometimes more. I remember going back to school after lunch and sleeping off a beer binge at my desk while the lessons continued interrupted only by my snoring. Even though the drinking age in Britain is 18 I had been going in pubs unchallenged from the age of 13. I had began shaving at the same time and I knew I looked older than I was. I also remember when about 14, sitting in a pub opposite Beaufort Ballroom when it was raided by the police looking for underage drinkers. I sat at the bar on my own nursing a pint without receiving a second glance. Almost every other youngster in the place was questioned, marched out and taken to the police station. Strangely enough I learned more about British Wrestlers from some of the old timers in the local pubs. According to them wrestling used to be a bi-weekly occurrence in Abertillery a number of years earlier. Needless to say they had all seen Bert Assirati and I would listen spellbound as I got a blow by blow and a slam by slam description of every match they could remember. They told me of many other colorful sounding characters like 'Man-Mountain' Benny, 'Black-Butcher' Johnson, 'Bulldog' Bill Garnon, Ken 'The Bearded Monarch' Davis, Jack and 'Bully' Pye, Hassan-Ali-Bey, 'The Terrible Turk'. When I'd inform them that they would soon be able to watch me wrestle they'd explode with laughter,

"What! A little shrimp like you," they'd chortle, "they'd rip you in half and eat the pieces for breakfast – HO-HO-HO!" 'Never mind,' I'd think, 'we'll see.'

Bert Assirati's name popped up again. There was a photo of him in one of the Sunday news papers. He was getting smacked on the head with a wooden chair by his opponent 'Bully' Pye during a match in Manchester's 'Belle-Vue' Stadium. A few weeks later there was another photo of middle-weight wrestler, 'Gentleman' Jim Lewis versus the British Middle-weight Champion, Tommy Mann, also wrestling in 'Belle Vue.' That was when I learned that unlike America, in Europe they had different weight divisions. Starting with lightweights, who could weigh anything up to 150 pounds, to welter-weights, middle-weights, light-heavy-weights and then heavy-weights.

All of a sudden I seemed to be getting bombarded with Bert. There was an article in one of the daily newspapers about Marge Assirati, Bert's Wife, she had become a Wrestling Promoter. The article featured a photo of Marge, surrounded by huge heavy-weights. They included the 6' 4" 290 pound Zulu, 'Prince Kumali', Canadian, Lee 'Flash' Edwards, Charlie Green and of course 19 stone Bert himself. Then best of all I learned that in a couple of weeks time Bert Assirati would be topping the bill at the Stowe Hill Baths Hall in Newport. The only problem being, that the last train back home from Newport would leave about half an hour after the Wrestling matches started. My friend and family Greengrocer Mickey Jacobs came to the rescue,

"Don't worry Adrian," he offered, "If you pay for my ringside seat, I'll take you and bring you back in my car." WOW! For the exorbitant price of 12-shillings and 6 pence each for ringside seats, I would be going to watch Professional Wrestling. GREAT! And so was the wrestling. Although I must admit that I was surprised by and a little disappointed in the lack of color and drama displayed by these British Wrestlers. When compared with the American larger than life characters I had read about in the books and magazines I had got from the States.

The first Professional Wrestler I ever saw enter the ring was Ron Harrison, who a few years later became a friend. I can't remember who he was wrestling, but the match was quite good. The second match was between two large Heavy-weights, Angelo Pappini versus Ed Martinsen of Sweden. Angelo was a protégé of Bert Assirati and it showed. Poor Ed Martinsen didn't stand a chance and was bullied unmercifully from the first bell until he got knocked out in the fourth round. Then came the main event, Vick Hessel was the first to enter the ring, then came the man himself Bert Assirati. Bert had a head like a bullet, a neck like a bull, huge shoulders, massive arms, a sixty inch chest, a thick but hard looking waist and hips set on two short tree-trunk like legs. He weighed in the region of 270 pounds at a height of only 5' 6". if you can imagine a hairless Gorilla with short arms by Gorilla standards that would be Bert. To start off with, Bert seemed to be taking a terrible beating, but it eventually became apparent after watching him in action many times that, that was a vital part of Bert Assirati's strategy. He would virtually allow his opponent to beat on him until his adversary was utterly exhausted and couldn't beat on him anymore. Then it would be Bert's turn and believe me what would happen next was not for the squeamish. As usual Bert would win decisively. What was not usual, was for any of Bert's opponents to make it back to the dressing room under their own steam. The last match was between Young Milo of Greece and Johnny Kovacks of Hungary. It was only billed as a middle-weight preliminary match but in my opinion was the best action match of the night. Also I noticed that both Wrestlers upon entering the ring wore short, smart looking jackets. Nothing as flashy as I was used to seeing being worn by my favorite American Wrestlers, but nice. Much nicer in fact than all the Wrestlers I had seen in the previous matches. They all wore identical style of grubby looking dressing gowns in various drab colors. The kind that would have been worn by any old guy in the audience while sitting in front of the fire or the telly in his equally grubby slippers. But in spite of the total lack of imagination that went into the Wrestlers ring wear, I really enjoyed my first live show and couldn't wait to see another one. Unfortunately, although we were told that there would be more Wrestling in Stowe Hill it would not be on a regular basis. I would have to keep my eyes open for posters or newspaper ads to tell us when the Grapplers would be back in town. Next time wrestling was being discussed in a pub I would now have a story of my own to tell.

I have often wondered if 'film star' Tony Curtis appreciated just how completely 'over' he was with all of us teenagers in the middle fifties. My own 'short back and sides' hairstyle had evaporated in favor of the D.A. [ducks arse] style. What we called a 'Tony Curtis.' In those days I couldn't afford a 'Teddy-boy' suit that young men were reported to be wearing in London. But, a Tony Curtis hairstyle complete with sideburns were at least a step towards that style. I would still sometimes collect a nice sword or dagger if I saw one that took my fancy, but a lot of my hard earned pocket money was now spent on records. This was before the 'Rock 'n' Roll' era got started in Britain. It's strange to look back on it now, but we were all looking for and wanting something that didn't quite exist. I remember Dad moaning about the money I spent on records and it wouldn't have been Dad if he'd approved of my taste in music. He suggested that if I had money to waste it would be better spent on putting at least one tenth of it into the Tabernacle's collection box. Instead of Mam having to supply me with my usual Sunday sixpence. I responded by taking all the money I had out of my pocket and replying,

"I'm going to throw all of my money up in the air, anything God wants, he can take, - anything that hits the ground is mine!" Needless to say dear Daddy was not amused. Mam took more starch out of his sails by roaring with laughter. She never complained but I know she resented the amount of hard earned money that made its way out of her weekly budget and into the Tabernacle's collection box.

Days seemed to take weeks as I suffered the countdown till the end of term and the end of school forever. Not that I actually attended school much anymore, but I wanted it officially over. Sealed, signed, delivered, an ex-schoolboy, - in fact an ex-boy. I'd felt I was a man since the age of twelve and soon it would be a fact. I was getting excited, BUT! Then an awful rumor began to circulate. - They were going to put the school leaving age up to 16, WHAT! As tough as I saw myself I didn't think that I could endure another one whole year of waiting to leave school. - Then the rumor modified a little, a possibility of reprieve. It was only eligible school leavers who didn't have a job to go to that would have to stay in school for another year.

"I already have a job," I claimed, "I do a paper round." 'That doesn't count,' I was told, 'it has to be a proper job, - like working down the pit.'

"Yeah right, I said, "that'll be the day!" But at that time there wasn't anything else. There was no work available in the steel works or the rubber factory, nothing except the coal mine. I think I would have even got a job with Eric Barnes in the Slaughter house rather than submit to Dad's decade long threat of,

"You just wait till you leave school," I'll have you down the pit with me!" But it didn't look as though I had a choice. It was the pit or the possibility of another year in school. With a very heavy heart I chose the pit.

Mam's Father had been a construction engineer, but his Father had been a miner. Mamo's Father and Grandfather had been miners also and so had Dado's Father and Grandfather. With the exception of the 4 years my grandfather Dado spent in the army during World War 1 he had been a coal miner, from the age of 13 till he retired at the age of 65. At the age of 14 Dad followed in his Father's footsteps. He began work in the pit even though the prospect terrified him. In his autobiography he describes a feeling of dread and apprehension in his stomach as he walked across the colliery for the first time. Towards the cage in which he would, as Dad put it, 'be lowered into the bowels of the earth. A strange feeling as though my tummy was up in my throat. As if I were dangling in space on the end of a piece of elastic. It took quite a few trips up and down that pit before I eventually got used to it.' Wrote Dad and that was what he wanted for me. Once again I hated that ugly gleam of triumph and satisfaction in Dad's eye. As I conceded and submitted to the fact that I too was to become a coalminer. - Just like dear old Dad, "If it's good enough for me it's definitely good enough for you!" I'd heard him quote a thousand times. But, if he thought the prospect would terrify me as it had him, he would be very much mistaken as well as disappointed. I had been scurrying through the bowels of the earth for years in my beloved caves for fun and enjoying every minute of it. Well, I had agreed to work in the pit, but in spite of Dad gloating over his victory I knew I was only giving myself a breathing space.

This poem hung for many years in Llanhilleth Workman's Institute -

A Welshman stood at The Golden Gate, his head bowed low.
He meekly asked the Man of Fate the way that he should go.

"What have you done," St. Peter asked, "to gain admission here?"
"I merely mined coal," he said, "for very many a year."
St. Peter opened up the gate and softly tolled the bell.
Come choose your harp," St. Peter said, "You've had your share of Hell."

THE PIT

"Time to get up!" My Father barked as he opened my bedroom door, "It's almost 5 o'clock!" I knew that already as I had heard the alarm clock go off in his bedroom a few minutes earlier. I normally arose very early in the morning, but would always wait until Dad had already left the house for work before I'd go downstairs. That way I'd only have to listen to the bloody Budgerigar screaming. Dad hated working in the pit, as I remember him telling Ter. 'It's hard work, dirty, unhealthy and dangerous.' I knew he wouldn't be good company first thing in the morning while contemplating what the day held in store. Mind you, as far as I was concerned he wasn't good company anytime. I began my 16 weeks of training as a coalminer in Oakdale Colliery. To get there from Brynmawr, I would walk to the railway station which would have been a little over a mile away from my house and catch a train to Crumlin. From Crumlin I would catch a bus to Oakdale and walk about another mile to the colliery. Upon arriving at the colliery I would make my way to the clean clothes lockers Undress, put my clean clothes in my allotted locker then walk through the shower room to a mirror image dirty clothes lockers on the opposite side of the showers. I'd put my dirty work clothes on, including my miners helmet. Then I would go to the lamp room where I would exchange my lockers key for the lamp, which would fasten on the front of the helmet. There was a lot more to becoming a coalminer than knowing which end of a shovel to use. There was packing. Putting up wooden props that had to be notched and cut to fit with an axe. Securing steel flats with wooden or hydraulic props. Putting up steel rings and learning how to shore them. How to move the conveyor belt up and down as well as sideways so that it was level and the allotted distance from the coalface. After the day shift had advanced their usual four and a half feet further into the coal seam. In Oakdale we would be trained to perform a specific task from early in the morning until lunch time and then we would be told where to go after lunch. Where we would receive training on some other aspect in the art of acquiring coal. But, before we had lunch we were supposed wait in line to return our lamps to the lamp room in order to get our locker key. Go to our dirty clothes locker. Take off our dirty clothes. Take a shower. Dry ourselves before proceeding on to our clean clothes locker. Getting dressed in our clean clothes, make our way to the cafeteria and line up to buy lunch. Bolt our food down as quickly as possible so we could return to the clean clothes lockers, get undressed. Walk through the shower room to the dirty clothes lockers. Put on our dirty clothes again, take our locker keys to the lamp room to exchange them for our lamps. Then make our way to where we'd been instructed to go before we left for lunch in order to continue our training. Of course when we finished for the day and it was time to go home we'd do the whole locker and shower thing again. I did all that once, the very next day I came to work armed with a bag of sandwiches and a bottle of water. When lunch time came, I'd go and hide in the woods on a hill near the colliery while everyone else went off to perform the lunch ritual. I'd eat my packed lunch, keep my eyes open for the rest of the trainees and rejoined them when they made their way back to work. Only when work was completely over for the day did I do the locker/shower thing. I considered it a waste of time going through all that trouble to get clean for lunch, when I knew damn well that as soon as lunch was over I was going to get filthy again. There were trainees from dozens of different Welsh towns and villages ranging in age from 15 like myself to some who were in their late 20's. All hoping to get work in a colliery as close to where they lived as possible. For me it would be Beynon's Colliery in Blaina, where Dad worked. I didn't make any friends at all for the whole time I was taking my training. All the other trainees called me 'Tarzan.' I knew it wasn't meant as a compliment but I didn't mind as I realized that even though they were making fun they must have noticed that I was in good shape. I was getting a hard time from a little gang from Nantyglo led by a huge ugly brute they called 'Jack the Gypo.' If you remember, I'd had my clock cleaned by a miniature Gypo, so I wasn't going to go out of my way to tangle with a giant one. Especially as he was always backed up by two or three henchmen. On the way home I would stay outside the station in

Crumlin till the last moment before the train left hoping to get a compartment on my own. Nine times out of ten, Jack the Gypo and his band of thugs, would be on the lookout and would pile into the same compartment. I would then have to put up with Jack's verbal bullshit until they all got out just one stop before mine. Crumlin was no more than about thirty miles from Brynmawr but the journey would take about an hour and twenty minutes. It would wind through the valleys and stop at every little town and village on the way. I could have jumped out at any of the stops and got into another compartment but I wouldn't have given the giant Gypo the satisfaction of chasing me off. Plus they could follow me, which would have also given him satisfaction and for me an embarrassing waste of effort.

About this time, I found out that Wrestling was back in Newport. Unfortunately Mickey Jacobs wouldn't be able to take me as he was going to be away on business. I didn't know anyone else who owned a car who liked Wrestling but I was determined I was not going to miss the show. Newport was closer to Crumlin by train than Brynmawr was. So on the day of the Wrestling I went straight to Newport after work instead of going home. I also realized that I would not be able to get home that night if I wanted to watch the whole show. I made up my mind to stay all night in Newport railway station and catch the first train I could to get back to Crumlin next morning and then back to work in Oakdale from there.

The Wrestling was great, once again Bert was main event, the first match featured the first masked Wrestler I'd ever seen in real life. 'The Emerald Phantom' who wrestled ex-body-builder Lou Ravelle. Other Wrestlers on the card included Charlie Green and 'Flash' Edwards. It was a very enjoyable evening until the Wrestling was over and I spent a cold, endless, uncomfortable, sleepless night on Newport station.

I caught the first train out and got to the colliery extra early. I knew we would be training on a simulated coalface that morning. I took advantage of my early arrival to get to our worksite first in order to take my pick of the best shovels to work with that day. Some of the tools we were given to do our training with were in a very sorry condition. If you were unlucky enough to be left with one of the shovels with a split and twisted blade it made your use of it very much more arduous than getting one that was in better shape. Working in the simulated coalface was a real drag. We had about four and a half foot headroom which was crowded with elbow splitting upright props that supported the roof. There was hardly room to move let alone work. We would spend all day shoveling coal from an endless convoy of steel buggies. onto a conveyor belt that would take the coal down the face. The coal would fill the buggies that would go around a track in a circle to be tipped out so we could shovel it back onto the conveyor belt again. This would go on and on, shoveling the same coal that would keep coming back like a bloody boomerang. But, as I said, if you had a decent shovel to work with it made your day a little more wonderful and on that morning after the Wrestling I had a decent shovel. Even so I was extra tired from a lost night's sleep which makes me extra grumpy and I'm not safe to be around when I'm extra tired and extra grumpy. What started the ruckus that day began when I leaned my shovel against a support prop in order to leave my hands free to pick up a very large lump of coal and manhandle it onto the conveyor belt. When I turned around to pick up my shovel again I found it had been replaced by the crappiest conditioned shovel I'd ever seen, I was furious.

"Who's got my fucking shovel?! I shouted and I shone my lamp on all the faces that were closest to me. I didn't have to look far as a guy they called Mongo, but never to his face, was smirking openly. I had seen him swap his cracked shovel for a good one on many occasions and as he was older, larger and nastier than most of us he'd been allowed to get away with it,

"Give me my fucking shovel you stupid twat! I demanded,

"You shouldn't have put it down." He replied.

I was extra tired and extra grumpy; he wasn't going to keep my shovel.

"You'll give me my shovel, Mongo! I growled, "I won't ask you again!"

"This is all you'll get from me!" He responded and threw a shovel full of coal dust right into my face. In spite of the shock I immediately threw a shovel full of coal dust right back into his face. Then both of us began shoveling and throwing coal dust at each other like a pair of animated maniacs. Everyone in the vicinity was screaming, coughing and spluttering. We were both acting like idiots but I felt that I was getting the best of the coal dust battle as I was much smaller and could maneuver better in such a low cramped space. He suddenly rushed forward and grabbed my shovel with his left hand, pushed it down to the ground and tread on it with his left foot. I relaxed as I was expecting him to tell me he had had enough. Instead he began shoveling coal in my face again just using his right hand while keeping my shovel trapped with his left hand and foot. I responded by kicking him as hard as I could in the shins with my steel toe capped boot. He leapt away in agony and shock, I spun my shovel around and hit him full in the face with the flat of it with all the force I could muster. He went down like a log but despite his size managed to roll aside in time to avoid another slashing blow I'd aimed at him. He tore off down the coalface with me in hot pursuit swiping viciously at him with my shovel. We'd hardly ran a few paces when we almost collided with the foreman. We were both dragged before the Colliery Manager. He threatened instant dismissal if there was any re-occurrence of any physical animosity displayed between us. I was still totally pissed off, but that stupid and dangerous episode proved to have one favorable and advantageous repercussion. While standing on the platform in Crumlin station watching my train approach I suddenly locked eyes with one of Jack the Gypo's satellites. He was standing with another of Jack's mates waiting for the same train further down the platform. He immediately broke eye contact and they both moved further down the platform away from where I was standing. They seemed to pretend they hadn't seen me. There was no sign of Jack the Gypo and it was obvious that I wasn't going to get the usual verbal bullshit from them unless they were standing behind Jack. The reason I had not gone out of my way to stand up to the big Gypo already was due to the fact that there was always a few others with him and I didn't think I would end up fighting Jack on his own. It occurred to me now that they would be unlikely to back Jack up and risk the consequences if they ever found themselves in my vicinity on their own like they were today. It then occurred to me that I hadn't seen Jack the Gypo for a few days either. I had seen various members of his little gang about, none of them had spoken to me, or come near since that last time I'd seen them with Jack. As the train stopped I rushed down the platform to the compartment that Jack's mates were entering. As the last one was closing the door behind him, I ripped the door out of his grasp with all my might and as two pairs of wide, startled eyes shot around in my direction, I demanded,

"Where's Jack the Gypo?!"

"He's off this week!" They both stammered. I gave them my angriest face, their faces went white with fright, they were both ready to crap.

"When is he coming back?!" I demanded,

"Next week!" they both stammered,

"Good!" I replied with a growl, I slammed the carriage door closed and made it to the compartment next door to it and boarded just before the train chugged out of Crumlin.

****

At home things weren't going very well. By now I'm sure that it may have dawned on you that I didn't enjoy the World's best Father and Son relationship. Now, believe it or not things had got much worse. It started the first Sunday after I had begun work in Oakdale Colliery. I had made this decision long before I had left school and today was D-day. I'll get straight to the point -

"You'd better hurry up and get dressed or you'll be late for Sunday school!" Dad warned me. I was sitting on the sofa trying to hide behind the Sunday newspaper I was reading, waiting for the inevitable to happen.

"I'm not going to Sunday school." I answered from the other side of 'The News of the World.'

"What! What do you mean you're not going to Sunday school, why not, are you sick – are you injured?!" Dad inquired.

"Yeah, I'm sick of Sunday school," I replied, "and I'm not going anymore."

"What are you talking about, - What do you mean you're not going anymore?!!!" Shouted Dad, while trying to adopt a facial expression that would have been more suitable if he had just discovered Mount Everest in the drawer where he kept his clean socks. I lowered my newspaper and looked him in the eye,

"I have been working down the pit every day this week!" I reminded him, "It's been dark when I've gone down the pit and it's been dark again by the time I've come back up. Today will be the first time I've seen daylight since last Sunday and I intend enjoying as much of it as I can. I'm not wasting any of it going to Sunday school!" I had never in my life seen a face that registered so much bewilderment. The only reason I had been able to complete what I had to say was the fact that what I had said had left Dad temporarily too speechless with shock to interrupt me. Unfortunately that didn't last long.

"Get yourself ready at once!" He snarled, "While you're living in my house you'll do as I tell you and as long as you're living in my house you're going to Sunday school!"

"It's not your house it's our house, I've been bringing in money and pulling my weight for years," I replied, "but, if you insist I leave, I'll be glad to. As soon as I've saved enough money to go to London and start wrestling." I knew I'd slyly recruited a powerful ally with that line as I was well aware that Mam didn't want me to go.

"You are going to Sunday school and you are going now!" screamed Dad, "Get yourself ready at once!" I snorted and straightened the paper as though to ignore him.

"You can keep on saying the same thing over and over all day if it'll make you happy, but I've finished with Sunday school and I'm not going anymore." I replied as casually as I could. WHOOSH! Dad swept the newspaper out of my hands and my reflexes responded faster than my brain as I found myself standing facing him and waiting for him to attack.

"Alright," Mam shouted as she stepped between us, "I've had enough of this, let's have a bit more quiet from both of you. They can probably hear you down the Tabernacle with all the noise you're both making!" I think Mam must have realized she'd said the wrong thing mentioning the dreaded Tabernacle.

"While he's living in this hou---!" Dad started to say, Mam interrupted him,

"What are you going to do Em' drag him to Sunday school every week by his hair? If he won't go you can't force him!"

"Yes I will drag him there by his hair if ----!"

"Yeah that'll be the day!" I interrupted, "If God gives us free will, who the hell are you to change the rules?!

"You shut up too!" Mam shouted at me, "I don't want to hear another word from either of you!"

"I think I'll get myself ready and go for a nice walk down the valley road." I sighed, knowing I was throwing more gas on Dad's fire, "A nice bit of fresh air and daylight will help settle my diner."

****

"I loaded 16 tons and whaddo I get, Another day older an' deeper in debt.

So Brother don't you call me 'cos I can't go, I owe my soul to the company store. "I was born one morning, when the sun didn't shine, I picked up my shovel an' I walked to the mine, I loaded 16 tons of number 9 coal --- CHHRUPTCH!" SPLAT! YUCK!" I stopped singing, scraped my throat and spat the huge, black, slimy gob into the contrast of the newly fallen white snow. I made my way from the top of the pit to the lamp-room, at the end of another Oakdale day. The very sight of what I was coughing up and scraping out of my throat made me gag. Coal mining is not a healthy job.

"And the stall boss said well bless my soul, - you loaded 16 tons and whaddo you get, another day older and deeper in debt!" As I said this was just before Rock 'n' Roll and Frankie Laine's "16 tons" made him the patron Saint of all the young coalminers in South Wales. We felt the song had been written and performed just for us. The song played on my mind the way songs do. While I undressed, while I showered, while I got dressed into my clean clothes, rode the bus to Crumlin station. As I locked eyes with Jack the Gypo who was already on the platform waiting for our train.

"If you see me coming better step aside, - a lotta men didn't an' a lotta men died." Jack the Gypo's eyes assumed that glassy, vacant, 'I'm looking right at you but I can't actually see you' look. He turned and spoke to one of the guys I had confronted a few days earlier who had told me Jack was off work for a week. He flicked a nervous glance over his shoulder to check where I was without looking directly at me. I walked purposely and directly towards him. "I've got one fist of iron and the other of steel, - if the right one don't get you then the left one will." I mumbled to myself as I advanced, the song getting me in the mood for upcoming events. I stood right by the side of Jack. He scowled but still refused to acknowledge my presence and he moved a little further down the platform followed by his friend. - I followed too. It felt good that the shoe now seemed to be on the other foot and Jack was attempting to avoid me. I didn't realize at the time, but was told by Jack's friends months later that they had been close to where Mongo and I had our, by now famous 'shovel scuffle.' They had almost crapped with fright when they had witnessed my vicious performance and the fury of my temper. They had reported the incident to Jack the Gypo who hadn't been in work that week. So it seemed that Jack must have reassessed his chances. As I said, I was unaware of this, but I don't think it would have made much difference if I had been. I had never done anything, or said anything to offend Jack the Gypo or any of his friends. Yet they had gone out of their way to threaten, ridicule and humiliate me from the first time I met them. I've always been a believer in re-paying a debt. If someone does me a good turn I believe in returning the favor with interest. If anyone does me a bad turn the same thing applies. As I stepped into the railway compartment behind Jack and his friend, Jack turned around pushed past us got out of the compartment and entered another one. Much to his dismay I followed him, followed in turn by Jack's mate. I pushed Jack's friend into the nearest corner seat as he entered so I could slam the carriage door closed and so stop Jack from playing any more musical railway compartments. Jack's pal stayed where I put him and didn't move again. Jack sat in the other corner on the same side, I sat opposite him.

"Why have you got such a big sloppy mouth, Jack?" I asked him, "Is that what your Mother used to pick you up out of your pram?"

"Fuck off, Tarzan!" He snarled, I honored him with my sweetest smile but he wouldn't look at me, so I tore a button off the padded seat on which I sat and flicked it hitting him in the eye.

"I said fuck off!" screamed Jack.

"No I won't," I replied, "I'm going to carry on annoying you to see if you've got the guts to do anything about it." I smiled at his friend who recoiled and shrunk further back into his corner. I was sure I could trust him not to interfere with anything I intended to do. Jack refused to respond to any of the verbal insults I piled on him. Displaying an amazing degree of patience he ignored button after button that I tore off the seats and flicked at him to punctuate each verbal insult. They bounced off his face or head and if the button bounced where I could reach it I'd pick it up and flick it again. If Jack could reach it he'd snatch it up and add it to the handful he was slowly accumulating. All of a sudden he screamed, "Fuck you!" the same way a paratrooper would shout 'Geronimo.' He threw the handful of buttons at me as he launched himself right behind them and landed straight on top of me. If any of you have ever found yourselves being attacked while sitting back in a soft seat, you will realize what an enormous disadvantageous position I'd placed myself in. But, as quick as a flash I reacted and somehow reversed our positions. Before Jack could land a single blow, he was now sitting where I had been and I was on top of him punching his face off. It had happened so easily it was ridiculous. So Jack got his investment repaid plus a generous interest. When I finished I threw him off my seat onto the carriage floor as a final bonus. - I hadn't even broken a sweat. Jack was bleeding a lot. After he crawled off the floor back onto his own seat he began mopping it off as best he could with his cap. I now ignored Jack who actually sounded as though he was sobbing. I remembered I had a ham sandwich left in my lunch box and thought I'd celebrate by eating it now. I took my first bite as Jack got up and turned to the window and opened it. It crossed my mind that as he had disgraced himself so badly with his miserable performance, he might want to end it all and jump out. Instead he gave his face a last wipe with his cap and threw the bloody thing through the window. I took another bite of my sandwich and turned and smiled at Jack's friend who was still cowering in the corner. He had not moved or said a word. He repaid my smile with a wild stare and said,

"You'd better look out now!" He suddenly shifted his stare at Jack. It just gave me that split second warning to jerk my head back and watch Jack the Gypo's huge fist flash past my face in a blur. Jack's fist missed me by a fraction of an inch, thanks to an involuntary but timely warning from Jack's own friend. Jack launched himself on top of me again and even though both his fists were flailing his attack ended in a pathetic replay of his first attack. Not to be too repetitious, this time I threw him down between the seats, kneeled over him and punched his face until I got bored doing it. I thought I'd finish my sandwich instead but when I found it, it was in worse shape than poor Jack. In fact some of it was stuck to the side of my face, so I kicked Jack on the head in disgust. I looked in the mirror, wiped the ham and butter off my face and sat down. Jack hadn't moved yet and I hoped he wasn't dead. He lay very still but when the train stopped at the next station Jack got up off the carriage floor and got out. Jack's friend stayed on the train and we ended up chatting quite normally for the rest of the journey. As it turned out he didn't seem to be a bad chap. I admit I was feeling fairly good about the outcome and wished that I had brought the matter to a head a long time before, instead of swallowing all the crap I had. The thing that left me feeling a little hollow was that in spite of his formidable size and appearance. When it came to proving himself Jack was unable to deliver. I know it isn't proper or polite to badmouth a vanquished foe, so I will try to put this as kindly as I can and just say. When it came to fighting the Gypo was fucking useless.

****

I was obviously still body-building every day in spite of the hard physical work coal mining proved to be. I lifted weights mostly at home and two nights a week at the club in Ebbw Vale. The club's only claim to fame was the one 150 pound barbell and a few gymnastic mats that I was allowed to practice my wrestling on. I would often make a thorough nuisance of myself trying to persuade gymnasts and some of the other body-builders in the club to get on the mat and wrestle with me. Most of them knew by painful experience how viciously and seriously I took my training. Then have to suffer my modest proclamation, whispered at the top of my voice. That I claimed to be the club's undisputed wrestling champion and no one was man enough to argue the point. It was pointed out to me that it wasn't a wrestling club and I regularly responded with "Well that's not my fault!"

I would mostly be accompanied by Peter Inge and, or Dai Hughes. Wrestling with them both one after the other would give me a varied practice session. Peter was lighter than I was and although nowhere near as strong he was very fast and a fairly good wrestler. Dai was a complete contrast, he was taller and much heavier than I was, very strong and tough. He rarely complained even though I was often extremely rough with him. He was a bit on the ponderous side and not in possession of a lot of wrestling savvy. One evening I was on the mats with Peter after I had finished an hour or so with the solitary barbell. Dai watched and waited for his turn. I found the best way to handle Peter was to allow him to take a hold and then fight my way out of it. I could then grab him and make him submit within a minute. That beat the alternative of going on the attack from the beginning and having to chase him all around the gym trying to get a hold on him. That was the way I was playing it that night. We'd grapple and I'd allow Peter to take advantage, then immediately take it away from him as I had done hundreds of times before. On that night I was more than a little distracted by a new girl in the club who looked very fetching in her dainty shorts while she practiced gymnastics. Each time I caught her eye she smiled and I continued wrestling with half my mind on what I was doing and the other half on what she was doing. Even so, I can't blame what happened next on that lovely distraction. I bulled into Peter with my head down offering an invitation to grab it. Peter did in a very snug front choke hold. That brought him nicely within reach. I grabbed him in a low bear-hug so as to be able to lift him a little higher prior to slamming myself forward onto the mat with Peter underneath me. Trapped by my body and at the mercy of whatever hold I decided to punish him with next. That was my intention and that's what I did. It was only a slight variation from tactics that had proved to be very effective in the past. But, this time as I dumped myself down on top of Peter he slid his legs around my body in a body-scissors. He leaned back with his upper body to increase the leverage on the 'Guillotine' choke hold he had firmly secured. The sharp edge of his forearm bit deeply into my throat right under my

Adam's-Apple and completely cut off my ability to breathe. I couldn't effectively reach his head in order to pull him towards me and relieve some of the pressure on my flattened throat. When I tried to push him away from me I found I was only increasing the tremendous leverage he already had on my throat. Struggle and fight as I did I could not break the hold. There was no way that I was willing to submit and concede defeat to Peter who I knew I could beat in my sleep with both hands tied behind my back. Especially in front of the other club members who I knew would derive so much pleasure in seeing me taken down a peg or two. Even more especially, I was determined not to disgrace myself in front of the new girl that I had hoped to show off for. But try as I did, I could not escape from Peter's devastating grip. My head felt as though it was ready to explode and I knew I was ready to pass out. Realizing that I had no alternative if I didn't want to suffocate, I gave Peter a few sharp taps on the shoulder as a sign of submission. But, as I had never submitted to anyone before he didn't recognize my signal and if anything he increased the pressure. With the whooshing going on in my head I felt as though I was being swung around and around at the speed of a rocket. I tried to scream out "I SUBMIT!" But when I tried no sound came out of my mouth. I must admit that if I could have reached Peter's face I would have happily dragged both his eyes out to get his attention. I couldn't reach and there was nothing else to do. Completely helpless, I continued to spin like a top. I felt myself losing consciousness when Peter suddenly released me and flopped back onto the mat. I was barely able to hear him say,

"Okay, you win; you're too strong for me!" I crumpled onto my face then rolled onto my back alongside Peter gasping. Neither of us moved or spoke, until Dai, who had got bored watching us both laying down asked,

"Who's going to wrestle me then?"

"Adrian is," answered Peter, "I'm too bloody tired, he's worn me out."

'Adrian isn't,' I thought, 'I'm too close to death.' The gym tilted and turned and I felt like I was going to fall down even though I was already flat on my back. With a superhuman effort I managed the rub the side of my eye, which had started to itch with the back of my hand. I caught sight of the blood on my knuckles, I dropped my arm again unable to move or speak.

"Are you okay, Ade?" Dai asked me, "You've got blood in your eyes!" I was aware of Peter enveloped in a scarlet haze slowly sitting up and saying,

"Shit, are you alright?!" I didn't answer, because I couldn't. I didn't try to move, because I didn't want to. They both made a grab for me and hauled me to my feet. If they hadn't continued to support me I would have fell back down. Everything I looked at was a shade of red. I painfully nodded my head in the direction of the dressing room and with Peter and Dai almost carrying me, made my way there. Both of them asked me over and over if I was okay. I tried to answer once but still nothing was coming through. In the dressing room I tried to speak again and a croaking, hissing alien voice said,

"Fuck it, I'll never wrestle again." At that moment in time I really meant it. When I was able, I looked in the mirror and saw that all of my visible eyeballs were bright blood red. After taking a shower the new smiling girl crossed my mind. But I would have been too embarrassed to speak to her now after what happened and the way I looked. So instead of swaggering out of the club as usual, serenaded by my own ear shattering boasting, I slunk quietly away and went home.

It didn't take me too long to recover my desire to become a professional Wrestler. It had been an obsession for so long that without keeping that dream in focus, my life had no direction. There was absolutely nothing else I wanted to be. After the night of the choke-hold I thought that I would never be able to show my face in the Ebbw Vale gym again either. But the thought of that smiling girl soon made me change my mind.

Her name was Helen and she was in the gym looking fit and pretty next time I went there to train. I began lifting weights and wondered what I would say to her in order to get acquainted. She walked over and asked me if I would teach her to lift weights and of course I agreed to happily. We began going out and got together almost every evening.

Before that I would have any number of girlfriends at the same time. Most would be a one night stand, occasionally it might last as long as two weeks. Before I have you thinking that I fancied myself as Don Juan, let me admit something now, that I never would have admitted at the time. Not only was I still a virgin but I was convinced I would grow old and die before I could bring myself to alter my status. I very much wanted to and with the abundance of very willing girls available I could have been at it day and night, if only I had had the guts to try. If they'd allow me, I would fiddle and fondle all night, as long as they kept THEIR hands to themselves. I was a strong believer in hands down their knickers on the first date, if not there would not be a second date.

With Helen it was different, I was the perfect Gentleman, I even used to take her to the movies, which I had never done before. Especially as in those days a cinema ticket in the dear seats could cost as much as a hefty one shilling and nine-pence each.

One night while getting myself ready to go out and meet her. I became so preoccupied with pleasurable anticipation. That I found myself brushing my teeth with shaving cream, while I squeezed out a handful of toothpaste with which to shave. It had been about a month since the time she had asked me to teach her to lift weights and three weeks since we had began dating. One night I was walking her home and asked her,

"Where shall we meet tomorrow?"

"Oh, I'm going to be busy tomorrow." She answered.

"I'll see you Friday then." I said, as I began to walk away.

"No, I can't," she replied, "I'm still going to be busy on Friday and the weekend."

"Oh, okay," I said, disappointed, "Well, I'll see you in the gym on Monday."

"I'm not going to the gym anymore," she answered, "I've lost interest in it."

"Why have you lost interest in the gym?" I inquired, "I thought you liked it, - so where will I meet you, should I call for you after I finish training?"

"No," she replied, "I don't want to go out with you anymore either."

"What! Why not?" I asked, flabbergasted.

"Well, to be honest," she stated, "I was very disappointed with you."

"Why?" I asked, bewildered.

"I heard about your reputation with the girls," she told me, "and I thought that was very interesting. That was the only reason I went to the gym in the first place. I was so excited when you asked me out that I couldn't sleep the night before, wondering what you were going to do, and you didn't do anything."

"I didn't think you were like that." I protested.

"You didn't even try to find out!" She replied impatiently.

"Okay, well from now on I will!" I promised.

"No! I'm not interested now," she said, "I had to tell you and that's spoiled it."

"Come on then!" I told her, as I grabbed her arm and began to drag her after me, " I'll unspoil it for you!" She snatched her arm away and gave me a push,

"No, you're too late!" she screamed at me.

"Well piss off then!" I shouted and pushed her back. She flew backwards into her garden gate which smashed off its hinges and both the gate and Helen crashed to the ground. She rolled over it with her legs in the air. The light of the nearby lamppost highlighting the contrast of her pale shapely thighs and her black knickers. I realized it was the first time I had ever seen them, even though I had known her for a whole month. 'That's got to be a record,' I thought.

****

Talking of records, by now we were 'Rockin' round the clock,' as 'Rock 'n' roll had arrived and we thought it was great. Even more so when I found that Dad hated it. If Dad didn't approve of something it was definitely worth checking out.

The national newspapers had been full of reports of riots breaking out in London cinemas where Bill Haley's movies were showing. Teddy-Boys fighting, tearing up cinema seats. Rampaging and attacking the hordes of Police Officers who had to be called out to quell the violence and destruction being caused by overly excited Teddy-Boys. The media coverage was to blame for similar riots and disturbances that broke out in many other towns. It happened all over Britain where Bill Haley movies were featured. Local Teddy-Boys thought it was cool to mimic the

Londoners. As a result many cinemas refused to show the movies. When 'Rock around the clock' was shown in 'The Cozy Cinema' every teenage kid dressed up in their very best Rock 'n' Roll outfits. Or as close to the Edwardian style as they could manage and packed the cinema to capacity. But so afraid was the cinema manager and the local law, of copycat behavior every Police person in Brynmawr was on duty inside the cinema. Shoulder to shoulder they lined every inch of the walls that surrounded the cinema's seating area. I had never seen so many Policemen in my life. I felt as though their presence posed a challenge that could have provoked more violence than if there had been no Police present at all. Even so, we had all come to watch a movie and that is what we did with no unruly action taking place whatsoever. I was never really a Bill Haley fan, the music was okay but I didn't love his voice and didn't like the way he looked. But, as Dad didn't like him, I thought he at least deserved a chance. Then one of my friends asked me,

"Have you heard of this new rock 'n' roll singer from America? He's fantastic!"

"What new singer?" I asked.

"His name is Elvis Presley." He told me.

"Elvis Presley?!" I guffawed, "What kind of a bloody name is that?!" I thought that that was the silliest name I'd ever heard and that my friends were trying to rib me. They didn't seem to appreciate that I wasn't as enthused with Bill Haley as they were.

"Yeah, they call him 'Elvis the pelvis,' one of the others chimed in, "because he shakes his arse all over the place when he's singin'. Yeah, he's great!"

"Elvis the pelvis!" I snorted indignantly, "Now I know you're taking the piss!"

"No, honest Ade," they assured me, "Elvis Presley is real, he even looks a bit like you, even got the same sideburns."

"Bullshit! I proclaimed, "If you think I'll believe that crap, you're all nuts!" I was convinced they were pulling my leg. But it did play on my mind. If there wasn't an Elvis Presley that looked like me, there ought to be one. Next time I was in my favorite record shop in Ebbw Vale I would find out for sure. Once in the shop, I couldn't see anything that said Elvis Presley. With a shop full of customers I wasn't about to make a fool of myself by asking the proprietor. I hung about the store for about an hour and in order not to appear to be loitering I picked up a record called 'Shifting whispering sands.' It was performed by Eamonn Andrews who spoke the lyrics while a lady with a very beautiful soprano voice sang in the background. Eventually, when there was no one within earshot of the proprietor I went up to the counter and as quietly as possible asked him,

"Hurum, er, do you have anything by Elvis Presley?"

"Elvis Presley?!" He replied, making me blush with his too loud voice, "We're sold out of 'Blue suede shoes' but we've got a new one in today called 'Hound Dog.' Would you like to listen to it?" Even now I wasn't convinced and wondered if he could possibly be in on the joke.

"Yes, please." I answered quietly, deciding to take the risk. He handed me a record and sure enough, there it was written on the label 'Hound Dog' performed by Elvis Presley. I walked to a sound booth put on the turntable and almost got blasted back out again. I had never heard anything like it. IT WAS FANTASTIC! I can't say anything better than that, as all those groovy 'Rock 'n' roll' sayings hadn't been invented yet.

"I'll take it!" I yelled at the proprietor, "When are you going to get something else by Elvis Presley?!" I knew Dad wouldn't like Elvis. Especially if he resembled me and the fact that he wore sideburns, it was almost too much. I wore sideburns as it was a part of the Teddy-Boy fashion and my friends and I were all devout Teddy-Boys by nature. Even if we all lacked the Edwardian costumes that would have completed the image. I was envied by all the guys my age as I had been shaving since the age of thirteen and my sideburns were quite magnificent. The other guys would brush part of their hair down in front of their ears and have it styled to look like sideburns. But, when the wind blew, which was all the time in them thar hills, well I'm sure you can imagine.

Dad's reaction to my sideburns was,

"Get those stupid things shaved off, you look flaming well ridiculous!" Needless to say they had to stay. I had always gone to the same barber from my very first haircut up until my early Teddy-Boy days. I used to sit in the barber's chair and let him get on with it. But ever since I became fashion conscious, I always told the barber exactly the way I wanted it cut and he complied.

"Take a bit off the top, just enough off the sides and back for a good D.A. look and don't touch the sideburns." I would recite this every time I sat in the barber's chair. One day I had no sooner got to the bit about 'and don't touch the sideburns' when, with clippers in hand the demon barber shaved my left sideburn completely off. I stared at the mirror in complete disbelief at my reflection. I actually saw my jaw drop with shock and the barber smirk with satisfaction.

"What the fuck are you doing?!" I screamed, "Are you deaf, you stupid bastard?!"

"Sit still and shut up, you little whipper-snapper!" He snarled at me, "Your Father's been in and told me exactly how to cut your hair, so ---!" I shot out of the chair grabbed the barber by the throat and ran him backwards across his shop. I slammed him so hard into the wall that the whole shop shook, rattled and rolled with the impact.

"You stupid, fucking arsehole!" I shouted, I crushed his throat with my left hand. I brought my right fist back ready to beat his face to a pulp. Just then his glasses came unhinged off his left ear and dangled down over his mouth. That caused me to arrest my fist mid flight. Instead I grabbed him again with both hands and hurled him right across his shop into the corner. He cringed and whimpered like a whipped dog. I wanted to stamp on him so badly it hurt. I couldn't stop myself from hurling myself at him, but managed to check myself before I made contact. I transferred my aggression by sweeping all the barber's tools, bottles and jars from in front of the mirror all over the shop.

"I'll never come to this shit-hole again!" I barked at him, "And neither will any of my friends!" As I slammed the door behind me with a force that shook Brynmawr.

I was furious, with one hand covering the side of my face where I had a one sideburn deficit, I strode towards home as though I had springs on my feet. I couldn't wait to have it out with Dad, but then I checked myself once more. I spun around and marched back down Beaufort Street. On the corner stood Bernstein's Tailors shop which I entered and asked Mr. Bernstein to show me his fabrics and to take my measurements.

By the time I got home, I had simmered down enough to

inform Dad that I wouldn't be visiting his stooge barber again. I also reminded him that my hair grew very quickly. 3 weeks later I was gratified by Dad's scowling countenance as I brushed my much longer and thicker than ever sideburns. They set off the first Teddy-Boy suit I had ever seen in real life that Mr. Bernstein had made to my exact specifications. The suit was black and the jacket was finger tip length and also had a shawl collar of a contrasting maroon velvet with cuffs to match. The pants were described as 'drainpipe trousers' as they were worn as snug and as narrow as the size of the wearers legs would allow.

"Well I've seen it all now!" Dad grumbled, as he watched me preening in the mirror, "Do you realize how flamin' ridiculous you look?!" I had purposely dragged the preening out and waited patiently for this very response. I paused for effect and gave Dad's reflection that look. Then without uttering a word I walked over to the sideboard, opened a draw and retrieved a photo that I had planted there earlier. I placed it on the arm of Dad's chair. It was a photo of Dad aged seventeen wearing a big trilby hat and a suit that would have probably been the height of fashion in the late twenties. He looked like James Cagney on steroids.

"If I want to look flamin' ridiculous," I informed him, "I know exactly where to come for advice."

As I strode into the dancehall in Ebbw Vale later that evening, everyone stopped dancing as they saw me. By the time I had crossed the floor and assumed what I imagined was a suitable Teddy Boy stance, even the band had stopped. Every person present stood in a half circle around me, just to gaze at the first real Teddy-Boy suit they had ever seen. Looking back on this period I realize I was already learning many valuable lessons.

On the day I brought my first Elvis record home, I was for once pleased to see Dad was home. I put both records on so that 'Shifting, whispering sands' played first.

"Oh, isn't that woman's voice lovely," Dad said approvingly to Mam, "she sings like my Mother used to when she was young." He sat and listened blissfully. he sighed as it ended. Seconds later 'Hound Dog' hit the turntable and Dad nearly hit the ceiling,

"Good night alive!" He shrieked, "What the blazes is that?!"

Well 'Rock 'n' roll' was here to stay. I loved Little Richard,

Chuck Berry, Jerry Lee Lewis, Buddy Holley, Fats Domino, The Platters, The Everley Brothers and all the rest, but even then as far as I was concerned, ELVIS WAS THE KING!

THE SCREENS

When I first began work in Beynon's Colliery, it wasn't underground but on the screens. It was called the screens as everyone working there had to screen the coal that came down a huge metal conveyor. We took out any slag, rocks or ironstone before the remaining coal was dropped onto a revolving spiked metal drum we called the 'crusher.' It was called the crusher as it crushed the coal into small particles before it was dropped again into 13 ton railway trucks. The trucks shuttled continuously along a railway track which ran under the elevated screens building. It was horrible, like something out of a B rated science fiction horror movie of the World after Armageddon. A row of stooped, gaunt, dirty, miserable men on either side of the 6 foot wide, clanking, squealing, thundering, metal monstrosity. It spewed an endless supply of coal and rocks that was tipped from above, crashing down onto the metal conveyor with deafening force. It filled the air with dense clouds of black coal dust from endless lines of buggies that were disgorged from the bowels of the earth. It continued for the whole of our back breaking, lung corroding 8 hour shift. The foreman's name was Mr. Summers. And if this had been the set for a B rated science fiction horror movie, Summers would have been type cast as the creepy Arch-villain. Tall, raw boned, stooped shoulders and a face that would have frightened a ghost. I'm sure that he must have sensed my revulsion when we first met and we were both aware that we hated each other before we even spoke. He told me he was putting me on sledge and passed me an 8 pound sledge-hammer. I bragged sarcastically that it was too light. I should have kept my mouth shut he walked away and returned with the biggest sledge-hammer I had ever seen. I would be wielding it all day, 6 days a week. There were two of us on sledge, I was on the right side of the conveyor looking up towards the advancing coal. A big, burly, black haired, pale faced man who very rarely spoke was on the left, directly opposite me across the conveyor. We were both the last two men that the coal passed before the conveyor curved up to a height of about 10 feet above us. From there it dropped the coal onto the revolving spiked drum. Everyone else was divided equally between the left and right sides all the way along the conveyor. Summers always stood next to my sledge bearing counterpart across from me and always looked up the conveyor. That was not only to see any rubbish that may have been left by the screeners further up the belt, but also to keep his eye on them to make sure that they were all working hard. I started off very conscientiously, pulverizing every morsel of coal that came by. If a large piece of ironstone which often looked like coal passed by everyone else's notice, I would throw a piece of coal in front of Summers to gain his attention. Then point to the offending ironstone, Summers would turn and press a button that would stop the conveyor and I would jump onto the belt and remove the ironstone. Then Summers pressed the button to restart the conveyor. Ironstone was so called as it was as hard and as heavy as iron. If a large enough piece got by everyone's scrutiny and fell onto the revolving spiked crusher drum it could jam it, or even damage the machinery that drove it. Needless to say even if it only got jammed it would only take a minute to dump a ton or so of coal on top of it from the conveyor. That would not only stop work in the screens. If it took long enough to remove the coal on top of the crusher and fix the damage, it could also back up the buggies all the way down to the bottom of the pit. As I said, I started off very conscientiously. But one day I noticed a particularly large piece of ironstone chugging by. The quiet guy opposite, caught my eye and gave his head a little shake as I grabbed a small lump of coal and braced myself to throw it in front of the foreman. I stared at him for a few seconds, a little confused. He shook his head once more and it dawned on me that he wanted the ironstone to go by unmolested. With my heart in my mouth I let it pass and I saw the quiet guy smile for the first time. Two minutes later there was a loud, grinding, shuddering screech. It could be heard even above the normal thundering, crashing and clashing. Summers spun around in a flash and stopped the conveyor, but not before the spiked steel crusher was well and truly jammed.

I looked back guiltily at the quiet guy who returned my look of consternation with another quick smile and a wink. He walked over to a corner where he sat down for the next 40 minutes while the crusher was being cleared and un-jammed. It then dawned on me, that my shift was 8 hours long whether I was slogging my guts out the whole time. Or, whether some of it was spent resting while the crusher was being cleared and fixed after getting clogged by something that was allowed to pass by. From then on I would wield my hammer like a maniac, until Summers attention was on the belt in front of him. Then I would prop my backside on the side of the conveyor to take my weight off my legs, lay my hammer on my shoulder in readiness and watch Summers back. The second he glanced around in my direction I would throw my arse off the conveyor and smash at anything that might be in front of me with my hammer in one movement. That would look as though that was what I had been doing all along. The only person that was aware of my new lazy game was the quiet guy who was doing likewise. He would occasionally give me a little nod of approval.

'Great idea' I thought, 'I can reserve more of my energy for body-building when I get home.' It turned out to be a great idea that almost cost me my life.

****

I had seen a movie a few years earlier when I had first became interested in becoming a Wrestler, called 'Night and the City' starring Richard Widmark and Herbert Lom. The film was about professional wrestling and also featured Stanislaus Zbyszko, Mike Mazurki and British Olympic wrestler, Ken Richmond. I thought it was a great movie but in 1956 I saw two movies that really had a lasting impression on me.

The first was 'Somebody up there likes me' Starring Paul Newman. He played the part of the great Boxing champion, Rocky Graziano. Tony Zale, Rocky's nemesis played himself in the movie. The scenes depicting their legendary trilogy were almost as exciting as they had been in real life. The part that appealed to me the most, occurred before Rocky became a Boxer. He goes scrounging around a boxing gym hoping to make a few bucks for sparring. Rocky is in the ring sparring with a Boxer who is training for an upcoming main event. During their session he becomes unnecessarily rough with Rocky. Rocky gets pissed off, spits out his gum-shield and retaliates by laying the future championship contender out! In so doing, he catches the amazed eyes of the managers, trainers, promoter, etc, who are present in the gym. Oh wow! That was how I saw myself. Just wait until I get to London and the Wrestling World gets a load of me, they are not going to believe it! I couldn't wait.

The other movie was 'A kid for two farthings' starring Britain's Blond Bombshell and answer to America's Marilyn Monroe. The gorgeous Diana Dors. Wrestlers, Primo Carnera and 'Tiger' Joe Robinson, MC Francis Blake and referee Lou Marco were also in the film. Little did I realize at the time that many years later Britain's premier glamour girl, Diana Dors would become a very good friend of mine. I went to the cinema every night they were showing the above mentioned movies, I've also watched them many times since and never tired of them.

I then discovered to my delight that Wrestling was regularly held in The Drill Hall, in Dumfries Place, Cardiff. The awful drawback was that the last train from Cardiff left about an hour before the wrestling ended. I began going to Cardiff whenever the wrestling was on. Then had to run the couple of miles as fast as I could from the Drill Hall to the railway station as soon as the second match was over to catch the last train. That meant that I would miss the main event and the last match. Can you imagine how soul-destroying that was for me? To feel the audience starting to buzz with excitement, in anticipation of the upcoming Main Event and then have to leave. My imagination working overtime as I ran like a blue arsed fly through the streets of Cardiff to the station. Knowing that as I got further and further away, two of the biggest names in Wrestling would be entering the ring to do battle?

In Beynon's as the other workers began to learn that I was into wrestling and body-building I began to hear the names of two local body-building brothers, Colin and Dave Thomas. Colin, who I was told was the oldest and more accomplished of the two, had won Welsh body-building contests such as Mr. South Wales. One day at Brynmawr's outdoor swimming pool I saw a very well built man walking around the pool on his hands and rightly assumed he was Colin. I waited patiently until he once again became the right way up. I introduced myself and asked him if he was the fairly famous Colin Thomas.

"Yes, I am," he answered spreading his lats and smiling with pleasure at being recognized, "how big do you think my chest is?" With diplomacy in mind I estimated his chest was probably a couple of inches larger than my own.

"About forty-seven inches?" I answered.

"No it's forty-nine inches!" He informed me, "I can get it over fifty when I bulk up, - where do you train? – Would you like to work out with me? – I'm going for a workout right now, do you want to come?" That is how I began training with Mr. South-Wales. I remember writing to Ter who was still in the army and stationed in Germany that I was now training with a genuine, titled Body-builder. Soon after Ter came home from Germany, he left the army and began working again in Beynon's Colliery. He also began body-building and we worked out together.

Some of my friends were talking about getting tattooed and were wondering where they could get them done. I remembered hearing about a new tattoo club that had just opened the last time I was in Bristol and we decided to go and check it out. By the time I was on my way I found that I was the only one who hadn't chickened out and I journeyed to Bristol alone. Les Skuse of Bristol had become Britain's tattoo champion the year before in 1955. I admired thousands of designs all over the walls of his studio. I chose a Black Panther that left the bloody impression of its claws on my left forearm as it clung there while it battled with a multi-colored python.

By this time I was alternating between three different Teddy-Boy suits whenever I went to a dancehall. Now to show off my first tattoo I went back to wearing brightly colored skintight jeans and my old, black, V-necked, Weider T-shirt. That left my arms bare and my tattoo visible. My tattoo attracted so much attention that my friends were now begging me to take them to Bristol so they could get illustrated too. But, as I was enjoying my picturesque uniqueness I kept them waiting for almost a year.

The night I unveiled my tattoo in the dancehall my friends and I had grabbed ourselves a bag of 'fish and chips' each and was eating them as we made our way to the bus-stop. As we walked along the pavement I noticed coming towards me a face I hadn't seen for some time. It was Helen of the black knickers, arm-in-arm with a soldier. She was wearing his hat and was laughing hysterically as they both weaved about the sidewalk. She seemed to be carrying on like a real slag and I don't know if it was jealousy, but the sight of her antics sickened me. They both almost collided with me before they were aware of my presence and I seemed to react without thinking.

"Have a chip!" I grunted as I flung my bag of greasy fish and chips right into Helen's silly face. The soldier was very fast, he got as far as saying,

"What th----?!" before I decked him with one punch in the face. He bounced once on the flagstones before Helen squawked with fury and leapt at my face with clawed hands. I checked her mid flight and gave her a mighty shove that sent her crashing down to the pavement. She landed arse first on top of the soldiers head, rolled backwards over him with her shapely legs in the air and gave me an action replay of her black knickers in the lamplight. Even though Ebbw Vale is only about 3 miles from Brynmawr, I never set eyes on Helen again, BUT - my last view of her is one I shall always cherish.

****

One would imagine that as the screens were not underground, it would be, - apart from the awful dust and terrible noise, a comparatively safe place to work.

Tom Porter worked on the same side of the conveyor as me, but closer to the middle, about a dozen or so yards away. Poor Tom wasn't right in the head, he seemed be in a world of his own. Although he was capable of working on the screens as proficiently as the next man, he would not have been considered mentally fit for work underground. Tom would talk to himself constantly and his arm waving, gestures and facial expressions suggested he was continually having a very heated argument with an invisible being. If you spoke to him he would look at you a little dazed and smile. Then you would probably need to repeat what you said. Once you had his attention he was very capable of carrying on a normal conversation, with the exception of his ability to believe almost anything anyone told him. The incident involving Tom happened as simply as this. He just reached across the conveyor as he did countless thousands of times a day and dragged a huge, heavy chunk of ironstone towards him in order to roll it off the conveyor. As he pressed his thighs against the guard to give himself more leverage he unconsciously squeezed his genitals over it. As he heaved the massive lump of rock towards him it crushed his genitals between the ironstone rock and the steel guard. I don't know if he mashed his dick, his balls, or the whole set. I saw the agony on his face and watched in horror as the whole front of his trousers filled with blood. I don't know if he was lucky enough to pass out but he was still rolled up into a tight ball as they lifted him off the ground and carried him out to where he could be transported to Hospital.

The second incident concerned me. Whenever Summers' lack of attention in my direction allowed. I would prop my backside on the guard and would happily allow any huge crusher clogging lumps of coal, ironstone or slag to sail by. The place where I always sat was exactly where the steel conveyor began its upward curve. With the tremendous wear and tear exacted on the conveyor by the constant dumping of ton after ton of coal, rock and slag onto it from above, eventually damaged most of the steel plates. But, as long as they were not twisted enough to impede the movement of the conveyor, the damage was completely ignored. This resulted in some very bad luck for me. I sat on the conveyor guard watching the back of Summers' head on the day in question. A badly twisted steel plate caught my trousers and almost the whole left cheek of my arse as it began to curve upwards. It squeezed tightly together with the plate in front and dragged me bodily backwards up the inclining conveyor. I glided towards the drop and the spinning, spiked crusher. The agony of having the whole of my left buttock crushed between two steel plates was enough for me to exercise my powerful lungs to their utmost capacity. I hollered for attention, but even lungs as powerful as mine was no match for the consistent thunderous crashing of the screens. I sat there in agony, slowly creeping backwards watching as everyone including the quiet man was looking up the belt while I was traveling in the opposite direction. I was horrorstruck to think that within a few more short minutes, I would be crashing down onto a huge revolving, spiked steel drum. The Crusher was designed to crush large lumps of coal into granules and dust and there wasn't a damn thing I could do about it. I couldn't have been much more than a yard away from the end of the conveyor and the end of me, when I drew level with a couple of iron scaffold pipes. The pipes helped support the elevated part of the conveyor and then carried on upward to help support part of the roof. I made a grab for it realizing it was my one and only chance to save myself from something unimaginable. I twisted and held onto it with both hands and then managed to hook my right leg around it. The pain I suffered as I managed to tear the cheek of my arse from between two steel plates was a very small price to pay in order to avoid the alternative. I was about 10 feet above the concrete floor and when I landed it was flat on my back knocking the wind right out of my body. The back of my head also crashed onto the rock hard floor, but luckily I was still wearing my helmet. I must have lain motionless and completely winded for about 20 minutes. No one else knew a thing about what had just happened to me. That in itself made the whole thing worse. No one came to my aid. No one offered any sympathy. Nobody did anything. At that very second I could have already been minced into ground meat and mixed into 13 tons of small coal. Not one single soul on earth would have known anything about it. Even my family would probably have thought that I had run away to the bright beaconing lights of London and away from the aggravation of Dad and the coal-mine. Eventually I got up on my own. I staggered back up the screens until I was level with Summers. Threw a rock at him to get his attention. Opened the tear in my tattered trousers to reveal my mangled arse. Watch as his mouth as it dropped in unison with his risen eyebrows, I pointed to the exit and left the screens for the first aid room. The whole of my left buttock was a navy blue bruise decorated with scratches caused by the tearing of my flesh from between the steel plates. I was made furious by the lack of attention and disbelief in the story of my adventure when I related it to everyone who would listen. But I suppose in fairness to the unbelievers, the years of tall tales of charging Buffalo and bloodthirsty Grizzly Bears may have tarnished my credibility a tad.

I was still smarting both physically and mentally as I stood poised with my big sledge-hammer. I was opposite Summers when Tom Porter who had just started back to work entered the building and I heard Summers say to no one in particular.

"Oh, the idiot is back!" I flew into an almost uncontrollable rage and called him all the 'fucking stupid bastards' I could lay my tongue on. He hadn't turned the conveyor on for the day so everyone on the screens, much to Summers embarrassment was witness to my savage outburst. The best part of it was that no one including Summers himself was aware of the reason for it. Summers blanched and left the building. When he returned he informed me that the Colliery manager was waiting in his office to see me, so I left the screens never to return.

****

I was desperate to get into a real wrestling ring. I began to inquire if there was a club anywhere in any of the towns in our vicinity that taught wrestling and had a ring to practice it in. None of the little gang of Teds I usually hung around with had a clue. There was Beynon Jones, Graham Foot, who we called 'Footy,' Brian Heath, who we called 'The Black Rat' and Mower. Mower's whole family were known for being very tough and proficient Boxers in the ring and very dangerous, quarrelsome thugs in every bar they frequented. Mower, although also renowned for his Boxing skills, seemed to be the 'white sheep' of his family. He was always a very nice, friendly and funny guy to be around and we always had a lot of fun together. But I became so desperate to get into a ring that I even asked Mower where I could learn to Box. It was for no other reason than I wanted to know what it felt like to stand in a ring. Mower made some inquiries but didn't seem to have any more luck than I did. Soon we both began to meet after work and travel to a different town in our area every day in search of a Boxing club. This must have gone on for weeks but no luck. We both became so frustrated that Mower told me he had plenty of boxing gloves he could borrow from his home. They belonged to him, his Dad, Brothers and Uncles and we could Box each other any time we wanted to. In our frustration we both seem to have lost sight of what I'd wanted in the first place and that was a real ring to wrestle in. Mower and I met as prearranged the following Sunday in a small park they called The Welfare. As promised he brought with him a couple of pairs of Boxing gloves. He helped me tie my gloves, as I had never ever worn boxing gloves before. He then squeezed his fists into his own and we began to circle each other. We began sparring on a large green area and I soon realized there was much too much room to suit my limited boxing skills. Mower immediately began throwing stiff straight jabs, which I managed to block skillfully with my face. When I went on the attack I missed him with every vicious haymaker I threw. Although I could see that the wind from my fists as they whizzed harmlessly by was really beginning to weaken him. I also knew that his own fist could never survive the savage punishment they were receiving as they bounced off my eyes, nose, mouth and granite hard jaw. I knew without a shadow of a doubt that he was mine for the taking; it was just a matter of time. Two hours later, with a head like an overcrowded Bee hive. Every single Bee a point of pain. With a face that only Lon Chaney could love. My fists were still in pristine condition and that's the way they remained. As I attempted for the 939th time to charge him he stopped me dead in my tracks with an almighty punch! I thought it had broken my neck and killed every Bee that was buzzing in my head. A volcano erupted in my skull and spilled red hot lava out of my nose and mouth in the form of a fountain of blood.

"OUCH!!!" I said. That concluded my first Boxing lesson. Although my performance may have left a little room for improvement, I did learn a lot, - first and foremost - don't Box.

Later the next week after work, I was taking a shower and covered with huge clouds of black and grey soap suds that I hadn't yet began to rinse off. Mower with a towel around his waist and already as clean as a new pin after his shower came sauntering by on his way to his clean clothes locker.

"How that Devil are you Mower old chap?" I said to him as I playfully slapped him on the back covering him with filthy, grey black suds.

"FUCK OFF, YOU IDIOT!" He screamed in my face, "I'm in a hurry and I don't have time for your shit!" I was more than a little taken aback. What I had just done to him was normal behavior for us. I'd done the same thing to him and my other friends dozens of times before as they had also done to me. His attitude shocked and annoyed me. I also noticed it turned a lot of heads in our vicinity, but I simply said to him,

"Hey, Mower what's wrong with you today?" He glared at me savagely,

"Not as much as will be wrong with you if you ever do that again!" He threatened in a voice loud enough to cause a landslide on Mount Everest. Already he was causing interest all around us.

"What will you do about it if I do?" I asked him.

"Beat the fuckin' shit out of you, that's what I'll do!" He shouted his voice getting louder still. He obviously wanted everyone in the Colliery to hear his threats, which made it impossible for me to let it go.

"Who's going to help you?!" I inquired, "Your Father, Brothers and Uncles?!"

"I don't need any help from anyone to kick your arse!" He boasted, "And if you've got the guts, I'll see you on the slag tip!"

"Okay I'll be there." I told him.

"Don't keep me waiting!" He warned me as he marched off to dress. I was amused to see he still had the filthy suds on his back. My blood soon started to boil as I heard his voice still threatening what he intended doing to me in his quest to gather an audience. I knew that his new found bravery was a direct result of the beating he had given me in the Park where he hadn't had an audience to satisfy his ego.

When I arrived at the slag heap which was on the Colliery land, I found that his loud vocal promoting had really paid off for him. More than half the pit's miners were waiting to watch me get my comeuppance. I had always been a very cocky, boastful, arrogant kid. I was never stuck for an answer and gave back any insult as good if not better than I ever received. So no one wanted to miss the punishment I was about to receive. I realized that even though I had been the one who had been challenged, I was going to be regarded by most of the onlookers as the bad guy in this confrontation. I was strangely comforted by the thought. The reason being I felt I had nothing to prove. It was going to be up to Mower this time round to make the play. Instead of me having to chase him all around the place and get picked off in the process. I

213

was also happy to see no sign of Dad or Ter as that would definitely have cramped my style. Mower was standing waiting for me and couldn't wait to get started and was unable to conceal his excitement. I walked to within a few paces of him and then just stood and folded my arms.

"Okay, Twat!" I challenged, "Let's see what you've got!" Straight away I knew that I had an advantage now that I hadn't had a few days before. I had placed the ball neatly in his court and to prove himself to all his new supporters he had to come to me.

He put up his fists and began his bobbing and weaving. I just stood and sneered,

"Ouch! That hurt," I sniggered sarcastically, "tell me when the fight starts so I'll know when to scream." A couple of onlookers chuckled which caused Mower to throw caution to the wind and he rushed at me slugging.

"Yahoow!!!" He screamed, "Okay-okay, I give up!"

"Are you sure about that?!" I asked him, adding a little bit more pressure as I pulled back on his jaw.

"Yeah, AAAAAHH!" He shrieked. I was kneeling on his back as he lay on his stomach where he had been slammed. I was dragging his head back with my hands locked under his jaw till the back of his head was level with his arse.

"What was that?!" I asked him again for good measure, "Have you had enough?"

"Yeeeees!" He screamed. The moment Mower had put himself within reach I grabbed him and hurled him face first into the slag and coal-dust covered ground. I knelt on him and yanked back his head. He had not even come close to landing a blow.

But, when I let him up he was furious and totally unrepentant, "Come on let's go again!" he shouted dramatically, he got a cheer from all around, off miners who didn't want to be short changed for action.

"It's up to you," I warned him, "but if we fight again, I am going to hurt you." He came at me swinging.

"Yahoow!!!" He screamed, "Okay I've had enough!"

"No you haven't, not this time!" I told him, "This time I'll tell you when you've had enough!" I had him in exactly the same position as he'd been in previously. This time I pulled his jaw back with my left hand while I battered his upturned face with the edge of the other as though I was stabbing it with an invisible dagger. When I tired of that I smashed his face down into the slag and rubbed it back and forth for good measure.

"Let him up!" Demanded one of the onlookers.

"Yes, that's enough! Shouted another one, "Leave him alone!"

"Would any of you like to take his place?!" I challenged and as I eyed them all, I savagely continued punching Mowers face in emphasis. Then I rolled him over in order to get to work on a new angle. When I did get up I was greeted with looks of disgust while Mower looked as though he'd been run over by a Bulldozer.

"Why don't you learn to fight properly?!" One of them demanded.

"What, like him?!" I replied pointing down at the bloody heap in the dust, "No thanks, I think I'll stick to my own game plan!"

"You're a bad looser, Streety!" Another one added.

"Losing is something I don't intend becoming good at!" I told him, "And I didn't lose, - he did!" I added as I pointed again at Mower, then to Mower I said,

"Go get yourself a shower and clean yourself up, you filthy, disgusting bastard!"

The strangest thing about this story, was the fact that Mower, who I'd considered to be a friend would behave in the manner that he did. What was even stranger for me still and this is a real Ripley's, - we soon became friends again! Not only did he apologize to me in front of the rest of the gang. He even described the fight to them with great emphasis on my skill and savagery and his own naivety in thinking he stood any kind of chance against me in a serious fight. He admitted blatantly, unrepentantly, even cheerfully that after our Boxing practice he was sure he could beat me. He thought that if he did it again in public he would enhance his own tough guy reputation even though it would be at my expense. – But Hey, what are friends for?!

I forgave him, as his eloquence when relating my easy but devastating triumph over him appealed to my ego, but at the same time I came to the conclusion that if you have friends and family, you sure as hell, don't need enemies!

Talking of enemies, the war on the home front was still going strong with no chance of a cease fire. I had stopped going to Sunday school the moment I had started work in the pit. Dad and I had a flaming row over it and as far as I was concerned that was the end of it, but Dad would not leave it alone. Each weekday was bad enough. Every time I saw him he'd find something to moan about. Rock 'n' roll music, What time I came in last night. The way I dressed. My hair, especially my sideburns, My body-building. I noticed he never criticized Ter when we worked out with the weights together. But, if he was a drag to be around during the week, Sunday was murder. I've got the feeling, even now that Dad was a very reluctant Christian and would also have preferred to stay at home himself but didn't have the guts to risk God's wrath.

Mam was a great cook and Sunday dinners were the most important event in a Welshman's week. But the days were gone when I could sit at the table with the rest of the family and enjoy my Sunday dinner in peace. Dad without fail would start nagging as soon as we were seated. He would say grace, then resume his nagging between and around every mouthful. It didn't improve my appetite. It didn't improve my digestion and it certainly didn't improve my mood or my disposition regarding Dad. It wasn't long before I would take my dinner off the table, carry it upstairs and eat it while I sat on the edge of my bed. WITH the door firmly locked, just in case grizzle guts crept up to impart any more little gems of wisdom. Or any of the other bullshit he was capable of.

"Which one is mine?" I'd ask Mam - and if Dad looked too smug when watching me depart, I'd hesitate, turn my eyes up to the Heavens and say,

"OY God thanks for the grub, mind you, you didn't cook it, - Mam did!"

I remember one day, standing in the living-room, warming my arse by the fire. I was facing the open door of the kitchen where Dad was helping Mam with the meal she was preparing. Mam was cooking, Dad was buttering bread. I can't remember what he was grousing about on that particular occasion, but I was getting it full blast. He'd come out of the kitchen nagging and as he had the butter-knife in his hand, he was using it instead of his usual forefinger to do his gesturing. I stood watching him in dejected silence. He'd go back into the kitchen carry on with his buttering, think of something else he wanted to impart, come back and nag some more. Just when I thought I couldn't take any more he came in poking away with his butter-knife and I noticed a huge lump of butter on the end of it. The sight of his red angry face as he parried in emphasis with a knife and a lump of butter looked so ridiculous that I burst out laughing in his face. Dad's face turned from angry to furious and he charged and tried to stab me in the stomach with the knife. I grabbed his arm and wrist with both my hands but the force of his charge and thrust, pushed me arse first into the fireplace and completely off balance. He added the strength of his left hand and then the weight of his chest to push the knife into me. I managed to drop sideways onto one knee onto the hearth which gave me back some balance and placed the end of the blade past my body. I was still in a hot position both from the fire in the grate and the fire of Dad's horrible temper. As I pushed myself back to my feet Mam who came running from the kitchen and added her weight. She tried to push her way between us and we all staggered in a weird, wonky waltz across the room until we hit the sideboard. Mam succeeded in calming Dad down and he retreated to the kitchen. He was still nagging and still gesturing with the butter-knife. Strangely enough still had some of the butter on the end, but for me it had somehow lost a lot of its comic qualities. - Oh well, I can't say I didn't get a good Christian upbringing.

If you imagine Dad had to be in a bad mood to get a little murderous, let me give you another example of what he was capable of.

Dai Hughes had come to call for me to go the club. Dad who seemed to be in a good mood was chatting with him amiably while sitting in his favorite armchair beside the fireplace. I was looking in the mirror above the fireplace whilst combing my hair prior to leaving the house with Dai.

"Are you two going wrestling Dai?" Dad asked Dai, who was standing against the wall across the room.

"Yes, Mr. Street." Answered Dai.

"Are you getting any good at it?" Asked Dad.

"Yes, I think so Mr. Street," replied Dai, "but not as good as Adrian."

"Have you seen this hold?" He said to Dai, as he grabbed my right leg and upended me onto the carpet in front of the fire. He chuckled away with triumph as he caught hold of my foot and ankle and twisted it while he was still sitting in the his chair. I had been taken completely by surprise, by his jovial mood and by his sudden move. I made a grab for Dad's left foot and applied a similar hold. We both laughed as we began to engage in a leg twisting contest with Dai as referee. This went on for a couple of minutes and I was happy to take advantage of one of Dad's very rare displays of congeniality. Then he suddenly cried out in pain, his face became furious and as I quickly let him go in response he kicked me viciously in the stomach and shouted,

"You stupid fool; you've twisted my knee out!"

I jumped up, both shocked and embarrassed, especially as Dai had witnessed it.

"I thought we were playing!" I shouted at him, "Don't you ever do that to me again!" My outburst was as much to try to save face in front of Dai as anything else. But Dad shot out of his seat like a jack-in-the-box. I checked him with both my hands on his chest and pushed him back into his chair. Almost like a rebound Dad hurtled out of the chair in an explosion of action. Like lightening he had gathered the steel poker from the fireplace all in one movement. He carried the momentum around in an ark, almost a full circle and brought it down on my head with a force that filled my vision with a million electric sparks. As the poker rose for strike number two I made a grab for it even though I could feel a sickening swoon enveloping my body and the strength drop out of my legs. Somehow as we both grappled for possession of the poker it ended up still in Dad's hand but trapped under my left arm. Dad struggled to pull it out and I struggled to keep it there. I managed in spite of my wobbly legs to push Dad back against the fireplace. He must have used it as a leverage to push back with one of his feet as I found myself suddenly flying backwards. I landed on my back on the settee which faced the fireplace with Dad on top of me. The poker which was still locked under my arm ripped right through the back of the settee and Dad was still fighting furiously for possession of it. He managed to extract it enough to twist it across my throat. Although he was on top of me baring down with all his weight with the poker across my throat my predicament wasn't quite as bad as it sounds. Luckily for me the back of the settee was just firm enough to support my elbows. I locked them like props as I held the poker in both hands which helped prevent it from crushing my throat and completely cutting off my wind. It also gave me a chance to gather my scattered thoughts. Dad was concentrating on pushing down on the poker and retaining possession of it. I brought up my legs and wrapped them around Dad's waist high enough to crush the sides of his lower ribs. I've always had very strong legs, they were no longer wobbly and as I began to squeeze Dad's advantage began to evaporate – and brother, did I squeeze. Every time I squeezed, he'd gasp in air, I'd relax but keep the pressure of my legs tight and wait for him to breathe out. When he did I'd tighten my grip a little more. This would make him gasp and as he'd breathe out again I'd squeeze again, - bit by bit, tighter and tighter. When I felt the time was right and I was certain he had other things on his mind. I pushed with all my might against the poker straightening my arms which gave me the room I needed to release my grip with my legs. I brought my feet up into his body and pushed with all the strength of my legs while I yanked the poker back towards me. Dad crashed into the fireplace and didn't even have time to burn his arse before I was on him poker in hand. I came so close to hitting him with it. Instead I beat it on the fire in a display of fury that an Alfa-male Silverback would have been proud of. I whisked Dad back onto his feet with my left hand, raised the poker in my right, just to show him the possibilities. Instead I spun him around and hurled him back into his favorite armchair. He gave me a look of sheer loathing and I echoed it right back at him as I stood above him weighing the poker in my hand.

"Get out of this house; I never want to see you again." He hissed. I gave him one of my best sneers, hurled the poker into the fireplace, stepped back in front of the mirror picked up the comb from where I had dropped it and began resuming my grooming.

All this time poor Dai had been standing against the wall and pretended not to notice what was going on. I could still feel the hatred of Dad's glare boring into me but continued tidying myself up and ignored him completely. As Dai and I were walking out of the house, I turned to Dad and said,

"I've told you before this isn't your house, it's our house and if you don't like that you can piss off yourself. I am going to leave and it can't be too soon for me, but I'll leave when I'm ready, not when you say!" I left the house before he could retaliate, slamming the door behind me.

****

After my outburst at Summers, the creepy foreman of Beynon's screens who had ordered my march to the Pit manager's office. You may wonder how I still came to be working in the Colliery. The only reason, I was told by the manager, was as a special favor to Dad, who he told me was a respected worker of long standing --- bla-bla-bla! And so on. Obviously I wouldn't be able to work on the screens anymore if Summers was to preserve any face after our screaming match. So until they could decide what else to do with me I was put to work unloading slag and rock out of railway trucks. I was a temporary replacement for some of the regulars who were taking their summer holidays.

I was given two 13 ton trucks to unload and a whole working day to complete the job. A piece of cake I thought. Most of the other men working on the trucks were skinny, scrawny specimens. I stripped to the waist, flexed a bit for their benefit and began to show them how to unload rocks. I'd been doing it in the garden for Dad since I was 7, after having to dig them out of the ground first. Plus I was a very strong body-builder and they weren't, so this was a perfect opportunity to show off my rock moving superiority. That's what I thought, but then somehow, something got lost in the translation! While I was still struggling to finish off my first truck most of the others were half way through their second. They were all completely finished by the time I had made an impression on my second truck. Every one of them finished unloading both their 13 ton trucks then sat on a grassy bank, while they enjoyed watching me try to race with the clock. Would I complete my work by the time the two-thirty p.m. hooter blew to end our shift? I did with about 45 seconds to spare, but was almost too spent to climb out of the truck. In spite of all my body-building and supposed physical superiority I ached everywhere and wondered after my first day if I was going to make it to the shower room. By the time I had worked on the trucks for 3 weeks I was able to keep up with the best of them. But, I never surpassed them or ever finished first, as I'd made it my secret and private goal to accomplish. By then all the regular workers had returned from their vacations and I was transferred to moving logs. I quite liked that job. The foreman would show me which pile of wooden props he wanted moved and where they were to be re-stacked first thing in the morning. I wouldn't see him again until my shift was almost over for the day. I always worked alone and worked hard as I always got a kick out of the surprise the foreman would display at the amount of props I had shifted. I was quite content, but it didn't last long. An extra hand was needed in the maintenance of the Colliery's wind-roads, so I began work with Gurnos. Gurnos Jones, although being ex Mayor of Brynmawr had also been the sole maintenance worker in the wind-roads for years. Gurnos was growing older and the worse for wear and so were the wind-roads. The purpose of the wind-roads was to supply the whole of the many miles of underground workings with fresh air. The circulation also helped to prevent the buildup of toxic gases. The air was pumped down an old disused shaft from the surface and by way of the wind-roads to every part of the pit. It was our job to keep all the tunnels in good repair and working order. A Colliery fireman would periodically inspect different sections of the wind-roads and then give us a list of the repairs required. Or old abandoned tunnels to be blocked off, so as not to waste air and keeps it flowing where it was most needed. He would then come and inspect our work, usually towards the end of each shift. Gurnos was a lazy, wily old git and I was soon to discover that I now had two jobs. The first would be performing whatever task the fireman had set us for that day, - on my own. The second would be to keep an eye and a ear wide open for a possible unexpected visit from the fireman, so that I could warn Gurnos and prevent him from being caught sleeping. Which in the coalmine was a very serious offence. It turned out to be the easiest job I ever had while working in the pit. In fact the hardest part very often was trying to stay awake myself in order to wake and warn Gurnos that I could see the fireman's lamp light flashing in the distance. Each day I would finish whatever task was set for us as quickly as I could. Gurnos would find somewhere to make himself comfortable for a hard days snoozing. If I was tired I would join Gurnos, or more often go for a walk and explore in every direction, the farthest reaches of the very extensive wind-roads. Most people would imagine the miles of dank tunnels in the coal mines to be a dark, dusty, dangerous, depressing, unhealthy, black hell-hole – and they'd be correct. But, some of the sights I witnessed on my wanderings were wonderful to behold. There was fungus in all shapes and sizes. Mostly growing like fluffy clouds or snow drifts which sometimes seemed to flow for dozens of yards across the ground. Up the walls, hanging from the ceiling in every conceivable shape and design. Sculptured by the constant wind, you only had to gaze at it to see anything that you wanted to see. Some of the colors were breathtaking, from the whitest white, to every pale pastel shade imaginable. Where those gorgeous shades originated I can only wonder at, from various minerals, old rotting timbers? I don't know, but what I do know is some of the sights I saw was almost worth the ordeal of working at Beynon's Colliery. Sights I appreciated that I shared with very few people on earth. Even the other coal miners, most of whom were not even aware that the wind-roads existed let alone my fabulous, fantastic fungus. It was on such a walk, or on this particular occasion a run. That I hit my helmet lamp on an overhead beam with such a force that it almost turned me upside down and plunged into the blackest darkness that it's possible to experience. My lamp was completely smashed and I must have been almost a couple of miles away from where I had left 'Sleeping Beauty'. I was lucky that where I had been running there was still an old buggy rail on whose ties I had been pacing myself as I ran. I used it to crawl along and feel my way back to where I could once again see Gurnos's lamp light.

I found that working with Gurnos was as agreeable to me as it was possible to get in Beynon's Colliery. When I had left school I stood a little over 5 feet, 5 inches and weighed 135 pounds. In order to become a professional Wrestler I wanted to get as big as I could. Although I ate like a horse in order to help achieve more size, I had been working far too hard in the pit to be able to gain any weight. I was also body-building every day when I got home. In fact I had gained no weight at all until I began working with Gurnos. In the few months I was with him I gained exactly 40 pounds. My chest now measured 45 inches, 2 inches bigger than Dad's and I also grew a couple of inches taller. Things seemed to be getting on track - until I got transferred again. It must have been my extra size that decided them that I was ready for the coalface.

A few days after starting work on the coalface I had called into the Blacksmith shop at the head of the Colliery to pick up my mandrill shaft that I had brought in the afternoon before to be sharpened. As a result I barely caught the last cage down the pit before the 7 a.m. hooter blew. After that empty buggies would be the only things allowed to go down the shaft. I had a couple of miles to walk from the pit bottom to the coal face that I had been assigned to. As I was a little later than normal I was not surprised to see that the entrance to the face where the miners usually gathered before starting work was deserted. But as I approached the entrance four figures shot out of the darkness. They grabbed me, lifted me into the air, slammed me into the ground and pinned me down with the weight of four heavy bodies. I hadn't even recovered from the shock when I recognized 'Big' Claude's voice as he demand of one of my other assailants, - "Okay Billy, give me the razor!"

****

Back at home I had still been suffering 'The Wrath of Dad'. Sister Pam told me a story recently concerning him, that I had never been aware of before.

I had came home from work ravenous as usual and had found that the dinner wasn't quite ready. Dad was late and Mam was holding it back for his benefit. There was a big cream sponge cake sitting in the middle of the table that was for dessert. I cut myself a slice to tide myself over till dinner was ready and then went out into the back garden to lift weights in order to pass the time. In the meantime Dad came home as Mam and Pam were preparing the table for our meal. Instead of saying hello, he asked,

"Who's been eating the cake?!"

"Oh, Adrian had a slice when he came in from work, he was hungry and dinner wasn't ready." Mam told him. Dad glared, grabbed a knife and divided the whole of the remaining cake into four huge wedges, one each for the rest of the family.

"Right he's had his now, so he's not getting any more!" Declared Dad with satisfaction. When Mam called me in for dinner and we all sat down. Pam said she sat there on tender hooks hardly able to eat as she waited for the confrontation to begin that Dad had devised. I apparently sat enjoying my meal, quite oblivious of the storm that was waiting to erupt while poor Pam was almost bilious with apprehension. Dad was poised ready to pounce. While I'd been eating I had been idly thumbing through a 'Boxing and Wrestling' magazine and was unaware of the tense atmosphere. I pushed my plate away and reached out my hand automatically for a slice of cake, that was the moment Dad had been waiting for,

"Put that back! He boomed, "You've already had yours and there's one slice each for the rest of us!" My cake bearing hand hovered between the plate and my mouth as Sister Pam, not knowing how else to defuse the situation said,

"Oh, I don't want any cake, Adrian can have my piece."

PLOP! The cake went into my mouth and I carried on eating it, as I carried on thumbing through my magazine. I was oblivious of Pam's sigh of relief and Dad trembling with frustration at the foiling of his latest master plan. It fell well shy of his spiteful intention to piss me off. Pam told me that her mouth had been watering with anticipation all day at the very thought of eating a slice of one of her favorite treats. But suffered the supreme sacrifice in order to avert the row that Dad was hoping to instigate. What proves how miserably his little plan failed was that I was still completely unaware of it until Pam enlightened me over 40 years later.

****

My love of colorful and flamboyant costumes didn't begin with my love of professional wrestling. From my earliest memories of my obsession of Red Indians. With their feathered headdresses, beaded and fringed buckskin and ferocious painted faces. To my blond haired, blue painted Celtic ancestors. Armored medieval Knights and right up to the colorful Hussars, Cuirassiers, Dragoons and Lancers of the 18th and 19th century. I have always been totally fascinated. I have often been asked why I was never interested in becoming a soldier myself. But from the time powerful and accurate rifles made colorful uniforms obsolete, only to be replaced by drab khaki and earth colors any former appeal evaporated. "Anyway I wouldn't look good in camouflage," I told them, "I was made to be seen." - That's always been my opinion, but as you may guess, not everyone shared my viewpoint.

From the time I went to school face painted and done up like an Indian I had received criticism, if not ridicule for the way I dressed. The Teddy-boy or Edwardian suits worn in those days by my friends and I were either admired or hated and I found that criticism could be amusing or very insulting. According to who was doing it, - I'll give you a couple of examples.

A few of us were walking down Beaufort Street, when a large woman stepped out of a shop doorway blocking our passage. She stood in front of me scowling. I felt it would probably take too long to walk all the way around her so we stopped and observed her expectantly. The street was quite crowded and as she was aware she had an audience, the woman heaved up her huge chest, placed her fists on her sidewalk blocking hips. Looked me up and down for effect and bawled at me in a loud voice,

"Huh - and where's the rest of the Circus?!" She got a few gratifying chortles and sniggers from surrounding pedestrians but not as many as I got when I answered,

"They are all gathering in the Market Square for a parade Madam - and if you hurry up and waddle on down there you'll find yourself in luck. The Ringmaster is desperately looking for a new Fat-Lady!"

So we thought the insult we got from fatso was funny, but on the other occasion. I was standing in front of the Market Hall Cinema one evening and had just met with a girl on a first date. I was startled by an exaggerated, screeching laugh which exploded right behind me. I turned to discover the author of the disturbance and came face to face with Bobby Wilkins and his fiancé. The fiancé was blatantly pointing her finger at me and both she and Wilkins were shaking with laughter and obviously at my expense. I wouldn't have taken kindly to that sort of behavior at the best of times but right in front of a new girlfriend made it doubly offensive. What made it triply offensive was the fact that Bobby Wilkins was a very skillful amateur Boxer and must have thought that his reputation would be sufficient incentive to dissuade any retaliation. But to me that made it worse. I forgot about the new girlfriend and advanced menacingly on Wilkins,

"Who the fuck are you laughing at?!" I roared sweetly. That sobered Wilkins' face a little, - but only a little. Still with a sickening smirk on his face he replied,

"Watch your filthy mouth when there's ladies present Street. Or I'll punch all the teeth out of it!"

"I'd love to see you try!" I roared charmingly, "And what fucking ladies are you talking about?!" For the first time I got a straight face from him which was the only satisfaction I got. He narrowed his eyes, clenched his jaw and said pointing his finger,

"I've warned you, if I was on my own I'd spread you all over the square!" and with that Wilkins turned on his heel and disappeared with his fiancé into the Cinema. - I was furious! If I had been on my own, I may have even followed them into the Cinema. But realized in spite of my fury that the Cinema was hardly an appropriate battle ground. I dearly wanted to commit grievous bodily harm on Boxer Bobby Wilkins. 'Never mind,' I thought to myself, 'Brynmawr is not a big town, there'll be another time.'

****

I struggled in vain as Billy fished out the open razor and handed it to 'Big' Claude, who then flicked it open and brandished it in front of my face for effect.

"What the hell are you doing?!" I wheezed apprehensively. The weight of the four heavy bodies held my arms and legs securely as they pressed down on my chest and constricted my heaving lungs.

"What your Father asked us to do!" replied Big Claude, "Shaving off your stupid sideburns!" My temper immediately exploded. Even though I had been pinned to the ground helplessly one second the mention of Dad's ridiculous plan to deprive me of my prize sideburns sent me into a raving fit of fury. First I managed to free one foot from one of my captors and I lashed out viciously with my steel toe capped boot it connected with one of the other miner's heads. His helmet protected him from any damage but it flew off his head with the force of my kick. The impetus of the kick helped to twist my body around and one of my arms became free. - The arm whose fist still held the freshly sharpened pick shaft. WHAM! I smashed it right at Big Claude's fat, sloppy face, but luckily for him it caught the rim of his helmet. With a leg and a hand wielding the deadly pick shaft free my four assailants leapt off me and ran. There was only two directions they could go. Two dived into the coal face and the other two, one of which was Big Claude ran back up the tunnel, I went after Claude. Although Big Claude was under 6 feet in height he weighed in excess of 230 pounds and the pit bottom was about 2 miles away so we both knew he couldn't escape. But I was still so furious that I stopped in mid charge and flung my needle sharp pick blade after him with all my might. Sparks flew and the whole tunnel rattled as the steel missile struck one of the supporting steel rings. It bounced on striking the next and the next and the next. Big Claude screamed like a big girl and the shock that I may have killed him stopped me in my tracks and brought me back to my senses. But only temporarily, when I ran to where my pick shaft had landed fearing the worst, I found that Big Claude's bloodcurdling scream had indicated fright not death. Although I was relieved I hadn't killed him I still felt he hadn't been punished enough, so I went after him again. I may have missed him altogether in the darkness and ran right past where he was hiding if I hadn't caught the sound of him gasping and wheezing for breath. I spun on my heel, looked to where the gasping was coming from and found him cowering in a manhole with his lamp turned off. I shone my own lamp in his face and advanced menacingly.

"I'm sorry!" the cowardly Claude whimpered, "Your Father

put us up to it."

I looked at him in disgust, he wasn't even worth kicking.

"You fucking pathetic pussy." I growled at him and walked back to the coalface leaving him blubbering in his hole.

When I got home that day I was happy for once in my life to see Dad was already there. I gave him the filthiest look I could muster, walked over to the mirror and made a big deal out of combing my magnificent, undamaged sideburns. Dad sat and watched in silence. I was still combing away when Mam walked into the room.

"Hey Mam!" I called to her, "I've decided to grow my sideburns right down to here," I indicated a spot two and a half inches below my ear lobe, "what do you think?"

"I think they look fine as they are." Mam answered. I turned to Dad and was gratified to see him wearing that glowering expression I had expected and I said to him,

"In future, don't tell anyone else to do what you can't do yourself!" I saw Mam's eyebrows rise with curiosity as to what I was talking about as I walked out. I didn't bother to explain, - Dad knew what I meant and that's all that mattered.

A few nights later I was laying in bed asleep when I was awakened by a tapping on a door and Mam's voice saying,

"Em,' open the door, come on, don't be silly!" Apparently Mam and Dad had had a flaming row about something and Dad had childishly locked Mam out of the bedroom.

"Emrys, come on open the door!" Mam said knocking louder. Then Dad's voice,

"Go away, clear off, I'm trying to sleep!"

"Stop being so childish and open the door, Emrys." Mam asked again.

"No I won't! Dad shouted, "You clear off now, you're not coming in here tonight!" The sound of Dad's voice and him barring Mam from the bedroom infuriated me and I was out of bed like a shot. I marched into the hallway and pounded on their bedroom door with my fist as hard as I could.

"Open this bloody door at once or I'll kick it in!" I shouted.

"You can clear off for a start!" Dad shouted back, recognizing my voice, "Nobody's coming in here tonight and that's the end of it!"

I lowered my voice till it was just loud enough for him to hear clearly,

"This door is opening by the time I count to 10, either because you've opened it, or because I've kicked it in. I don't care which, it's entirely up to you, but if you don't open it yourself you'll have to put new hinges on it tomorrow. One – two – three-." The door opened and I heard Dad jump back into bed.

"Thank you, Ade." Mam said to me as she entered her bedroom and closed the door. I went back to my own bedroom and it was quiet for the remainder of the night.

Next morning was Sunday so I didn't have to get up early for work, when I did get up as I didn't see Dad about I assumed he had gone out early to the Tabernacle.

"No he hasn't gone this morning," Mam informed me after I had inquired, "he's still in bed sulking."

Dad's sulking sessions were legend he could keep it up for over a week at a time when he was pissed off about something or other. In their early days Mam told me, she used to try for hours or even days sometimes to coax him back into a more reasonable frame of mind. It wasn't too long though before she realized that the attention he received as a result of a tantrum was something he was loath to relinquish and would drag out the agony even longer. Mam's remedy for that was to take as little notice of him as possible and go about her chores busily and singing to herself just to exaggerate her supposed unawareness of his filthy mood. It would piss Dad off even more but he would always get over it all the sooner as it dawned on him that no one was impressed. If any friends or family visited whilst Dad was in one of his moods he could become instantly friendly and chirpy until they left. Then he would lapse back into his former 'I'm not speaking to anyone, I hate the world mood'.

As Dad was still in bed and everyone else was downstairs I decided it might be a good time to clear the air as far as he and I was concerned. I went upstairs and walked into his bedroom to confront him about the previous night. To be honest I was still smarting over the underground attack on me and my sideburns that he had instigated. I didn't want to bring it up, and draw any more attention to the incident. I wanted to give the impression that his failed attempt had been so insignificant that it was beneath any further concern to me. He was laying in bed and glaring murderously at me, as I said.

"Don't you ever, EVER! Lock any door in this house on my Mother again; if you do I'll smash it to pieces!"

"I hope to God you go to hell!" He replied, viciously.

In spite of myself I felt an involuntary intake of breath as though he had kicked me in the guts. I gazed at his hate filled eyes. If anyone else had said that to me I probably would have taken so little notice that I would hardly have been aware of its utterance. Coming from Dad with all his so called chronic Christian beliefs it was a hard pill to swallow.

"I hope I don't," I replied, 'it would mean having to spend eternity with you."

****

My little gang and I would frequent every dance hall in the area and every little town around had at least one. None of us ever actually danced as that would have compromised our dignity, which in turn would have dented our self promoted tough guy images. We'd just swagger in, then prowl, scowl and growl, hopping to appear tough enough to attract admiration from the girls and trouble from the guys. Since Ter had come back home from the army it became much harder to get into a fight. If they knew who my Brother was they would keep right out of my way. I may have got to the stage in an argument when the very next stage would be violence and some idiot would say,

"Hey, I'd leave him alone if I were you, do you know who his Brother is?!" And that would be that, no one wanted to get on the wrong side of Terry Street. His viciousness bordered on the bestial. He had all the ingredients to make an excellent boxer. Great boxing skill, lightning speed, a killer instinct and brutally hard knockout punches with either hand, especially his left. Which would explain his only weak point. His punches were so powerful it was not unusual for him to break bones in his fist on impact. Advice that would warn off any potential opponents from engaging me in a bout of violence was well founded. If Ter heard of anyone threatening me he would go after them. Whether it was a display of Brotherly love or just a good excuse to break some body's nose, I'm not certain. Knowing Ter, it was most probably the latter. His self appointed protection of me was not only unwanted, but especially suspect by the fact that it was no more unusual for him to take a poke at me than it was for him to take a poke at anyone else. There was the time he and I were standing together outside a candy shop across from the Market Hall. Ter was telling Brothers Dougie and Loshin Hughes, how wrong it was for Brother to fight Brother. Doug and Loshin had got into a scrap. And Doug who was almost a rival to Ter when it came to violence, had made the poor usually good looking Loshin look more like the twin Brother of the 'Elephant Man' than kin of his own. After administering his advice about Brothers sticking together he went on to tell Doug and Loshin about some of our conflicts. All of which I noticed were pretty ancient, where I'd fared about as well as Loshin had against Doug. All of our latest battles had been a much closer call and all had lacked a conclusion due to premature intervention. So I interrupted him and reminded him of our last confrontation.

Ter and I used to lift weights together and we had an agreement. Whenever we came home from work, either one of us could tell the other,

"Okay let's have a workout." And the other would have to comply whether they were up to it or not. After a hard day's work in the coalmine it wasn't very unusual for neither of us to feel like training and we would play a cat and mouse game each hoping that the other would keep quiet. But we could both also be cruel and might feign extreme tiredness and see what the other one would do about it. Woe betide the one who fell asleep first. No sooner would he be deeply into dreamland when the other would suddenly shake the hell out of them and shout,

"Okay, it's time to train!" Then much to the other's amusement the poor victim would leap up not knowing what day of the week it was. Then shaking with fatigue and still asleep fall all over the weights trying to exercise with them. That was what caused our most recent fight. Ter had looked totally disinterested in exercising and I was totally exhausted. When he wasn't looking I snuck upstairs to bed, he just gave me time to sink into a really deep sleep, and then burst into the bedroom like an explosion.

"Okay, let's go!" He shouted at the top of his voice. I jumped out of bed bounced off the wall a couple of times before I found the door and then trembled my way down the stairs like an unset jelly. I cleaned the barbell to my chest and barely managed to press it above my head then staggered all around the kitchen stubbing my bare toe on a dumbbell while trying to control my balance. Ter began to shake with laughter. I must admit I have a very poor sense of humor when I'm very tired. So I threw down the barbell, punched Ter, picked him up and slammed him onto the kitchen table. I brought back my fist to punch down on him when Dad dived in from behind and grabbed my arm before the blow fell. That gave Ter an opportunity to escape off the table and hurl a punch of his own. It narrowly missed my face thanks to Dad pushing me back as he forced himself between us. Ter had just got to that part in his narration to Doug and Loshin and then added as he got caught up in the story,

"It's lucky for Adrian that Dad was there to stop me or I would have killed him!"

"What?!" I shouted, amazed at his cheek, "If Dad hadn't stopped me, you would have never got off the kitchen table while you were still conscious!"

WHAM! That bloody Brother of mine was fast. I never saw him move, but his fist hit me right in the middle of my face with such force that my head shot back and smashed the candy store window behind me.

"Twat!" I shouted, with shock and fury. I shook my head and tried to focus my eyes so that I'd know which way to charge. WHAM!!! His fist hit me a second time so hard that I was smashed backwards and right through the damaged shop window. By the time I disengaged myself from a display of boxed chocolates and leapt back heroically into the street to do battle Terence was nowhere to be seen. - I told you he was fast.

"Where did he go?!" I wanted to know,

"He ran across the other side of the square!" answered Doug and Loshin together.

"Right!" I shouted and marched off in the direction they had indicated.

By the time I reached the other side of the square I felt like the 'Pied piper of Hamlin' as I must have had half of Brynmawr behind me in order to see the action. There was only one thing that traveled faster in Brynmawr than my Brothers left fist. And that was news of a fight. I saw him walking towards me with two packages in his arms.

"Are you okay Ade?" He asked, "I've bought you some fish and chips," He added, passing me one of the packages as if nothing was amiss.

****

What we called the Valley Road was the walkway down through the picturesque Clydach Gorge. Every Sunday evening, weather permitting it would be crowded with groups of teenage boys and girls. They would walk up and down with no other purpose than to make new acquaintances with the opposite sex. A few of my mates and I were on our way there one weekend when we met a gang of guys from Ebbw Vale. We were all eying each other as we drew level when one of them pointed at me and said,

"You're the bastard that beat up Norman last week!" Where we came from you couldn't call anyone a bastard and not have a fight, as we took that insult very personally. All the same I was curious, so I asked him,

"Who the fuck is Norman?!"

"The bloke you nearly crippled outside the dancehall in Ebbw Vale last week! He replied.

"Oh, that Norman!" I smiled, remembering the incident. I didn't know the name of the guy that I'd fought with but did remember that I had been especially brutal.

I shall call him Norman as that is what his nanme seemed to be. He was the most unlikely bully you could imagine. He was very large, but he squinted through eye glasses that were so thick that I thought at first they were binoculars. He had an old fashioned short back and sides hairdo, wore baggy trousers and a paisley cardigan. Hardly a fashion icon in our Teddy-boy era. Norman appeared to be about thirty years old and couldn't have looked more out of place amongst all the rock 'n' rollers. He looked like the most nerdish nerd but acted as though he'd just swallowed a quart of testosterone. Norman seemed to single me out and purposely barged right into me, which we recognized as the most straight forward way to pick a fight.

"Watch where you're going!" He warned me, although I hadn't actually moved. 'He's new at this,' I thought. "You're the one who needs to watch where they're going," I corrected him, "but I suppose with eyesight like you have you probably couldn't see me."

"Oh, I can see you alright, Janet," he answered, "and there's nothing wrong with my eyesight!" He blinked furiously through two inches of glass like a constipated Owl.

"I stand corrected," I agreed, "You must have terrific eyesight to be able to see through those fucking things!"

"Let's finish this outside!" He growled, conceding the verbals. So out we went and found ourselves a dark alley.

"Will this do?!" He asked, as he turned to face me he took off his glasses and placed them carefully in his pocket.

"Just fine." I answered, as I grabbed his head and ran it into a tall, solid wooden garden gate. The gate flew open and we both found ourselves airborne above a steep fight of stone steps. We landed knocking the wind out of both of us. I had let go of his head before we both landed, with the result that he ended up halfway down the stairs and landed close to the bottom. As I turned and scrambled towards him he threw a kick towards my face as he still lay on his back on the steps. It was a poor effort and I grabbed his foot and dragged him underneath me as I advanced up the steps. Then it was all me punching down onto his face and him shouting he wanted to quit. Uncharacteristically I let him up and we both stepped and back into the alley, he turned to me and said,

"I'd better put my glasses back on." And as he did so he punched me in the face. I couldn't believe I'd let him get away with such a corny sucker punch. It was the first time he'd hit me, - it was also that last! There wasn't much left of him as I started to walk away. As I did I noticed on the ground in front of me, glinting in the lamplight, completely unscathed, his thick pebble-lens eyeglasses. I stomped viciously on them, instantly reducing their condition to that of their owner.

"Yes, that Norman!" Replied the leader of the Ebbw Vale thugs, looking ugly.

"So, what's it to you, are you his Mother?!" I inquired.

"No I'm not his Mother," he answered, "I'm the man who's going to beat the shit out of you for beating the shit out of him!"

"Okay come and get it." I invited.

"Not here," he stated, "let's go somewhere quiet, where we won't get disturbed."

"Do you want to fight or cuddle?!" I replied, getting suspicious.

"Are you getting frightened?!" He accused.

"Lead on." I invited, "But you arseholes stay put!" I demanded pointing my finger at the rest of his gang. "And you lot make sure they do!" I added pointing the same threatening finger at my friends. So off we both walked down the Clydach Gorge in search of a suitable battle ground. It was quite dark, so by the time we had walked several hundred yards both our gangs were well out of sight. Then I heard a sound I had been half expecting, - the sound of feet running towards us from behind like they were going for a world record. I barely had time to make a half turn in that direction. When someone slapped my shoulder and actually used it as a launching pad to dive right past me. Then land like a ton of rocks on top of my future adversary, - not what I expected. I thought that one or more of his gang had slipped away to reinforce my enemy. Instead it turned out to be 'Terrible' Terence, poaching my catch. The force with which Ter hit him was so hard that by the time they hit the ground the Ebbw Vale guy ended up on top. Instinctively I kicked him in the ribs knocking him right off Ter. I was not proud of the fact that I had just delivered what I regarded as the cheapest of shots. But in spite of the fact that Ter and I were often at each other's throats, we were both extremely protective of each other where other people were concerned. It was a hard kick that completely winded the guy. Feeling guilty as soon as I had acted, I quickly jumped in between him and Ter to save him from an unfair and savage beating that he would have received at the hands of my Brother. Slightly embarrassed, I asked him if he was okay and that if he was still up to it we could go off, - alone this time and finish what we hadn't got the chance to start.

"No!" He replied and then added ominously, "But I will see you both again!"

Give Ter a couple of drinks and he can be both amusing and

uncharacteristically talkative. Give him a couple more drinks and he can become downright evil. We were in the Beaufort Ballroom and we were both at the couple of drinks stage. I was screaming with laughter at Ter's crazy cavorting dance. He was right in the middle of the dance floor and performing slam dancing about a quarter of a century prematurely. There were men and girls bouncing off him in all directions. Then all at once a big hand from nowhere grabbed him by the scruff of the neck and hauled him backwards. Once again reacting protectively and instinctively I lashed out at his attacker. I then watched in horror as a very large Policeman bit the dust as he crumpled under the impact of my punch. Ter spun around and spying the policeman's helmet that was still spinning on the floor after it had flew off the downed copper's head. Gave it an almighty kick and scored a field goal with it as he sent it into orbit and spinning again as it soared over the heads of the band who were playing frantically on stage. We then made ourselves scarce. We were both drunk, but not enough to be so dumb as to hang around under the present circumstances.

A week or so later, Dai Hughes and I were walking through Ebbw Vale fairly late at night after a Scrumpy session in one of our favorite pubs. Scrumpy is what we called the roughest hard cider imaginable and at only 8-pence a pint you could get completely paralytic for 2-bob. We were wobbling along, hoping we still had time to catch the last bus to Brynmawr. We didn't relish the thought of walking about 3 miles over the mountain in the dark in the condition we were both in. I was carefully carrying a bottle of Peach Brandy, which was meant as a Christmas present for Dad. He liked the sickly, sweet, fruity liqueurs and I had bought him both Cherry and Apricot Brandy for his Christmas or Birthday presents in the past. I knew they were always a safe bet to please him and as he had never sampled Peach Brandy, to my knowledge, I thought it would be a nice surprise. As we passed the police station which was on the opposite side of the street I called over to a policeman who was standing outside the front door. I inquired if he knew if we were still in time to catch the last bus to Brynmawr. He placed his hand behind his ear to indicate that he couldn't hear my question from across the street. So Dai and I walked over to him and I repeated my question. Instead of answering he asked,

"Are you old enough to be buying alcohol?!" I was quite taken aback as I had never been asked that question before. Even though I had been drinking alcohol in pubs since I was about 13 and I was now just a few days shy of my 16th Birthday.

"This isn't for me," I answered, "it's a Christmas present for my Father. I don't drink alcohol myself." I added with forked tongue.

"No, I can tell!" He said sarcastically leaning forward and sniffing at my breath. He took the bottle of Peach Brandy out of my hand and said,

"We'll settle this inside, - stay here!" He barked at Dai, as he nudged me in front of him into the police station. As I stepped inside I saw one policeman leaning over the desk in conversation with three more coppers sitting or standing around the station room.

"This is the little Monkey who took a poke at me last Friday in Beaufort Ballroom!" he announced to my utter amazement, as he interrupted the other policemen's discussion. I certainly hadn't recognized the policeman I had punched and how the hell he recognized me under the circumstances will forever be a mystery to me. But I wasn't given much time to contemplate the puzzle. He slammed my bottle of Peach Brandy down on the station desk with his left hand and slammed me right across the back of the head with his right. The impact sent me stumbling into the middle of the room. Without further ado all the policemen in the room piled into me. Even the one from behind the desk ran around and joined in. I was punched slapped and pushed from one to another all around the room. What I was most worried about was the ripping and tearing sounds I heard as they grabbed large handfuls of my prized Teddy-boy suit. I had to think fast.

"AAAGH!!! My nose, you've broken my nose!" I groaned loudly and dramatically. I knew they probably wouldn't believe me. They had hit me everywhere except the face, but I relied on the fact that although each one knew that they had not punched my nose. They couldn't be certain that one of their colleagues hadn't. I knew I hadn't convinced them but it was enough to call a halt to the beating. They threw me through the station doorway with such force that I landed on my arse at Dai's feet. I soon realized to my surprise that the only thing that was actually hurt was my dignity and the only clothes damaged was my shirt. There was not one button left on it.

Partly in an attempt to save face in front of Dai and partly because I am an eternal optimist I picked myself up and marched right back into the police station.

"Excuse me!" I said politely, "But I had forgotten my Peach Brandy!" I walked towards the desk, hand outstretched, but the desk-sergeant snatched it away before I could reach it.

"Get out and don't come back or I'll charge you with unlawful possession of alcohol!"

"It's for my Dad, not me!" I argued hopefully.

"You're a minor!" He screamed at me.

"I know I'm a miner," I conceded, "So is my Dad!"

"Get out!" He screamed, "Or you're nicked!!!"

****

It was at the Beaufort Ballroom that we first saw Tom Jones performing. Of course he wasn't known as Tom Jones until after the Albert Finney movie of that name that came out years later in 1963. I was amazed to find out that it was the same guy that I saw prancing about the stage trying to look like Robert Mitchum and sing like Little Richard. I found his performance hilarious and I don't mean that in an insulting way, it was his absolute air of confidence that was both exhilarating and charming. Whenever I see anyone put so much of themselves into a performance irrespective of their talent it makes me want to laugh or cry. I was watching him cavorting like a Dervish, one evening from the back of the Ballroom. I began to walk across the dance-floor to take a closer look, when a man who was dancing with an attractive girl deliberately barged into me. It was so blatant that I was obviously meant take offense and after exchanging the usual preliminary niceties we agreed to settle the matter outside. I was surprised, and it occurred to me that this bloke must enjoy fighting even more than I do. To leave such an attractive girl alone, just for the sake of a little violence. Once outside with our taunts, threats and insults behind us we walked towards the hills in silence until he said,

"You haven't got your Brother to help you tonight!" And I realized he was the one who I had been prevented from fighting by Ter's untimely intervention.

"Good," I replied, "hopefully we won't be interrupted this time." We walked into the nearby hills and found ourselves a shelf of flat earth which was halfway up a hill. It had a steep incline on one side of it and a very steep decline on the other. There was plenty of room for what we had in mind. In fact I would have preferred a lot less. He attacked, I was driven back a few paces and stepped into a hole which caused me to lose my balance and fall flat on my back. I received a vicious kicking before I managed to grab him and slowly haul myself up. It was a costly ascent as blows were rained on me from left and right until I pulled him into a headlock and hurled him into the stony ground. He struggled like a maniac and although he was very strong he couldn't break free of my hold. Unfortunately, although I had control of him I wasn't in a position where I could hurt him or do any further damage. Eventually he conceded defeat. Otherwise it seemed we would be there all night. It felt to me more like a standoff than a victory. Although I wasn't getting anywhere with the advantage I had gained I was loathe to let him up as I had been the one who had received a beating. All I had succeeded in doing to him was to hold him down. I released my hold and stood up, my mind in a jumble. I certainly didn't feel much like a conqueror and I was cut and bruised everywhere. Other times when people noticed and commented on any wounds that might be apparent the day after I had had a fight, they would receive the same retort,

"Yeah, but you ought to see the other guy!" This was one time when I would have hated them to see the other guy; - he didn't have a mark on him!

"Give us a hand up!" His demand cut into my thoughts and I numbly reached for his proffered hand and hauled him to his feet. 'SHIT!' I thought, 'Will I never learn?!' He came up fist first and I hit the deck again like a ton of crap!

'You stupid arsehole!' I thought and that was me I meant, not him, I should have known better. More kicks, more cuts and bruises but I managed to find my feet and got a few good kicks and punches in of my own, 'fucking take that home with you!' I thought. His treachery demanded revenge and I flew at him with a renewed surge of energy and fury. I gave him everything back that he'd given me, 'now for the interest!' I thought but was suddenly stopped in my tracks by a new surge and vicious counter attack from my opponent. I gave a little ground and he charged me to re-close the gap. I turned on impact taking him over in a beautifully timed hip-toss. But with the tremendous impetus caused by his furious charge it sent us both flying into space over the very steep decline that bordered our battleground. I realized immediately what had happened but as we hurtled through the darkness I wondered when we were going to make contact with the ground. It came quickly enough but only lasted long enough to batter us before we were both sailing through the air again and back into space. Our fall was finally checked when we hit a fencepost strung with three tightly strung strands of barbed wire. The post snapped like a toothpick under the impact of our bodies and we both rolled right into and over the sharp spiky wire of the broken fence. As I placed my hands on the ground to push myself up my left hand impaled itself on the barbed wire and my right hand closed around a large round pebble.

"Fucking shit!" I heard the other guy complain. That was all he got to say before I turned and hit him in the face as hard as I could with the pebble.

A rough night indeed, from 'rock 'n' roll to 'roll and rock', it wasn't a clean victory but it was decisive and I'd prefer to be a bad winner than a good loser any day!

****

Back in Beynon's I was still working on the coalface. Each miner had a five yard width to cut out. It was undercut to a depth of four and a half feet and the height we were working in was usually about four to five feet. We would put up our own hydraulic or wooden props to support the roof to replace the coal we had cut away as we went along. I had almost finished when there was a sudden uproar at the head of the face. At first I thought I was hearing things and then I thought I was dreaming when I heard the shout,

"Cave-in in district H!" 'That's the district Dad works in.' I thought apprehensively. "Cave-in in district H." They repeated, "Emrys Street is trapped!" Now I was sure I was dreaming but I took off running for district H. As fast as my heavy steel toe capped boots and the dozens of dark, shadowed hidden obstacles would allow.

The only cave in that I knew anything about at that time had trapped and killed a man I had worked with, before he had gone on the afternoon shift. He had been pulling the conveyor belt nearer the coalface that had been extended during the morning shift, with a Sylvester. He had secured the anchor chain to one of the wooden props which supported the roof. That was against the safety rules and for good reason. The rules were that an independent prop had to be used as an anchor when using a Sylvester to move a heavy object. And not one that was supporting the roof, because if a supporting prop was accidentally pulled out, it's obvious what could happen. It was a rule that was rarely adhered to and almost everyone took a chance. It was a chance that cost this man his life as the weight of the conveyor proved to be too much for the prop. Out it came, down came the roof and he was buried. When they had finally dug him out they said his face was purple and his tongue was hanging on his chest. Caused by the handle of the Sylvester being pressed into his throat by the weight of the rocks that had fallen on him.

All this had been going through my mind as I raced through the ink black tunnels for over a mile before reaching the head of district H. I had to drop onto my hands and knees and crawl as the coalface was no higher than a kitchen table. It was constantly flooded with a few inches of water that was fed by the constant dripping like rain through the cracks that were etched in the roof like cobwebs. I was soaking wet and had crawled almost the whole length of the coalface before I came to the fall. And there was Dad sitting with his back against a prop looking quite casual and relaxed. Two or three miners toiled to free the bottom part of his body which was still partially buried. There was not really room for anyone else to help free him. But I pushed my way in and began moving debris as I had to do something to help myself unwind. When we finally got him free he said he suspected that one of his legs was broken. It was impossible to be able to bring a stretcher up the face as it was too low and had too many props which were necessary to support the incredibly cracked, weak roof. They decided that our only alternative was for him to get onto my back. I would have to crawl on my belly all the way back out of the coalface until we reached the exit tunnel where a stretcher would be waiting for us. Dad wasn't as big as me, but damn, he felt awfully heavy before we got to the stretcher. When we got to where we could stand they rolled Dad off my back onto the stretcher while one of them supported his injured leg. I had to stand up a section at a time as having Dad on my back for so long had buckled my whole body.

"You can get off there for a start!" I told Dad, "You've had your ride now it's my turn. I need the stretcher more than you do!" Everyone laughed at my quip, surprisingly, even Dad, who seemed to be uncommonly cheerful, especially under the circumstances. We had 2 miles to walk to pit bottom and by the time we got there I was exhausted. I had been carrying the head-side of the stretcher for the whole journey. The relief I felt when I finally stood under the shower was indescribable. By the time we had showered and dressed an ambulance had arrived for Dad and I accompanied him in it to the hospital. Dad had his leg x-rayed and as he suspected it was broken. But instead of becoming morose and despondent as I would have been under those circumstances he actually became even cheerful. 'Funny fellow' I thought.

When Dad and I arrived home from the Hospital, his mood changed dramatically. As the ambulance men delivered him into Mam's care he began to grimace and groan with pain for the first time. I was quite startled, as I would have thought, that as Mam would obviously be very distressed when she heard the news of what had happened. He could have, at least stayed as brave and as unconcerned as he had been before he got home. Then it dawned on me. There was only one thing Dad liked more than attention and that was sympathy and attention. I wouldn't have called him a hypochondriac. It was just that he played every affliction to the hilt. A simple head-cold, or headache would be life threatening and you should see what he could do with a tooth-ache or the flue. No one ever got an ache, pain or sickness like Dad as long as he had a sympathetic audience. Given cushions and pillows to make him more comfortable as he sat in his favorite chair. Waited on hand and foot, friends, family and members of the dreaded Tabernacle visiting to pay homage and 'tut-tut' their sympathy. Dad would thank everyone for expressing their concern and smile bravely, but would be unable to completely hide the pain behind his eyes, - Damn! What a drama Queen. He had it down to perfection. He could have given Lawrence Olivier advanced lessons. I've never seen him happier or more content. Struggling in agony to the Tabernacle must have been the summit of self-righteous bliss,

"Oh, make way for Brother Emrys!" Megan would coo.

"Ar' ew comfortable Emrys?! Chimes in Blodwyn, "There then, sit down there comfortable an' let me take your crutches for ew!"

"God must 'ave been lookin' out for ew, Emrys!" Said Megan, when she heard the whole story.

"Yes!" agreed Blodwyn, "It was God who protected ew an' delivered ew from danger, Halleluiah praise the Lord!" I wouldn't call being buried alive and having a broken leg as a result being protected and I also wondered what Megan and Blodwyn would say behind Dad's back,

"Oh, I wonder what Emrys done to deserve that punishment from God?!" And, "Oh yes, he must 'ave sinned somethin' awful for God to allow that to 'appen!"

In spite of what Megan and Blodwyn thought, hobbling to the Tabernacle in such exaggerated agony must have really built up Dad's Heavenly brownie points. But for me back on earth, Dad's wish came true and I went to Hell!

The cave-in in district H. had to be cleared while the coalface was still being worked so more men were needed there. Unfortunately for me, I was one of them. I was given a stent on the coalface to help fill the void and soon found out what the H. stood for, yes, Hell. As I reached the head of the coalface and dropped onto my hands and knees to crawl to my stent. I kneeled in about six inches of water and sloshed my way forward as huge drops of the continually trickling water soaked me as it seeped out of the roof just a few inches above my head. By the time I reached my stent I was soaked to the skin and then when I began hacking at the coal with my pick I found that the coal in district

H. was as hard as ironstone. Usually when I swung my pick at the coal I would bury the shaft right up to the hilt. But here the coal was so hard that the shaft would ring like a bell and I would feel the impact vibrate right down through the handle of the pick into my hands. Without making much of an impression on the coal. My hands were hard and heavily calloused as a result of working in the mine, but it wasn't long before the leathery calluses were torn and bleeding as I hacked away hour after hour at the unyielding coal. The coal was hard and the roof was weak. Every time I managed to hack out a sizable section of coal I would have to support the roof with more and more props. Which gave me more and more obstacles to pick and shovel around. All the while I would be suffering the drip-drip-drip-drip of the water seeping through the roof. Pieces of rock falling out of the roof. And if they didn't fall on me, they would fall in the water which covered the ground and splash me from bellow. While I was being drip-drip-drip-dripped on from above like the victim of that infamous Chinese torture. I was so bloody miserable I felt I could have just lain down in the water and died. And this is where Dad had worked for years. No wonder he was so cheerful when the cave-in broke his leg. I was ready to quit the pit after one day working in district H.

But it's said every cloud has a silver lining and even H. proved to have one too. I made friends with two middle-aged Brothers who both worked near me and they turned out to be avid Wrestling fans. - Avid Wrestling fans who hadn't missed any of the matches in the Drill Hall in Cardiff for years and drove there every show in a car that belonged to one of the Brothers. And best of all they invited me to accompany them anytime I wanted, just by sharing the price of the gas with them. Which would cost me no more than a return fare train ticket. Now I would be able to watch the whole show instead of just the first two matches. Also I would be able to discuss Wrestling all the way to Cardiff, then all the way back home, with two knowledgeable fans who had been watching British Wrestling for years. And were happy to talk about the Wrestlers for hours. The work in the pit was horrible but if I focused on the next show in Cardiff I managed to get through it.

****

I still held a passion for armor, swords and daggers and as well as collecting them, I also enjoyed practicing fighting with them. A friend of mine whose real name was Mike James but for some strange, Welsh reason was known as 'Shikey' would often practice with me. This day after we had both chosen our weapons from my now, extensive collection. We went up into the field above my house for a session, on my way out Mam warned me to be careful.

"I know what I'm doing!" I assured her, "I've been practicing for years!"

Shikey and I had both chosen a 19th century field-sword each, which I joked was appropriate considering we were going to practice in a field. I had been playing with my swords for years and had taught myself what I thought were some neat little tricks. One of which enabled me to poke holes through my opponents shirt under either of his arms without harming his body. Shikey was wearing a red shirt with matching jeans. I was wearing a black shirt with matching jeans. So he became the 'Red Knight' and I became the 'Black Knight' and we all know the Black Knight always wins. True to form I was hacking and then jabbing as he tried to counter and hole after hole appeared under the armpits of Shikey's prized shirt. Much to my amusement and Shikey's chagrin. But I must have became over repetitious as well as over confident with my little party piece. Just as the umpteenth hole appeared in Shikey's shirt he brought his own sword up at an angle and the point went right into my arm just below my elbow and hit the bone. The pain was like an electric shock and the reflex sent my sword spinning out of my grasp. It ended up further away from me up the field than I could have possibly flung it. Even if I'd thrown it on purpose. My whole arm felt as though it was paralyzed, from the tips of my fingers right up into my shoulders and into the muscles of my chest.

There was no way that I would ever believe a Robin Hood movie again. When brave Robin would fight on valiantly even after he had been wounded half a dozen times by the evil Sheriff of Nottingham. Lord of Sherwood Forest my arse, I was in bloody agony. I tried to hold my arm up in an attempt to stem the flow of blood that was pouring off my hand it felt as though my arm had been tied to my side.

"I know what I'm doing; I've been practicing for years!" I'd cockily told Mam when she warned me to be careful with my swords. I could just imagine what she would have to say about it. Luckily for me although my arm had been pouring blood, it didn't show through my black shirt and jeans. With the help of Shikey I cleaned up my hand with bunches of grass. I put both of the swords under my left arm, walked back home and managed to slip past everyone to the bathroom without attracting any attention. In the privacy of the bathroom I cleaned myself up as best I could. I put on another black shirt and then one of my black Teddy-Boy suits and went out to meet Hazel who I had a date with that evening. We walked up into the hills at the base of the Milfraen Mountain. But by the time we reached our usual courting spot my right forearm had swollen up like a pumpkin and threatened to burst my shirtsleeve. My arm was throbbing murderously and in the end I had no alternative than to go home and own up.

Mam did give me that 'I told you so look' but gratefully didn't elaborate on the subject. We had to cut the sleeve of one of my favorite shirts in order to examine the wound which we found had turned black. Ter accompanied me to the same Hospital that had fixed Dad's leg. They told me it needed stitches but as my forearm now looked as though it belonged to Popeye the sailorman it was no longer possible. After cleaning it up they fastened the edges closer together with clips. I was given an anti-tetanus injection in my shoulder and then told by the nurse to drop my trousers for the first of a series of penicillin injections. I was still very shy in that area so I asked the nurse,

"Don't you think I've been stabbed enough for one day?!"

"No!" She replied, "Not if you want to make sure you keep your arm, you could easily get a very bad infection, especially from an old sword."

"Well can't you inject me somewhere else?" I inquired. I was loathe to drop my trousers in front of the nurse especially in front of grinning Terence, who was enjoying my discomfort no end.

"Where would you like me to inject you then?" The nurse asked chuckling along with my Brother.

"In the eye if you like!" I told her disgustedly. Both the nurse and Ter burst out laughing, but she stepped forward and yanked down my trousers.

"You might as well get used to it now!" She told me, "You'll have to come back and get one every day for a week!" But they also told me that I wouldn't be able to go to work until my arm was better, so even that cloud had a silver lining too, - NO DISTRICT H. TILL FURTHER NOTICE! YIPEEE!

****

Just like dear old Dad, I was happy to be taking time off from district H. Even if it was due to an injury. Brynmawr was a desperately boring place the best of times. And hanging about the streets of Brynmawr on my own on a weekday morning while all my friends were in work only made it worse. I had just got back from the hospital where I had received my fifth and final penicillin injection. And was leaning on one of the four metal pillars that supported the front entrance to the Market Hall. I scrutinized my surroundings and wondered what I could do to entertain myself for the next few hours.

I didn't have to wonder for long. I had been watching the big red, double-decker buses coming in and going out when all of a sudden, who should step off one of them, was none other than 'Boxer' Bobby Wilkins. He didn't see me at first and he walked straight towards me.

"About time you turned up!" I snarled at him, "Where have you been hiding?!" I hadn't seen him since he and his fiancé had pissed me off and then left me without anything to hit. So I had been dreaming about this meeting for a long time. He looked down his nose at me with a sneer and intended walking past without even answering me.

"Hey you, you deaf bastard I'm taking to you!" I shouted at him. He stopped placed his hands on his hips and said with a sigh,

"Yes, what do you want?!"

"You, you stupid git!" I answered, "We've got a score to settle!"

"I've got better things to do than to beat up on some silly

snot-nosed kid!" He replied, "So piss off in case I change my mind!"

"Well change your mind now!" I advised him, "Because I'm not pissing off until I've sorted you out!" He walked towards me and tried to look down his nose menacingly. It didn't really have the effect he was looking for, as he wasn't much taller than I was and was probably a few pounds lighter.

"Thank your lucky stars that I've got nothing to prove by beating the likes of you!" He hissed dramatically,

"Why don't you prove you're not shitting yourself with fright?!" I asked him.

"Frightened! – frightened of what?!" He sneered.

'This is going to go on forever,' I thought, 'time to change tactics.'

"Where's your girlfriend?" I asked him, "I'll bet she's worn out."

"You'd better leave my fiancé out of this if you know what's good for you!" He warned me. 'That's his Achilles heel,' I thought and pressed on, happy to hit below the belt if it got me what I wanted.

"I hear she's working nights down Tiger Bay!" I sniggered, "I suppose that's why I haven't seen her around lately." Tiger Bay was Cardiff's infamous dock area and sleazy red light district, it was a cheap thing for me to say, but hey, it worked.

"Okay, that's it, you've done it now!" He roared, "Where do you want to settle this?!" All of a sudden I began to feel a sense of unreality as I had been rehearsing this scenario over in my mind for months.

"Let's go!" I told him, "I've got just the place." And I did too. Here was my little fantasy unfolding right before my eyes. We walked down Alma Street and cut along a lane that took us to the railway line and then we turned left and walked along the track until we reached my destination.

"Are you trying to walk me to death?" Wilkins complained impatiently.

"No, we are here now." I replied and indicated the fence by the side of the track. I crawled under the wooden fence and waited on the other side for Wilkins to follow me. He crawled halfway under the fence when I stepped gently but firmly on his right hand. Wilkins looked up at me with a startled expression on his face, realizing the possibilities.

"Oops!" I said, smiling down at him, "That could have been a mistake." Relief spread over his face as I removed my foot and let him through. He followed me down a narrow pathway that led to a space between two small but prominent hills. Known locally as the 'Camel's Hump.' It divided the railway track from the Clydach Gorge which it overlooked more than 100 feet below. It was a spot I had fantasized over for this very purpose, with this very person, ever since he had annoyed me in the first place.

"Here we are," I smiled, "nice and quiet with no one to disturb us for miles." I made it sound as though it was our first date. My attitude couldn't have done much for Bobby Wilkins' overblown confidence. I was really beginning to enjoy myself and didn't mind it showing. I didn't have to think about tactics or strategy. I'd done that over and over months ago and now was my chance to try it out. As expected Wilkins adopted his most menacing boxing stance, which was probably a pathetic attempt to intimidate me. I walked almost carelessly into the punching rang of his fists and as he threw his first punch I grabbed him. Down we both went with Wilkins held securely in a front choke hold. I could have finished it there and then, but I wanted to try a few things out. I spread my legs wide and purposely rolled myself onto my back and still using the choke hold to control him easing Wilkins on top of me. I hesitated just long enough for him to think that he might gain advantage from the position I had placed us both in. Then I clamped my thighs around his body and let the weight of my upper body force the sharp edge of my left forearm up into Wilkins' throat. It was the very same hold that I had suffered – and I do mean suffered, at the hands of my friend Peter Inge. I had wanted to try it out on someone else ever since that time, as I knew from personal experience how effective and painful that chokehold was. Wilkins submitted as soon as I relaxed a little to give him a couple of breaths of air. I explained to him that it wasn't time yet and reapplied my grip with renewed vigor. I repeated that treatment for a while longer then rolled Wilkins over and underneath me. I released the choke hold altogether and could have passed the time punching him in the face as he lay pinned beneath me. But there were a few more things I wanted to try. I stood up and positioned myself imitating Wilkins' boxing stance and I waited patiently for him to be able to stand up. I was curious to know how well he could box after choking for a while.

"Take your time," I told him, "we've got all day." When he did stagger to his feet I charged him fists flying and sent him tumbling back to the ground. When he got up again I knocked him down again. This was repeated again and again. At last Wilkins managed to land a retaliatory blow which just grazed by my left cheek. It also decided me to stop playing this stage of the game. I had picked my battlefield carefully. When I stood up after choking him I had positioned myself so that when I faced Wilkins again his back would face a sheer drop of about 6 feet that was directly behind him. Before I even blinked away the sting on my cheek I charged Wilkins backwards right over the edge of the drop. I hesitated just long enough to watch how he landed before I launched myself after him and landed with a foot on his chest knocking him completely unconscious. I hadn't really exerted myself very much so far but decided to take a break anyway. I sat on a bank near Wilkins and waited for him to regain consciousness while I checked my injured forearm to make sure it wasn't worse for wear. Eventually he began to stir and he sat up and squinted stupidly at me through his badly swollen eyes.

"Oh, are you still here?!" He croaked.

"Yes I am you lazy bastard!" I replied, "Are you ready for round two?!"

I've got to hand it to him, he was game. With a big sigh he heaved himself to his feet, but he still looked tired. So taking pity on him I knocked him out again in order to let him have a little more rest. This was repeated a few more times, with Boxer Bobby Wilkins taking longer rests between each session. I felt like a nasty, spiteful, little boy who would pull the wings off a fly for fun. I knew I had nothing more to prove and was surprised by my own cruelty. But each time I decided to call it quits the thought of Wilkins and his fiancé blatantly making fun of the way I looked made me want to smash him again and again. I do have a nasty temper. I decided eventually that he had had enough. And next time he resurfaced I would help him up and escort him safely back to Brynmawr. I hoped that later on that day I wouldn't give myself a hard time for letting him off so easily. I was sitting beside the prone Wilkins thinking along those lines. When all of a sudden like a flash Wilkins sat up and threw a punch that caught me flush on the jaw. Unbeknown to me he must have been conscious and waiting for such an opportunity to launch an attack of his own. I suppose from the angle he threw the punch while still sitting down, plus the poor condition he was in. Contributed to the total lack of authority in the blow delivered. But I had to admire his guts. I jumped on top of him and beat his face to a pulp. I then retired a little further away from him when I'd finished. So he wouldn't try to surprise me again and give me another excuse to hit him some more. I didn't want to leave him here on his own, but I was getting bored sitting about with no one to talk to. So I dragged him up the pathway and rolled him back under the wooden fence onto the edge of the railway track. I was finding it very difficult to pick him up while he was in such a relaxed state. Fortunately he came around enough to hold onto the fence while I stood him up and I was able to drape him across my shoulders. It probably took more energy to carry him the mile or so back to the Market Square than it did to fight him. I dumped him on one of the benches by the side of the Market Hall and decided to go home as fighting always gave me an appetite. Mam was home when I arrived and as soon as I walked in through the door she looked at me and said,

"You've been fighting again!" I was amazed. Although I shouldn't have been, as Mam seemed to have an uncanny knack of always knowing when I'd been fighting.

"Yes I have," I admitted, "but it wasn't much, look I haven't got a mark on me."

"How is your arm though?" Mam asked, "You know you shouldn't be fighting with your injured arm."

"Its fine, it doesn't bother me at all." I assured her, taking off my black shirt to show her the prime condition of my wounded forearm.

"Oh my God, Adrian, what have you done?!" Mam yelled with a look of sheer horror on her face. Her exclamation and expression panicked me and I looked apprehensively at my arm, almost expecting to see that the clips had burst open. I looked in the mirror and immediately saw the reason for her distress. Under my black shirt I had been wearing a white T-shirt that now looked as though it had been left over night in a bath full of blood, it was soaked. But as with my forearm injury the blood didn't show through a black shirt. I had to stay hungry for quite a while longer while I attempted to pacify Mam and reassure her that I hadn't killed anyone and all the mess on my T-shirt was caused as a result of a nasty nose bleed.

Whenever I happened to bump into Boxer Bobby Wilkins and his fiancé again it seemed as though they had both gotten over the amusement my appearance had caused them. If I caught their eye, the most I would get was a straight faced nod, - never a smile?

****

All too soon, I was back at work, that was the bad news. The good news was my place had been filled in district H. Now I would be working as helper to two miners who would be opening a new coalface, but that turned out to be more bad news.

They were on piece work which meant that the more yardages they took out, the more bonus money they made. As their helper I didn't get any extra bonus paid directly to me from the Colliery. But it was a recognized practice for the miners I was assisting to pay me a bonus themselves out of their bonus money. The set up was like this, they would be extending the future coalface. And were both working on the face which gave them only a little over four feet of headroom. They would both be throwing coal back to me and the only advantage I had over them was that I was outside the coalface in the tunnel and must have had eight feet or more headroom to stand up in. That was my only advantage. Because all the coal that they shoveled back to me, I had to throw with my shovel as far up the tunnel behind me as I could. The large lumps of coal I would carry or throw. When there was a big enough pile of coal. I had to go and throw it further up the tunnel to within range of the track that ran at right-angles to my tunnel. There an endless line of buggies would stand waiting for me to fill. So that it could be hauled eventually to pit bottom and from there to the surface. Whenever I filled up a couple of buggies I would press a button that would alert a hauler. He was operating the hauling machines about a quarter of a mile up the track. So that he could turn on the huge wheel and steel cable that would pull the full buggies past the exit of my tunnel and a couple more empties within range. Then I would fill them and press the button again. When I had no coal left near the buggies. I would go back to the end of the coalface. Where there would be an Everest sized mountain of coal waiting for me, that the two miners had been throwing back all the time I had been gone. So then I would have to shovel it from there back up the tunnel twice before loading it into the buggies. Plus I had to supply them with wooden support props whenever they needed them from a pile that I would periodically unload from the same line of buggies. The pair of tight arsed jerk-offs never ever gave me one bloody penny of their lousy bonus money the whole time I worked for them. And their excuse was, that I wasn't getting rid of the coal they threw out of the face fast enough. I know that they had to use their picks to break the coal from the face and erect their own props before they threw the coal out to me. But there were two of them throwing the coal once to me and I was throwing the same coal three times in order to load it into the buggies. That is what I was complaining to them about, one day as we made our way back to pit bottom at the end of our shift. And in describing to them the way I felt about the situation and about them in particular I had used every four letter description I had ever heard. And a few I made up on the spur of the moment so as not to get overly repetitious. Unfortunately for me. Also walking to pit bottom and following me in the darkness by no more than a dozen or so paces was Daddy!

Boy did I hear about that when I got home and Dad being Dad made sure that he tackled me on the subject in front of Mam. Obviously in order to maximize my embarrassment. But Daddy made a mistake. There were plenty of old miners who had memories of Dad before he saw God and they weren't shy in telling me that self-righteous Dad used to F and blind with the best of them in those days.

"You didn't hear me say anything that you haven't said yourself!" I told him.

"You've never heard me using that filthy language!" He

declared.

"No I haven't!" I agreed, "But all the older men in the pit have and they told me so!" Dad blushed, I almost felt like going to the Tabernacle next Sunday just to change the verse I used to recite and instead of saying 'Jesus wept' I could say 'Dad blushed.' Just to watch his face and to see the looks of speculation spread over the drooling chops of Megan and Blodwyn. With his face full of guilt he glanced at Mam and she just gave him that 'look' it was really great. There was a long-long-long silence and then Dad remembered something one of the Tabernacle members had told him that provided him with a comeback.

"Oh, Brother Noble told me he saw you coming out of a pub at the bottom of Beaufort Street last week!" He accused in an effort to change the subject.

"Yes, he probably did," I replied without hesitation, "I went in there looking for Terence." I winced a little as through the corner of my eye I saw Mam's hand cover the smile that had appeared on her face.

"Oh, try to keep away from places like that Ade," he said in a nice gentle Fatherly manner, "or one day you might be tempted to take a drink."

That was it, Mam and I both fell down laughing.

****

After holding out for almost a year, I finally relented and took my little gang to get themselves tattooed in Bristol and at the same time get a couple more done myself. I had a Tiger's head being attacked by a Snake on my upper forearm and a Peacock perched on a branch below it with its tail draped over my wrist. I always remember getting that tattoo done whenever I hear Larry Williams' song 'Bony Maroni' as that was the first time I had ever heard it. I was wearing a ring on every finger, each one with a huge rhinestone set in it and the vibration of the tattooist's needle on my wrist bone made every rhinestone dance in time to the music. I had started the huge rhinestone ring craze, which soon caught on. The guys fancied, with one of a different color on every finger they looked like they were wearing a garish, glittering knuckleduster on each hand. After that, some of them went overboard got one ear pierced and began wearing earrings to match the rings. I remember The Black Rat Brian Heath and Beynon Jones squabbling like two bitchy girls over which pair of rhinestone earrings they were going to buy between them. So that they could wear one each. I wasn't interested in getting my ears pierced myself as they would have got in the way while I wrestled. But I came very close to changing my mind when Terence who was disgusted with the earring craze told me,

"Don't you ever even think of getting earrings, if I ever see a Brother of mine wearing them, I'll pull them right through your ears!" That for me was a challenge that was very hard to ignore, as I refused to let anyone tell me what I could and couldn't do. His threat placed me in a dilemma. I didn't want to wear earrings, but that was my choice, not his. Fortunately a situation arose that resolved my dilemma without my having to resort to getting my ears pierced in order to exhibit my defiance.

Although we both worked in different districts in the pit, Ter and I would always get up together at 5 am. Grab a bite of breakfast then hurry down to catch our bus to Blaina from near the Market Square. We would both be inclined to be grumpy that time of the morning. Especially with the thought of work to look forward to and it wasn't unusual for us to get a little testy with each other. On this particular morning Ter decided he didn't want to converse and my constant attempt to do so sent him scurrying out of the house before I was ready to accompany him. Our boxes of lunch, bottles of water and our bus fares would always be waiting for us on the kitchen table. They were the last things we would grab to take with us when we left the house. In his haste to get out of the house before me Ter had taken his water and lunch but left behind his bus fare. I noticed this and I should have collected it for him when I took mine. But under the circumstances, I thought, 'Sod him, serves him right.' By the time I was approaching the bus stop I could tell by Ter's agitated demeanor that he had realized he was missing his bus fare. I made sure he could see me walk towards him, but then purposely stood as far away from him as possible. Before the bus arrived he had edged his way right up to my side and I heard him clear his throat nervously. He didn't speak and I pretended I didn't know he was there. I knew that under normal circumstances, when he was in a dodgy mood he would keep as far away from me as possible. When the double-decker bus stopped I boarded and ran upstairs. Ter was right behind me. I sat down in the back seat and my Brother sat next to me, but still didn't speak. Again I heard that little nervous cough as we heard the conductor's voice on the lower deck calling,

"Fares please, everyone get your fares ready!" Ter still sat there as silent as a wooden Indian and so did I. Any minute now the bus conductor would be coming upstairs to collect our fares and Terence didn't have any. - 'He-he-he!' Finally he had to break the silence as he had all but run out of time.

"Did you see my bus fare on the kitchen table before you came out of the house?" He asked me.

"Yes I did." I replied.

"Well where is it then?" He asked, looking relieved and holding out his hand.

"It's still on the kitchen table where you left it." I told him. WHAM! Here it came, but I was expecting it. His fist brushed past my temple and Terence ended up underneath me on the back seat of a double-decker bus. I clobbered him a few times before I threw him down between the seat we had been sitting in and the seat in front. I forced him down flat with both of my feet. Then I grabbed him roughly by the hair and his throat and although I didn't hit him I let him digest the fact that I could have. And that he couldn't do one damn thing to prevent me smashing his face. I didn't have to ask him if he wanted to continue, I could see it in his face. I let him feel my strength as I hauled him back up and sat him back in his seat. He now realized that he had chosen the wrong battle field and if he tried again he would end up back on the floor of the bus. It must have had the desired effect as after 16 years of being on the wrong side of his nasty temper and his vicious fists he never, ever tried to strike me or even threaten me again.

So at least on that score it was going to be easier for me to live with me. As both Terence and I knew now that if I decided not to wear earrings it was because I didn't want to wear earrings and not because someone else thought they could influence my decision with threats. Well I had finally put an end to any future violence from both Dad and my Brother so I was feeling pretty smug and confident, but if you think that it was finally safe to go home you'd be as wrong as I was.

Just as he had done a hundred times before, Ter shook the life out of me after I had fallen asleep and invited me to lift weights with him. And just like every one of those hundred times it would put me in the worst of moods. When the weather was good we would always have our workout in the back garden. When it was bad we would do it in our very small kitchen/dining room. Today we were training deltoids and Ter began by pressing a barbell overhead for his first set. When he completed it he stepped aside to make room for me to perform mine. Still shaky from being woken up I bent over and grasped the barbell prior to cleaning it to my chest. Mam walked out of the sitting room and passed close to me on her way to the kitchen. I stood up with a sigh and let her pass, then bent forward again and gripped the bar. I drew in a huge lung filling breath of air before grabbing the barbell as Mam comes trotting back out of the kitchen and interrupts my lift again. I stood back impatiently and let her pass and as I bent forward for the third time here she comes again. Ter who was aware of my mood and my agitation began to chuckle, which didn't help improve my mood or my agitation. When Mam came back out of the kitchen I was readying myself for the fourth attempt at lifting my bloody barbell I said to Mam, somewhat snappily,

"Don't keep running back and fore when I'm trying to lift weights, this is the fourth time you've stopped me!" Mam's face registered an apologetic expression and she stepped back into the corner of the room. With another sigh I bent and heaved the 165 pound barbell to my chest with effort as my body was still half asleep. With much gasping and struggling I managed to press the barbell to arms length and that's when my face exploded. SPLAT! I stood swaying under the barbell with blood gushing from my shattered mouth and both barrels of my nose. When my tear fogged eyes began to refocus I looked down at my 4 foot, 10 inch Mother's angry face, which seemed to be swimming in its own galaxy of stars, sparks and fireworks.

"Don't you ever speak to me like that again," she threatened, waving her tiny balled up fist in front of my face, "who the bloody hell do you think you are!" I couldn't believe the enormous amount of force there was behind that one devastating punch, but I guess I should have, - she was Big Jim Arnold's Grand-Daughter!

Instead of putting down the barbell, when Mam stepped out of my face, I pressed it a record 23 reps which was almost twice of what I was usually capable of in those days. I've often thought that Mam really took a chance throwing such a huge punch when I had a heavy weight above my head, if I had dropped it, she would have probably ended up being a lot shorter than 4-foot 10. That was also the last time Mam ever hit me but it did give me something to think about. All I needed now was for my 10 year old Sister Pam to beat me up to make everything complete. I knew that was unlikely as we love each other very much. But it wasn't impossible as she can be a feisty little package and also a typical Street family member!

****

He had a dodgy looking face, a largish nose and no chin. Also his blond hair looked as if it had been dyed that color. But in spite of all that he had managed to make himself look fairly magnificent. His light green Teddy-Boy suit was trimmed with darker green velvet, which matched his green suede shoes a treat. As he saw us scrutinizing him enviously he opened his jacket and displayed his waistcoat which was green and gold brocade. The pair of open razors one each in his waistcoat pockets were half exposed for effect. We had heard that the London Teddy-Boys were reputed to carry razors or bicycle chains as weapons. Razors were also used by gangsters and Street gangs in London. The Gorbals in Glasgow, Tiger Bay in Cardiff and anywhere including kindergarten in Liverpool, but I had never seen anyone carrying them in our area.

He sneered at us down his caricature of a conk and I was drawn to him like a moth to a flame.

"You ought to be more careful shaving with those razors of yours." I advised him, "It looks as though you've cut your chin off."

"I don't use them for shaving." He replied menacingly.

"Well not since you've cut your chin off anyway," I agreed with him, "what do you use them for now?"

"The way you're talking, you're going to find out." He threatened, then added, "Do you know who you're talking to?!"

"No!" I replied, "I don't know who I'm talking to and the answer to your next question is also no, if you ask me if I care."

"Oh, you'll fucking care!" He promised me, "You'll care for the rest of your life, when you have to see my name carved on your face every time you look in a mirror!"

"Now you're asking me to believe you can actually spell your name." I countered. It's strange, sometimes I couldn't wait to get to the rough stuff and other times I enjoyed the foreplay which preceded the violence almost as much as I enjoyed the following fight. But this time my future opponent seemed to tire of it before I did and he concluded,

"If you'd care to step outside, I'll give you a lesson in spelling I'll make sure you'll never forget!" So as the Rock 'n' Roll music rocked on, we walked past the prancing dancers out of the Dancehall and went off to consummate his promise. Followed at a discrete distance, by his gang and mine who would witness the ceremony. I began to experience a slight sense of unease, as he seemed to be leading the way to what appeared to be his own prearranged battleground. At the same time, I was not at all worried by the fact that he carried razors. I was convinced they were merely for show and I was certain that he wouldn't attempt to use them. On the contrary, his dangerous and flamboyant image didn't intimidate me at all, in fact it made him an irresistible prize. It would add spice to the stories that I would tell and retell for a week or two to come. Before newer and hopefully bigger confrontations would finally eclipse this battle as it faded into legend. A drizzly rain began to fall and the dark dismal streets began to gleam dully as we walked along the pavement. It all added to my irritation as I now felt like I wanted to get on with the main event.

"Are you going to start your spelling lesson soon?" I asked him impatiently, still adhering to his chosen theme, "There are girls back at the dance that are getting lonely."

"I hope you've got a photograph of yourself 'cos they won't recognize you when I've finished with you!" He replied. I didn't like the way he seemed to be taking charge of the situation and I liked it even less when he suddenly stopped and then vaulted over the 4-foot high stone wall that we had been walking along. The wall was about a foot thick and the top of it was encrusted with broken glass. He seemed to know exactly where he needed to put his hand to prevent cutting it when he placed it on top of the wall to vault over it. This, I thought, placed me in an awkward position. I didn't want to appear hesitant in front of him or the guys that were still following closely behind us, but I didn't want to cut my soding hands either. He stood expectantly on the other side of the wall and in the lamplight I saw that as he posed with his hands high on his hips. He was again exposing the twin razors in his waistcoat pockets. I became enraged at his consistent and blatant attempt at intimidation and decided to throw caution to the wind. But as I placed my hand on top of the glass covered wall and leaned my weight forward ready to vault over it I felt a burning sting across my upper left arm. The crazy bastard had slashed me with one of his razors, I felt the warm blood run down my arm inside my jacket and shirt sleeve. I had simultaneously lashed out with my fist and caught him a glancing blow just above where his chin would have been, if he'd had one. As I vaulted over the wall I lashed out again but with my right foot and caught another glancing blow in his left eye. It staggered him back a few steps and although it didn't knock him down I saw him drop his razor. Instead of going for the other razor he bent down and was scrabbling to retrieve his lost one amongst the wet grass. From my angle I could see it clearly gleaming in the light which shone from a lamppost behind me. But he had put himself in a dangerous position whilst searching for it. And taking full advantage I stepped forward and delivered an almighty kick which caught him flush in the face. It straightened him up and sent him flying backwards down a steep bank where he landed heavily across a gravestone at the bottom of the bank. There was a sickening crack as my foot had contacted his face and another sickening thud as his body crashed into the hard granite grave. My fury suddenly turned to concern. Which was multiplied as Dai Hughes, who had been one of my gang that night. Suddenly appeared over the wall and went bounding down the bank in aid of the fractured, green and gold Teddy-Boy. I snatched up the fallen razor and watched apprehensively as Dai attempted to lift the crumpled figure to his feet. As he succeeded I thought that Dai was acting out of compassion. Until he brought back his big fist and smashed the groggy Teddy in the chops. Which sent him hurtling back onto the gravestone that he had just been lifted from. Dai then began doing a shithouse shuffle on the Teddy's blond and bloody head. And I had to run down the bank and call a halt to Dai's frantic fandango before 'Chinless' Teddy became a permanent fixture in the graveyard. I jealously resented Dai turning my date into a 'ménage trios.' But I consoled myself when I robbed the chinless wonder of his second razor. Which with its twin was prominently placed in the top pockets of my black, maroon velvet trimmed Teddy-Boy suit to exhibit proudly when I returned to the dancehall as a trophy of war.

****

I discovered a Boxing Club in Ebbw Vale that had apparently been there for years. I immediately wanted to join, if only to know what it felt like to step into a real ring. I decided it might be a good idea to add Boxing to my arsenal at the same time. I had to go there three times before the Boxing instructor would allow me in the ring. Especially after my debut, when I lost a three round contest against a very skillful, hard-hitting and crafty speed-bag. Every time I managed to get a good haymaker in, the bloody thing must have flattened my nose about 5 times on the rebound. I didn't fare much better with the punch-ball at first but did manage to improve with practice. The heavy-bag was easy but boring. I couldn't wait to get into the ring and show the instructor what I'd got. I was highly flattered, after just a couple of rounds. When the instructor stopped the sparring session I was having with one of his Boxers and told me that I reminded him of a Bar-room brawler. At first I took it as a compliment until he added the bit about me being the worst prospect he'd had the misfortune to instruct. I told him that he wasn't too hot as an instructor if the truth be told. As every time I listened to his instructions and tried to bob, weave and jab, the guy I was sparring with crucified me. When I allowed my natural instincts take over I could rush him or hustle him into the corner. Then I wouldn't stop punching until he was in a heap. Then the damned instructor would yell "STOP!" Order me back to the center of the ring advise me what he wanted me to do and I'd get slam-dunked again. It just seemed to me that I managed to do a lot better when the instructor kept his mouth shut and let me get on with it. Looking back on it now I can appreciate the fact that I was pretty bad. I was too impatient and stubborn to take instruction, especially when my own methods of mayhem seemed to work so much better for me. There was an interclub contest coming up and the Boxers that would be taking part in it were training for it like lunatics. The Boxers who weren't taking part, myself included, had to serve as sparring partners for those who were. If I was so awful, I wondered why the instructor kept pairing me with his pet protégé who was the Club's best prospect. I also resented the fact that the instructor supervised all our sparring sessions and as a result I got a battering while we sparred and teachers pet got all the pats on the back and compliments when we finished. My resentment soon turned into a grudge and I wanted satisfaction. I got my chance soon after when one evening we were told to carry on training on our own, as the instructor was going to be late. 'wonderful' I thought. Teacher's pet was in the ring shadow boxing and gave me the come hither and get whacked look. So I hopped up onto the apron and ducked through the ropes.

"You've forgotten your gloves!" He informed me impatiently.

"I thought we might have a fight for a change," I suggested, "are you going to take your gloves off or leave them on?" He didn't answer me, he just adopted his boxing stance, as he probably realized I couldn't hit him whether I was wearing boxing gloves or not, - the thing is, I hadn't invited him to a Boxing match. By the time the instructor walked into the Club, his pet protégé was almost unconscious and once again the 'Peter Inge' chokehold had proved to be a more effective weapon than bob, weave and jab.

"WHAT THE FUCK ARE YOU DOING?!" Screamed the instructor, "LET HIM UP, GET OUT OF THE RING, GET OUT OF THE CLUB - AND DON'T EVER COME BACK!" – 'Now there's a bad looser.' I thought.

****

The Abergavenny boys were coming! – No, they weren't a local Rock Band, they were a rival teenage gang from Abergavenny, comprising mostly of Farm laborers. They were the Farmers we were the Miners, sworn enemies. - Or at least that's what we chose to think. In reality we'd never really had a gang war, it was just a childish fantasy that both sides played up after seeing American gang movies like, 'I was a teenage nutcase,' and 'Rebel without a brain,' type of thing. Like dozens of times before we were patrolling the Market Square. Watching the bus stop and waiting for the Abergavenny gang to arrive and like dozens of times before they wouldn't actually come, it would just be another rumor.

"They must be coming up here to steal our Brynmawr girls!" Stated Footy, that wasn't original either. That was the usual way we would rouse ourselves for the upcoming battle that would never happen.

"Yeah, but they won't be getting any today!" promised The black Rat.

"No, not after we've finished with them!" Injected Beynon Jones, squaring his shoulders. We were all bravely puffing ourselves up and boasting to each other what the Abergavenny boys could expect, if they just as much as dared to show their freckled, farmers faces in our territory. This would probably go on for an hour or more, till we decided that once again our sworn enemies had chickened out. Then we would congratulate each other's bravery, scorn the Abergavenny boy's cowardice, then go and find some other mischief to get up to. I had just thought of something original to say when Mower beat me to it,

"Oh SHIT, look at that! He shouted. We all looked and piling off a newly arrived bus was the Abergavenny gang. I opened my mouth to say something else, but it stayed open and silent. As I watched farmer after farmer stepped off the bus. There was about six or seven of us and dozens of them and still they kept coming. The bus put me in mind of one of those cars in a Clown's Circus act, where an endless army of Clowns appear out of one normal sized car.

"Okay, this is what we'll do!" I started to tell my gang, but as I turned to them to impart my strategy, I found I was standing there alone. It seemed as though, not only was my gang's strategy better than mine, they had also thought of it a lot faster than I had and had left. I thought, but couldn't swear, that I had just seen the last of them disappear into the 'Griffon Hotel' across the other side of the Square. Now it was my turn to say, 'OH SHIT!" To my dismay, it didn't seem to dismay the Abergavenny Gang to find that the Brynmawr gang consisted of me. I was loathe to surrender one inch of Brynmawr territory to these foreign invaders, but under the circumstances decided to give them as much room as they wanted. Surrounding the Market Square was a half circle of short concrete pillars, linked together with heavy steel chains. I ran to one of these and managed to unfasten one side of a chain from one of the pillars before I was surrounded by belligerent farmers. I began to swing the chain around my head daring any of the Abergavenny gang to approach me. It was very heavy and hard to control once I'd got it going. The fact that the other end of it was still fastened to another pillar didn't help much either and I knew I wouldn't be capable of swinging the chain indefinitely. I shortened the amount of chain I was swinging which was easier but it also shortened the distance with which I could hold my antagonists at bay. But it did enable me to reach the other pillar more easily where I managed to unlink the other end of the chain. All the taunts and baiting being heaped on me by the furious farmers who had been trying to reach me while my movement had been restricted. Was immediately replaced by wide eyes and slack jaws as I took off after them and lengthening my swing as I lengthened my stride. I went straight after the farmer who had appeared to be the Alpha-male amongst them and whipped his legs from under him with one tremendous swipe of the heavy steel chain. He went down like a tenpin. I had lost the momentum in the process and concentrated on getting the chain back into the swing of things before looking around for my next victim. There wasn't one, looking back across the square the Abergavenny gang was piling back onto the same bus they had arrived in only minutes before at a speed that even surpassed my own gang disappearing into the safety of the Griffin Hotel. I decided not to interrupt their departure and instead walked back across the square to re-hang the chain, passing their fallen leader who was still lying groaning on the ground. I couldn't wait to find where my fearless gang had hidden themselves, so I could boast about my single handed victory of the Abergavenny gang. If my gang had stayed to fight the results may have proved painful for them, but not as painful as having to listen to me retelling the story over and over again until I had milked every last drop of mileage out of it. The only thing that finally shut me up, were the rumors that began to arise from the incident. - The police were investigating. I had broken one of the Farmer's legs. I had broken both of his legs, I had broken both his legs and he had concussion. I finally thought it best to shut up and hope the story died before rumor had it that the farmer had done likewise.

****

There must have been about a half dozen of us sitting in the cheap seats of the Market Hall Cinema. None of us were taking any notice of the movie as there were three young girls sitting in front of us who had already evolved well into the giggling stage that would be a prelude to us splitting them up and choosing our partners. As usual I was doing as much yapping as the rest of my gang put together. But as a result had more or less established my claim on the girl I fancied the most. And would let the rest of the guys squabble over the two who were left. I was just about to suggest a little seat trading when I was interrupted by the noisy entrance into the Cinema of a group of guys who all seemed to be shouting loudly at each other at the same time. As they hustled and shuffled their way into their chosen seats across the aisle from where we were sitting, one voice rose above the rest. It was a voice with the coarsest, crudest, ugliest accent I had ever heard, - 'well that wasn't quite true,' I thought. - I had heard that very same voice and accent for the first time three and a half years before and many, many times since in my imagination. A cocktail of emotions swept over me with such a force that I think I would have thrown up. If my racing heartbeat, my pounding head and the icicles fighting with the molten lava in my guts could have afforded me that luxury. I sat silently, temporarily incapacitated trying to control my breathing and my heart. I was vaguely aware of the girl sitting in front of me occasionally turning to glance at me with curiosity. No doubt wondering why I had suddenly appeared to have lost interest in her. She was a very pretty girl and I would have liked to come to grips with her. But not as much as I wanted to come to grips with the author of that awful voice. I had sworn we'd meet again, but as so much time had gone by in the meantime I had began to doubt that it would ever happen. But sitting across the Cinema aisle in the darkness, as completely unaware of my presence here, as he had been unaware of the fact that he had occupied a special place in my thoughts for over a thousand days and nights. It was 'Hairy' the Gypo.

My whole body seemed to throb. My mind was a turmoil of possibilities and plans that kept evolving, canceling themselves out, swirling, revolving. I seemed to be in a place alone, but aware of the fact that my friends hadn't noticed my change of mood. Even the girl had seemed to have forgotten my existence in the face of the renewed attention she was receiving from the guys still competing for her favor. My turmoil continued and I hadn't got any further with formulating a plan of action when Hairy the Gypo stood up and announced to his companions in a voice that informed the whole Cinema audience,

"Keep my place; I'm going for a piss!" I gave him about 30 seconds head start. Then without further ado got to my feet and hurried after him. As preoccupied as they were, my friends and the girls seemed unaware of my departure. Enveloped with a sense of unreality I seemed to fly in slow motion across the foyer towards the men's toilets. And as I had prayed, when I burst through the door the Pikey was alone. He was standing in a stall with his back to me when I entered, he didn't even turn to look at me. He seemed to have grown a little, but was smaller in comparison with me now, than he had been when we had last met. I remember looking at the back of his neck which was bowed as he was looking down and concentrating on his aim. His neck was a very grimy white and looked almost delicate. I had to remind myself who it belonged to and what he was capable of. "I'm sorry I hit yer boy Mister." Was the last thing I had heard him say all those years ago, words he had branded on my brain. I roared like a hungry Lion and fell on my prey like and alpine avalanche while he was still taking a piss. I smashed him face first into the porcelain ledge at the top of the receptacle he was pissing in with all the force I could muster. Then again and again right into the receptacle itself as he dropped to his knees. I grabbed two handfuls of his lank greasy hair and held him in a kneeling position while I stabbed him repeatedly in the back with the point of my right knee. Red blood had spattered over the white porcelain, but not enough. I wanted to see more of it. So I commenced smashing his face into the porcelain again. I wanted to punch him, kick him, stomp him and slam him. I wanted to do it all at once I wanted to be a one man band of pain and destruction. I didn't like Hairy and I wanted to express my dislike to the utmost of my ability. When I'd finished with him, - dept paid, interest rendered, I walked out of a toilet that looked more like a slaughter house. Every white tile was splattered scarlet, it was the most satisfying score I had yet settled.

I didn't return to my seat, instead I left the Cinema. I had lost my mood for movies, even for girls. I just wanted to walk and savor my newly found tranquility.

The only thing that had cast a small shadow over my satisfaction during the next few days when I reflected on my toilet triumph. Was the fact that Hairy the Gypo was completely unaware of who had pulverized him and why. But the realization that the mystery would undoubtedly plague him, as much as I had been plagued over the years, more than made up for it. However a new situation arose that even managed to eclipse the whole 'Hairy the Gypo episode' from my mind for some time to come.

****

Here is how my next war began, I was just about to leave the house to meet Hazel Masters, who was my girlfriend at that time. But Dad had a chore for me.

"I want you to take this bag of Books up to Mamo's house." he told me.

"I don't have time now," I told him reasonably, "or I'll be late for a date."

"What's more important, what I tell you to do or a date with some girl?!" He demanded.

"A date with some girl," I told him even more reasonably, "I'll take the books for you tomorrow if you like."

"I promised Mamo she would have the books today!" He insisted.

"And I promised Hazel I would see her at six thirty and if I don't go now I'll be late," I replied, "why don't you take the books up to Mamo's yourself," I suggested, "then we can both keep our promise." I could tell by the color of Dad's face that he was livid, - as usual, - so I left to meet Hazel.

Unless we went to a dancehall or the cinema to see a movie, we would both go back to my house where we could lock ourselves in the back parlor and enjoy complete privacy. When we got back that evening I was happy to find the house empty. - At least that's what I thought. Until I opened the door of the back parlor and found Dad snoozing on the settee I usually did my courting on. Now it was my turn to be livid as I knew Dad was only in there to spite me for not taking his books up to Mamo's as he had asked me to. Dad mostly went to sleep after he had come home from work but always in his favorite armchair in the front room and never in the back parlor. I refused to be thwarted by Dad's childish behavior, so I took Hazel up stairs to my bedroom. We had no sooner lay down on my bed when Dad burst in like an implosion from Hell.

"How dare you take a girl to bed under my roof?!" He screeched, "I never did anything like that when I was a boy!" He continued.

'No,' I thought, 'maybe that's the cause of what you've been like ever since.' But I said, "We weren't doing anything that we couldn't have done in the back parlor, but as you were in there, we came up here instead." It was a very long time before I'd heard the last of that incident. And even longer before I could induce Hazel to come to my house again as she had been totally humiliated and embarrassed by Dad's outburst.

****

I was still attending every Wrestling show that promoters 'Dale Martin' held at The Drill Hall in Cardiff, so that by now, even if I hadn't seen all of the Wrestlers that performed in

Britain, I was at least aware of them. Thanks to Dale Martin's official wrestling programs. There were many that I greatly admired. But of all the Wrestlers that I had seen so far, the Italian Heavyweight, Mike Marino was my favorite. I had made up my mind that on the next occasion he appeared in Cardiff I would try my best to speak to him. And ask his advice on how I could get started in the 'Grunt 'n' Groan' business. When I learned of the date when Mike Marino was going to return to Cardiff next I was on tender hooks with anticipation for days. All the way from Brynmawr to Cardiff I kept asking the two Brothers I rode with what the time was. I wanted to be at the Hall before any of the Wrestlers arrived, so that they would have to pass me on their way from the entrance to the dressing room. We arrived in plenty of time and I seemed to pace back and forth for ages before the first of them came. When I finally spotted Mike Marino come through the front entrance and stride towards me, I became so breathless with excitement that I feared I wouldn't be able to speak after all. But with what seemed to me like a superhuman effort I managed to get myself under control and blurt out,

"Hello Mr. Marino, I'm going to become a professional Wrestler. What should I do to get started?" He stopped and a smile broke through the most rugged features I had ever laid eyes on. His scarred eyes and badly broken nose were framed by a pair of cauliflowered ears that almost made him look as though he had three heads. 'That face looks as though it was built about the same time as Noah's Ark', I thought.

"Join a good Amateur wrestling club and become an Amateur champion." He replied without hesitation.

"I don't know of any in South Wales," I told him, "that's why I want to go to London."

"Yes, there are plenty of clubs in London." He answered and promptly disappeared into the dressing room before I could even think of my next question.

As I stood there chewing over what he had said, a loud murmur arose from the audience, I looked towards the entrance and immediately recognized the reason for it. - The huge Russian-Canadian, George Gordienko who would be Mike Marino's opponent that night had arrived. I scrutinized him and tried to estimate Mike Marino's chances, - Slim to zero I decided, as the 6 foot, 300 pound monster walked past me and I was correct. That was the first time I saw my favorite European Wrestler, Mike Marino lose a match. But I consoled myself as I looked around Dumfries Place Drill Hall and promised myself that one day I would wrestle in this very arena. I would be Main Event, just like Mike Marino and George Gordienko and then all my Great Welsh fellow wrestling fans and fellow countrymen would be cheering me on to victory. Oh boy, I just couldn't wait!

All the way back to Brynmawr that night I must have speculated on a hundred different ways of interpreting Mike Marino's two short sentences. But before we arrived I had persuaded myself that his advise had been that I should go to London soon and not to waste any more time doing it than I had to, I just couldn't wait. I had always said I was going to live in London. Even before I knew I wanted to be a professional Wrestler. But now more than ever I seemed to be unable to form a sentence without reminding whoever I was talking to that I was definitely going to go. I also knew Mam was very much against the plan and once again she suggested that I should wait until I was at least 18 before taking off on my own. It was a shame as Mam seemed to be the only person in the world who actually took me seriously. I didn't want to cause Mam any stress but I really wanted to go. What finally brought things to a head was the next time I went to make arrangements with the two Brothers who took me to the wrestling matches in Cardiff. They told me point blank that I couldn't go with them anymore. At first I thought they were joking with me as we had always got on so well together. Not only were we all rabid wrestling fans but I shared the price of their gas and even bought them all kinds of refreshments when we were at the matches. Just as my treat, to show them how much I appreciated them taking me with them. I was so disappointed that I became determined to know the reason why I was not welcome anymore. But they were both reluctant to discuss it any further. They started to walk past me indicating that our discussion was over, but I took a step to prevent them escaping with dignity and asked them again.

"If it was up to me you could come with us." Said one Brother.

"Well, who is it up to?!" I demanded, glaring at the other

Brother.

"Not me either!" He declared quickly, not liking the expression I was wearing.

"It is your car isn't it?!" I stated, "So tell my why I'm not welcome any more?!" All of a sudden a thought crossed my mind, "Hey, wait a minute, has my Father got anything to do with this?!" They both pushed past me and quickly walked away and I repeated my question at their retreating backs but never received an answer.

Dad I thought had not really punished me for the 'books, Mamo and girlfriend in my bedroom' incident. Whatever happened to 'Vengeance is mine, sayeth the Lord?' I thought. But then realized that Dad would be far too impatient to wait for judgment day.

I was furious, I was disappointed, I was hurt, I wasn't certain Dad had anything to do with it. - Not certain, but suspicious enough to make my mind up there and then that I was as good as gone. My summer vacation was coming soon and I determined that I would spend it in London making arrangements for my big move. I saved as much money as I could and hit the weights with a vengeance as a start to my preparations.

My plan was to go to London for my holiday and instead of touring around and seeing all the sights as I had done on previous visits. I would find a place to work, to live and to train to become a professional wrestler. By the time I got on the train to leave, a friend of mine we nicknamed 'Chewy' decided he wanted to leave Brynmawr and live in London too, so we set off together. After we arrived in Paddington Station we walked all the way to the London Y.M.C.A. We booked ourselves a room for the duration of our holiday. After dropping off our bags in our room we went down to check out the gym. It was by far the best gym I had ever seen up until that time. The weightlifting and bodybuilding equipment was situated in an upstairs gallery. From there we could look down on most of the other activities taking place in the main hall. Chewy wasn't in to anything strenuous especially lifting weights. But he watched me and waited patiently until I completed my first London workout. On our way to the shower-room we saw an indoor swimming pool and decided to play in the pool before taking a shower. At first

Chewy and I, were the only ones in the pool. But after we had been swimming for a while, Chewy began making funny faces and performing strange signals. in an effort to draw my attention to something he could see going on behind me. I turned around to look at what had caught his interest and saw a man wearing nothing but a white, rubber bathing cap, walking along the edge of the pool. We had already noticed that there was a large board that said 'Nude bathing allowed in the swimming pool.' Personally I couldn't think of any reason why anyone would want to take advantage of that fact. But the thing that really shocked the both of us was that the naked man had an enormous erection that he didn't seem to appear to be aware of. Neither one of us could hardly believe what we were looking at. Nor could we understand why he didn't run and hide himself. Or at least wrap a towel around his waist. I wondered why he would ever think of swimming in the nude if he couldn't control himself. Or why he didn't at least jump into the pool to hide it, where maybe the cold water would cure it for him. Instead he just paraded back and forth in full view of both of us. I really felt embarrassed for him, but as sorry as I felt, I would have been too embarrassed for myself to point it out to him. So we both ignored him as best we could and carried on swimming as though he wasn't there.

That was the one and only day I relaxed. After that we looked for a job. I tried to find one close to the area where Uncle Fred lived, as I knew that area of London quite well. My plan was to find a job before I looked for somewhere to live, so that I could then get somewhere close by and not have too far to travel each day. Once I'd sorted that I could check out all the wrestling and weight-lifting clubs in that area. We found that it was not easy to find a job in London. But after days and days of 'No, sorry, we are not hiring at the moment!" We finally both found work in the 'Acton Bolt Factory'. Acton wasn't as close to where I would have chosen to live as I would have liked, but it was better than nothing and anything had to be better than the pit! We would commence work in the factory in less than 3 weeks. Which gave us just a few more days in London before returning to Brynmawr and Beynon's Colliery where I would be working off my 2 week's notice. We found a bed-sitting room in Harlesden. After checking out dozens that were advertised in shop windows everywhere. We were surprised and quite shocked to see so many of the adds saying 'Whites only need apply.' 'No Blacks! or, 'No Blacks, Irish or Children!' We had never seen anything like that in Wales at that time. The bed-sit was a little more than a couple of miles walk from the Bolt Factory. So that was basically everything we wanted to accomplish before going back to Wales and kiss Beynon's bloody Colliery goodbye for good, I couldn't wait.

"Oh, are you back home already? We thought you were going to live in London, Ha-ha-ha!" With the gleeful looks on all the miner's faces the first day back after my trip to London, you would have thought that they were actually glad to see me.

"I'll be going for good in 2 more weeks," I told them and added, "I just wanted to come and take one last look at you stupid bastards to make certain that I never get the urge to come back to this fucking piss hole of a pit!" Well I certainly managed to steal the headlines for the whole period of the time I was working my notice. People had been saying for generations that they were going to get away from our area and make something of their lives, but never did. So no one had taken any notice of me when I said I was going. But now I was claiming I had a job and a place to live in London. And even though they didn't really believe me, they also knew I was too cocky to make such a claim if I couldn't follow it through. As I would have been setting myself up for a ribbing that would last me for the rest of my life.

The two guys I had been working with were both genuinely glad to see me back after my holiday. They told me that now that I'd had 2 long weeks of rest they both expected me to work like a bloody Beaver. Bad luck, I made sure that I hardly exerted myself, the coal that they threw out to me that I was supposed to shift on my own mounted up. And they had to come out of the face periodically to help me move it and load it. They complained bitterly, but I told them that I didn't want to work too hard as I wanted to gain more weight for when I started wrestling and if they didn't like it go ahead and report me to the manager,

"What's he going to do? I gloated, 'Fire me?!"

By the time I stood at the bottom of the pit amongst crowds of miners waiting to go up the shaft for the very last time, on my very last day, speculation was running high.

"So you are really going to London are you Street?! They asked me for the millionth time.

"Yes, that's right." I answered for the millionth time.

"He thinks he's going to be a wrestler!" Shouted one of them as he puffed himself up and adopted his interpretation of a wrestling stance, which looked more like a Chimpanzee taking a crap, everyone laughed encouragingly.

"Wrestler, huh, the first time he comes face to face with a real wrestler he'll run all the way home from London!"

"Just to change his trousers!" Said another.

"Yeah, he's too little to be a wrestler, have you seen the size of some of 'em?!"

"That's right," another chimed in, "they'd rip him in half without even blinking!"

"How long do you think he'll last up in London on his own?!" Someone asked.

"About 5 minutes," came an answer, "less than that if he bumps into a wrestler, Ha-ha-ha!" Everyone joined in the laughter, including Dad. Who had been standing opposite me in the tunnel and grinning like a Jackass with its gob full of Hawthorne.

"What do you think Emrys," they asked Dad, "do you think he'll make it in London?!" As strange as it seems, I found that I was actually interested in Dad's opinion.

"No," he replied, "he'll be back; he likes his Mother's cooking too much to stay away too long!"

"HA-HA-HA!" Laughed everyone obligingly, as expected. It was unusual for any of the miners to ask self opinionated Dad his views about anything. So I suppose that as the topic had suddenly given him a few seconds of limelight he didn't want to blow it by going against popular opinion now. I don't know why I was so disappointed; Dad had never supported me in anything I had ever wanted to do since the first time I ever remember meeting him. So why spoil it just before I was leaving home? I looked at him reproachfully, he grinned back triumphantly. Enjoying the chuckles and guffaws his little witticism had evoked from the other miners. I would have thought Dad of all people would have been the first to appreciate, if only from past experience. That if I said I would do something I would do it and if I said I wouldn't do something I wouldn't, - end of story!

"Oh yea of little faith," I said for Dad's benefit and then I told them, "Every time I've said I was going to London, you've all told me you've heard it all before and I believe you, because you are the idiots who've said it. But the difference between you and me is, that I have got the guts to do what I say I'll do and if you don't believe me just wait and see. I'll live my dreams not just dream them, every time I win another match I'll think about you lot down here rotting your lungs out!"

Their collective jeers was interrupted when the Colliery hooter blew to tell us it was time to move towards the cages that would take me up the shaft to the surface. Where I intended to stay for the rest of my life.

When I left Beynon's Colliery I had been one out of a workforce of six hundred and thirty-eight men who in that year produced 148,000 tons of coal, the Colliery finally closed in April of 1975 after an underground fire.

****

Well I was going and that was that, Dad never said anything to me, no words of encouragement and no words of wisdom or last minute advice. Mam didn't want me to go and was the only one who seemed concerned.

"You'll want to be careful living in London on your own." She warned me.

"Why?" I asked, hoping to reassure her, I added "I've been to London before."

"Yes," she replied, "but only for holidays, you've never lived away from home before and had to look after yourself."

"What's the difference?" I inquired, "I can cook, I know what I should eat and I've got a job and somewhere to live."

"You want to be careful where you go," she told me, "some places in London are very dangerous."

"Not anywhere near as dangerous as where I've been working since I left school," I countered, "there's nowhere in London as dangerous as the coal mines."

"Well you'll want to stay away from Soho for a start." She said.

"Soho! What's in Soho?" I asked.

"Jack Spot!" she warned.

Jack 'Spot' Comer was known as one of London's most vicious gangsters, famous for his brutal, razor slashing ways.

"Oh, I'm sure Jack Spot has heard that I'm coming to live in London and he's probably hiding behind a dustbin or in a shop doorway in Soho right now. Just waiting for me to visit Soho so he can jump out and get me," I replied sarcastically, "don't you think I'm a little bit too old to be frightened of bogeymen Mam?"

"Well there are women in Soho who would like to get hold of someone like you." She told me.

"Women?!" I said, "What women? If I'm not afraid of Jack Spot I'm definitely not afraid of any women!"

"No, that's what I'm afraid of!" replied Mam. - Soho?! Mmmm, I was intrigued, I would definitely have to check that out. But I was going to London to become a Professional Wrestler and I had no interest in gangsters or strange ladies. - But then that's all I knew. Only time would tell, 'that Mummy knows best.'

****

Will I make it in London? - Will I meet Gangsters and Strange Ladies? - Will I become a full time Professional Wrestler? - Or will I do as Daddy predicts and run back home to Mummy and the Mines? All will be revealed when My story continues in -

BOOK 2 - 'I ONLY LAUGH WHEN IT HURTS.'

PHOTOS

Great Grandmother Caroline in 1894.

Left: Dad, Age 17, in 1927. Right: Mam, Age 17, in 1932.

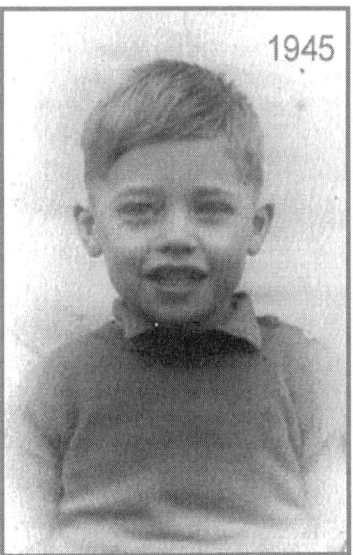

Left: Brother, Terence, and Me in 1941.
Right: Me after WWII in 1945.

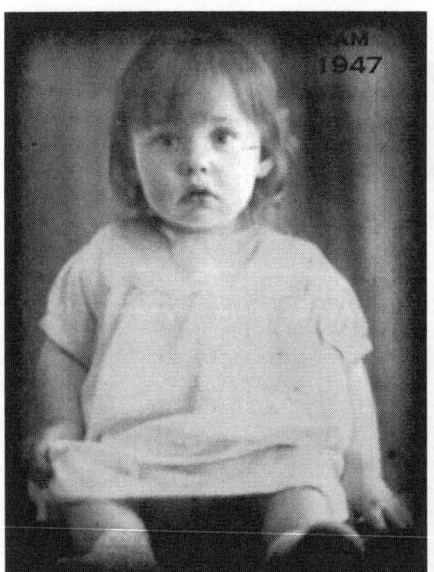

Left: Sister, Pam, in 1947. Right: Pam at 2 years old in 1949.

Dad (left) and Mates in Durban, South Africa, 1941.

Printed in Great Britain
by Amazon.co.uk, Ltd.,
Marston Gate.